Stories and Readers: New Perspectives on Literature in the Classroom

Edited by

Charles Temple
and
Patrick Collins
Hobart and William Smith Colleges

Christopher-Gordon Publishers, Inc.
Norwood, MA

Acknowledgements

The editors gratefully acknowledge the cooperation of all of the contributors to this volume. We knew that they had interesting things to say; but it was an added pleasure to learn that they were also very competent, dependable, and agreeable people.

Our editor deserves a special note of thanks for believing in this project from the beginning and helping us through every stage of it in her enthusiastic and caring way. Anyone who has despaired of finding an editor who still works closely with authors should write down this name: Sue Canavan; and that of her company: Christopher-Gordon.

A lot of good talk went into this book along the way. We thank many present and former teachers and colleagues: Edmund Henderson (now deceased), Tom Estes, Shane Templeton, Austin Quigley, Ronald Walker, David Tucker, Lynn Bevill, Ruth Nathan, Bill Teale, Bob Schlagal, Tom Gill, Jean Gillett, John Burns, Madeleine Grumet, Claudette Columbus, and Chris Vecsey.

Finally, we thank those who helped prepare the manuscript. They supplied a stunning range of literary, mechanical, and cybernetic skills in making one book out of twenty papers from many different time zones and computer languages: Nancy Curvin, Julie Fryer, Sharon Elder, Lee Skrzyniarz, Lois Polese, Lisa Berry, and John Vaughn.

Credits:

Chapter 3: This chapter is adapted from *The Empire's Old Clothes*, by Ariel Dorfman, translated by Clark Hansen. Copyright © 1983 by Ariel Dorfman. Reprinted by permission of Pantheon Books, a division of Random House, Inc.

Chapter 10: John Stewig's materials reprinted and adapted by permission of the publisher from Stewig, John Warren, *Informal Drama in the Elementary Language Arts Program* (New York: Teachers College Press, © 1983 by Teachers College, Columbia University. All rights reserved), pp. 89–90.

Christopher-Gordon Publishers, Inc.
480 Washington Street
Norwood, MA 02062

Printed in the United States of America

10 9 8 7 6 5 4 3 2 1   96 95 94 93 92

ISBN: 0-926842-10-2

Short Table of Contents

Long Table of Contents

PART I

How Do Stories Mean?

Introduction

How does an experience of meaning get from the page of a text into a reader's head? How do stories do their work? What is their work?

These are the kinds of questions that teachers are usually too busy to ask, let alone answer. Like most fundamental questions about teaching, however, if we don't ask them, we will never extend the limits of what is possible to accomplish with our students.

The reigning unexamined assumption about reading is that meaning somehow lies whole on the page of a text. Readers are supposed to take it away, just as it is, from their reading. Basal textbooks have been written as if there were a fixed amount of exact meaning in a story and good readers would fill themselves up with nearly all of it, and poorer readers with lesser amounts. The amount of meaning a reader takes in can supposedly be measured, like the amount of gasoline that is put into a tank. This assumption still guides much of the practice of teaching reading and reading literature, and the assumption is wrong.

Anyone who writes seriously knows that this "gasoline assumption" is mistaken in two ways. First, it is not true that meaning is envisioned by a writer and put down intact onto paper. As writers will tell you, even when they start out with a specific intention, the characters in a story can be counted on to come to life and dictate their own events to the author, and in the end, writing finds its own meaning, in the words of Donald Murray.[1] Second, when readers pore over the text, each with their own experiences, needs, and expectations, it is amazing what a variety of shades of meaning they find in it and even point out to the author.

So how does meaning arise from the mix of author, story, and child? Answers to this question usually proceed along four different lines.

1. *The structures of text.* We can explain the process of reading and the power of texts by exploring the unspoken rules that govern

1

the presentations of plots, characters, and themes in texts. Rules like these will be known by both authors and readers, and their knowledge will go a long way toward making reading possible.

In this section, Charles Temple's chapter sets out this line of thinking, as he presents four different kinds of patterns that commonly shape stories and the readers' experiences of them.

2. *Readers' responses to texts.* The experience of reading can be described as highly personal encounters between readers and texts, in which readers essentially construct meanings for themselves. Jonathan Lovell's chapter in this sectin shows a group of children constructing their own meanings of Roald Dahl's *Danny the Champion of the World.*

3. *Archetypal symbols with psychological power.* We can also stress the images and themes in stories that seem to speak to very deep human concerns, showing the ways that reading can lead to greater self-knowledge, especially of a mystical or a religious kind. Stephen Simmer's chapter in this section is written from such a point of view.

End Notes

1. Donald Murray, "How Writing Finds Its Own Meaning." *Teaching Composition: Theory Into Practice*, eds. T.R. Donavan and B.W. McClelland (Urbana, IL: NCTE, 1981).

1

Lots of Plots: Patterns, Meanings, and Children's Literature

Charles Temple

Charles Temple teaches courses on human development and literacy at Hobart and William Smith Colleges and writes about children's writing and reading. For the past several years he has been exploring the relation between literary theory and children's literacy.

Let me begin with an experiment. The following seven sentences are presented out of their original order. See if you can find a more satisfying order for them.

1. In despair, he went to the wizard for advice.
2. "I see. Well, try fishing in the lake next time," said the wizard.
3. He used the best bait, but caught no fish. He even bought the best equipment but still caught no fish.
4. "Can't catch fish?" the wizard asked. "Where have you been fishing?"
5. The fisherman took his advice and caught fish from that day on.
6. "In a swimming pool," replied the man.
7. There was once a fisherman who could not catch fish.

Many readers eventually arrange those sentences in a sequence that goes something like this: 7, 3, 1, 4, 6, 2, 5, and they say they are arranging them into a story. But how? Essentially, they must call up a story pattern that resides in their heads and then impose it on the lines as they find them. The reader must scan the lines, intuitively seeking a character with a problem who makes some attempts to solve it and eventually reaches a solution.

These patterns of characters, motives, and events have received a lot of attention in recent years as researchers have pointed out the existence of "story grammars" and teachers have shown their power in the classroom. In this chapter I want to explore some other kinds of story patterns that have not received so much attention in classrooms. Like story grammars, these patterns may exist both in the reader's mind and in the author's work: They can thus be seen as a set of unspoken rules that readers and authors both use to help them associate meaning with a text.

Let me first retell a story so that we can see these patterns in action. I'll use Jay Williams' "Petronella"[1] because it uses story patterns in interesting ways and is read fairly often in the elementary grades.

Figure 1-1. "Petronella"

In the mythical land of Skyclear Mountain the first daughter in many generations is born to a king. She decides to do what the males in the the family have always done: to ride forth to seek a prince and not wait to be sought. On the road with her brothers she finds a wizened old man rooted to a tree stump. The brothers ask which way to go to find their fortunes, but Petronella asks how she can help the old man. Her question alone frees him: She is the first person in sixty-three years to show concern. He points her to the castle of Albion, the enchanter. She finds a prince there, an empty-headed, lazy sunbather. He isn't much of a prize, but she decides he'll have to do. Before she can carry him off, however, the enchanter, a stern and powerful man, gives her a series of tasks to perform: to spend one night in a room with fierce dogs, another in a stable with wild horses, and a third in a loft with dangerous hawks. With kindness she befriends all these animals and saves her own life. Then she begins her escape with the prince, but the enchanter pursues them. She manages to immobilize him with a magic ring, but at once she feels pity for him and goes back to free him. He explains that he was chasing Petronella, the girl of his dreams, not the slovenly prince—this one was just a freeloading houseguest. The enchanter asks for a kiss to free him from the ring, and they go off together to ask her father's permission to marry.

Levi-Strauss' Opposites

Children enjoy this story for its many surprises. The author constantly sets up expectations and then thwarts them. The author also sets up interesting contrasts: between Petronella and the typical fairy tale princess she refuses to be; between Petronella and her brothers; between Prince Firebright and the typical princely hero; and between Firebright and Albion, the enchanter.

The French anthropologist Claude Levi-Strauss[2] argued that contrasts like these lie at the heart of what literature is all about. By nature, we humans seem to seek contrasts in experience—hot and cold, good and bad, rich and poor, brave and cowardly. In literature, contrasted images, situations, and characters can stand for the tensions between contrasts we make in real life. One valuable use of stories for any group of people is to encode and work out safely the tensions between opposites that worry people most, tensions that may be too painful or controversial to talk about directly. In ancient Greece, Levi-Strauss says, such tensions often focused on the relations between men and women. In modern-day North America, the focus has not changed much.

"Petronella" is a good example of a story that encodes and tries to work out sex role-related tensions. In "Petronella," we are invited to make many sets of contrasts. First, there are contrasts between the males and females in the story. Second, there are contrasts between the stereotypes we carry around in our heads of females and males and the actual males and females we are presented in the story.

To illustrate, let us take Petronella herself and the stereotypical female—the woman we expect at the beginning that she turns out not to be. Any traditional fairy tale princess will do; think of the Sleeping Beauty. We will call this imaginary person "S.F.," for "stereotypical female."

Petronella is strong willed; S.F. bends her will to suit others. Petronella is adventurous; S.F. is timid. Petronella is a seeker; S.F. is sought. Petronella does things; S.F. looks beautiful. Petronella is a vivid character; S.F. is an undeveloped facade of a person (see Figure 1-2).

Figure 1-2. Petronella vs. "Stereotypical Counterpart"

Petronella	"S.F."
Strong willed	Weak willed
Adventurous	Timid
Seeker	Sought
Focuses on actions	Focuses on appearance
Vivid character	Empty person

Of course, the character in the story who most closely resembles the stereotypical female is not a woman at all but the young man, Prince Firebright. When we see the set of weak and passive characteristics projected onto a male figure, we are shocked to see how undesirable these characteristics are in anyone, male or female. We may be led to wonder why females in traditional stories must have such limited personalities in order to seem attractive.

On the other hand, it is not quite the case that Petronella is cast in a traditionally masculine role. There is something essentially feminine about her, and it becomes clear when we contrast her with the stereotypical male hero ("S.M."), as we see in Figure 1-3.

Figure 1-3. Petronella vs. Stereotypical Male"

Petronella	"S.M."
Strong willed	Strong willed
Adventurous	Adventurous
Seeker	Seeker
Focuses on actions	Focuses on actions
Vivid character	Vivid character
Strives for others	Strives for self
Wins through care	Wins through violence

The contrast between Petronella and the typical male hero is pointed to several times in the story: first, when she asks the old man at the crossroads the question that frees him; next, when she uses acts of kindness to survive the ordeals put to her by the Enchanter; and finally, when rather than vanquishing her rival she unites with him. This contrast between Petronella's qualities and those of the typical male hero are important, and we will come back to them.

In the character of Petronella, Williams is showing us a woman who is as assertive and adventurous as typical males and yet has some admirable qualities that are essentially female. These characteristics are important, and we will return to them shortly. First, however, we must pick up some other loose ends in the story. For one thing, who is really the seeker in this story? Who is the sought? Etienne Souriau's approach will help us investigate the roles the characters in "Petronella" play.

The Dramatic Roles of Etienne Souriau

Did you notice as you read the synopsis of "Petronella" how you automatically put the characters into "slots" as you read about them? This one's the hero. That one's the desired one. That one's the bad guy. Whoops! That bad one's the desired one after all!

A French drama critic pointed out that being able to assign characters to dramatic roles is basic to our understanding of a story (much as assigning words to the roles of subject or predicate is basic to our understanding of a sentence).

Just as there is a limited set of grammatical roles that words can play in a sentence, there is also a limited set of roles that characters can play in a story. Souriau[3] claimed that he could describe what each character is doing in a scene of a story in terms of no more than six roles. We have found that the characters in children's stories can usually be accounted for by using no more than four of his six.

He gave each role a name and symbol from the signs of Zodiac:

The Lion Force. There is one character whose will directs the action in a story. We might call this person a protagonist. It is the protagonist's goal that mostly organizes the events in the story.

Sun—the Object. Something is sought—a tangible item, a new state of affairs, a quality, even another person (as in a love story).

Mars—the Rival. The rival opposes the efforts of the lion force to gain the object. The rival might be a person, such as a competitor for the same object, or it might be a set of circumstances to be overcome, such as isolation on the sea in a survival story.

Moon—the Helper. There is often a person (though it may be a quality or even a form of magic) who helps the lion force gain the object. In a story with many characters, the rival may have one or more helpers as well.

It is instructive to look for these roles in "Petronella." Who is the lion force? It seems to be Petronella, at least at first. Who or what is the object? Children tell us that it is a prince, but many add that Petronella seeks a more basic object—after all, Prince Firebright isn't much of a prize. Perhaps it is independence, adventure, or her own destiny she seeks. Who is the helper? The old man at the crossroads, many say; but here again, on reflection, the helper may turn out to be the qualities of Petronella's character: initiative, determination, and compassion. Who is the rival? The enchanter seems to be, at least so long as Prince Firebright is seen as the object. In a deeper sense, another rival is the whole weight of tradition that says a woman shouldn't go out and get what she wants.

This story flip-flops in the last scene, and these roles help us keep track of the changes. One reading is that Petronella begins as the lion force but ends up as the object. The enchanter, who was the rival, becomes the lion force; it is his will that wins out in the end. The prince becomes the helper to the enchanter, a kind of bait to catch Petronella. By this reading, the liberationist theme that opened the story is abandoned at the end, and Petronella reverts passively to the role of the pursued.

There are more loose ends. Why do these roles—the wizened old helper, the fierce patriarchal enchanter, the beautiful maiden—all seem so familiar?

Joseph Campbell's Hero Cycle

All stories partake of a very limited range of forms. As we noted above, cognitive psychologists in the last fifteen years have familiarized the notion of story grammar, a limited set of elements that combine in certain orders to generate the structures of the stories we hear and tell. Even before coming to school, children use something like these grammars to comprehend stories. Why, though, is the set of possible story forms so limited? And why are stories from different cultural settings so strikingly similar to each other?

No one has investigated this question in a more compelling way than Joseph Campbell. Campbell devoted his life to the study of myths and religious stories from all parts of the world. He was struck by amazing commonalities shared by so many myths. He concluded that all stories tell the same story, and in his book, *The Hero With a Thousand Faces*[4], he gave his version of the archetypical story from which all other stories are derived. Campbell's archetypical story is outlined in Figure 1-4.

Figure 1-4.

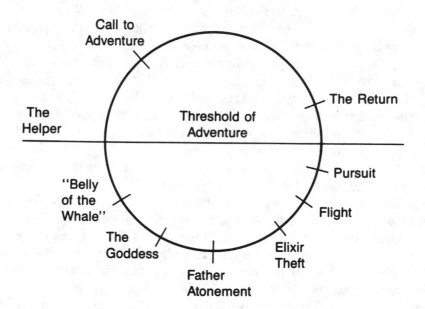

The hero at home doesn't know he (Campbell's "he" is supposed to stand for both male and female) is a hero. In the beginning, he is all latent potential. When he is called to adventure, he soon comes up against a barrier at the threshold of the land of adventure, the enchanted realm where great things are possible and people act larger larger than life. He is often aided by a helper to make this transition (Campbell tells us that this helper represents his own true self, the powers he didn't know he had). In the land of adventure, he soon finds himself in mortal danger, locked "in the belly of whale," as if dead. He escapes, however. He encounters a strong woman (an Oedipal mother figure) and a stern male (a father figure) who gives him tests so that he may prove himself worthy. He may find some elixir, some boon to help humanity, and he may have to steal it. Often the trip home amounts to a flight, with a dreaded enemy in hot pursuit. He arrives home eventually in a changed state: fully developed, often married (unifying the different parts of his personality), rich, perhaps recognized as the rightful king, or simply wise and at peace with himself.

"Hansel and Gretel," "Jack and the Beanstalk"—there are countless stories that conform closely to this scheme. Certainly, the self-conscious conventions of the story of "Petronella" fall into place when held up to Campbell's hero cycle. The call to adventure, the threshold, the helper, the testing by the father figure, the flight and pursuit, the return and presumed marriage are all there. There is one jarring element, however: the enchanter is clearly the stern father figure. Indeed, readers tend to exaggerate his sternness and describe him in fiercer terms than the author does. The enchanter's turning around and courting Petronella is somehow inappropriate. This courtship seems to bother male readers more than females although, on the other hand, males don't seem bothered by similar stories in which the hero wins the affections of an older but still beautiful queen.

With third, fourth, and fifth grade students, I don't think it is productive to talk about the hero cycle directly. Children find it more natural to compare the several stories for parallels in their events. We note that in "Hansel and Gretel" and "Jack and the Beanstalk" the heroes, too, leave home, are helped, seem irretrievably lost, and then manage to seize something valuable and bring it home with them. Then we compare how they are at the end—how they feel, how they are seen by others—with the way they were at the beginning. Were they secretly heroes all along, or was there something in their trials that made them heroes? We ask the children who the old man at the stump reminds them of or why the enchanter gave Petronella tasks that might have killed her—and what this challenge reminds them of in other stories. Or we ask them to compare a story about a heroic quest, such as "Petronella," or *The Book of Three*, with a more realistic story in which the gains are more ambiguous, such as *The Bridge to Terabithia* or *The Hundred Penny Box*.

Male and Female

The story of "Petronella" is a lot about male and female. How is a woman supposed to act to get by in the world? How is a man supposed to act? How have they been expected to act in the past, and what's wrong with these expectations? These themes are prominent in the story. How do we approach them? Here, as elsewhere, we like to start by giving ourselves some background to a discussion, even if we don't share this background directly with children.

Carol Gilligan[5] has put forward an interesting theory of male and female personality differences that goes a long way toward explaining the behavior of characters in "Petronella." Gilligan claims that males and females have different core themes in their personalities because of the earliest events in their lives.

Put briefly, when males are born to females, they first go through a period of a year or more of close attachment. Then, some time in the second year, they find it necessary to break away, to assert their own individuality. In the males' case, this striving for separation is particularly strong because they are not only different people from their mothers but are also different kinds of people, with different destinies. To a large extent, their self-definition will be based thereafter on otherness; the sense of separateness and isolation that begins with males in early childhood remains as a dominant theme in their personalities. It later disposes males to violence against others, which they often channel into competition. In Gilligan's view, males seek autonomy and competition and are threatened by relationships.

Females also go through an early period of separation. Because they are the same kind of person as the mother and share the same destiny, however, their urge toward autonomy is not so pronounced. From these early years on they stay related, and the organizing theme of their lives thereafter centers on relationships. Females seek relationships and are threatened by separation, according to Gilligan. The urge toward relationship is so strong in females, Gilligan believes, that they tend to be constantly putting their own interests behind everyone else's. The central developmental task of women, then, is to learn to balance their own interests with those of others. This does not mean they must accept the competitive struggles, with winners and losers, in which males typically engage. Females can continue to work within an ethic of care, in which everyone's best interests are taken into account.

Reminders of Gilligan's thinking are much in evidence in "Petronella." We asked a group of fourth graders why Petronella was the first person in sixty-three years to ask the old man at the crossroads the question that freed him.

"Because she's a woman," one girl said quickly.

"Why does that matter? Suppose she'd been a man?" we asked. "Men just look out for their own business without thinking about other people," the girl insisted. "A man would have found what he wanted to know and left the old man there, just like Petronella's brothers did." Two boys in the group reluctantly agreed.

"How about the tasks the enchanter put to Petronella? Would it have mattered then if she'd been a man?"

"A man would have tried to fight his way out, and he would have been killed," said another girl. "Petronella was able to get along with the animals because she was kind to them. That's the way she was: kind to other people—to people and animals, I mean."

In this discussion we talked about Petronella the girl, the female stereotypes she broke away from, and the female characteristics she embodied. I am usually inclined to center discussions solidly in the story so I might look at the ways these gender characteristics and stereotypes drove the story along, creating surprise at many points and lending interest and meaning to the actions of a character who was, really, very thinly drawn. We could, however, move away from the story and discuss gender roles themselves. The story makes us aware of many boy and girl stereotypes. What others can the children think of? Where do they come from? Which ones would we want to change, and how would we go about changing them?

Notes on Teaching

Levi-Strauss' opposites, Souriau's dramatic roles, Campbell's hero cycle, Gilligan's gender-based characteristics: We now have laid out four approaches to a better understanding of a story. How do we use them in the classroom?

The first consideration is "sparingly." As both Keith Stanovich and Paul Wilson have made clear in their chapters in this volume, the first goal of a reading program should be to cultivate the habit of reading for pleasure. If we accept that, we will encourage children to read widely and comment on what they enjoy about their reading, and just occasionally we will convene a group of them to inquire into their sense of the meaning of a story they all have read.

Then we can use the four approaches presented here in two ways: some we can use directly in discussing the stories children read and write; others will inform us as background—directing our curiosity toward a good question to ask or causing us to notice something a child has said about a story or written into a story of his or her own.

The dramatic roles of Etienne Souriau are used the first way. We can teach these roles to children explicitly—in my experience, from second grade on up. Typically, we remind them of a familiar story, such as "Jack and the Beanstalk," and then use that story to introduce each dramatic role, with its name. Then we invite the students to find characters that play these roles every time we discuss a story; nevertheless, once we've introduced them, we can readily refer to them from time to time when they seem to help us better understand the motives of a particular character.

We also talk to children in terms of these roles when the subject is the stories they write: Who is your hero, your lion force, in this story? What is her object—what does she really, really want? Who is her rival? Why is this rival standing in her way? Such questions have proven their worth in lending shape to children's stories.

Levi-Strauss' opposites are used to deepen discussions from third or fourth grade up. One session on "Jack and the Beanstalk," for example, had students contrasting Jack and the Giant. The students came up with a list like this:

Jack	The Giant
Small, young	Huge, adult
Seems weak, but clever	Seems strong, but stupid
Poor	Rich
Ambitious	Miserly
Nothing to lose	Everything to lose
On the way up	On the way down

Then they were asked to think of other contrasting pairs of characters that could fit into these columns. They thought of David and Goliath, Taran and the Horned King, Tom and Captain Najork, Tweety and Sylvester.

Even with younger children, we sometimes get at important contrasts by asking of one or more characters: What does this person really want? What does this person really not want? Petronella really wants to go off and fend for herself. She really does not want to stay home and wait for whatever turns up at her door. This question quite often takes us to what seems to be the heart of the story.

Campbell's hero cycle and Gilligan's gender theory are used rather as background. If we keep these theories in mind as we hear a student comment on a story or write one, we become more aware of their sense of the universals in literature, of the structural conventions that inform their understanding of literature.

Sometimes, however, a good question for discussion may be suggested by one of these theories. Campbell's hero cycle suggests questions that tap children's awareness of archetypes, deep-seated story conventions, in narratives. Asking questions like why Petronella was the first person to ask the old man the question that freed him explore the children's sense of what a helper is and their awareness of the gender-based stereotypes on which the story centers.

In any case, I believe the reader will find that the time spent in exploring these patterns—Levi-Strauss' opposites, Souriau's dramatic roles, Campbell's hero cycle, and Gilligan's gender themes—will be handsomely repaid in the light they shed on children's engagements with stories.

End Notes

1. Jay Williams, "Petronella," *Weavers,* ed. W. Durr. (Boston: Houghton-Mifflin, 1984).
2. Claude Levi-Strauss, "The Structural Study of Myth," *Structural Anthropology* (Garden City: Anchor Books, 1967).
3. Etienne Souriau, *Les Deux Cent Mille Situacions Dramatiques* (Paris: Flammarion, 1950). See summary in Robert Scholes, *Structuralism in Literature,* (New Haven: Yale University Press, 1975).
4. Joseph Campbell, *The Hero with a Thousand Faces* (2nd. ed.)(Princeton: Princeton University Press, 1968).
5. Carol Gilligan, *In a Different Voice* (Cambridge: Harvard University Press, 1982).

2

Reader-response Theory in the Elementary Classroom
Jonathan Lovell

Jonathan Lovell teaches in the English Department at the California State University at Santa Cruz. Trained in literature at Yale University, Lovell collaborated for several years with Diane Barone at the University of Nevada-Reno in a developmental study of children's responses to stories. They have published articles on their work in *Language Arts* and *The New Advocate*.

Grasping a Text

Teachers working with primary grade readers in "book-rich" elementary classrooms are in an ideal position to affirm the basic contention of reception-oriented reader-response theorists: Texts do not automatically imprint themselves on readers' minds; they trigger a process of reception that involves the reader in continuous interaction with the text. Any elementary teacher who has followed a beginning reader of an extended literary narrative through his or her sometimes startling, often unpredictable responses knows that while these stories set in motion a succession of responses we call reading, the product of that reading is as much a creation of the individual reader as it is a reflection of the text being read.

Wolfgang Iser offers one of the most extensive and detailed studies of how such a process might be understood in *The Act of Reading: A Theory of Aesthetic Response*.[1] In his fifth chapter, "Grasping a Text," Iser explains how literary narratives are uniquely structured so that they involve and engage readers in this dynamic interaction. Rather than presenting a succession of sentences, paragraphs, and chapters that build slowly toward a cumulative meaning, Iser argues that literary narratives are composed of successive segments, each of which requires a shift in a reader's perspective. Readers are led to enter the narrative first from one perspective, then a second, then a third, as their "wandering viewpoints" are alternately confirmed or challenged by what they have read.[2] Rather than simply flowing forward like a stream, a literary narrative situates readers in a sequence of viewpoints from which they project forward, based on what they have just read, and reflect backward, reexamining and transforming what they thought they understood.

Members of a group of readers reading along, chapter by chapter, in a work of literature will therefore come up with quite different understandings from each other of what they have just read, based on the different ways they have synthesized their new with their old information. These different responses can be compared and discussed, however, since each response will have been triggered, more or less fully, by the narrative's structure of shifting perspectives. Such discussions of differing interpretations will occur quite naturally, moreover, since part of the purpose of the narrative's shifting perspective structure is to nudge readers toward just such "gestalt-forming": relating different perspectives to one another in such a way that they make sense within a larger context that only the reader can supply.[3]

The reader's desire to resolve conflicting viewpoints and make sense of what he or she has read is labeled "consistency-building" by Iser, who calls it "the indispensable basis for all acts of comprehension"[4]. Literary narratives convey their sense of immediacy and "presentness" by constantly inviting readers to create consistencies out of the network of different perspectives they have introduced. "We do not grasp [what we have read] like an empirical object," Iser concludes, "nor do we comprehend it like a predicative fact; it owes its presence in our minds to our own reactions, and it is these that make us animate the meaning of the text as a reality."[5]

Reflecting back on the choice of phrase—'grasping a text'—that Iser uses to describe this process, we can experience one of those sudden shifts in perspective that Iser mentioned. Starting with the expectation that Iser will most likely be referring in his chapter to how readers learn to seize or embrace the meaning of a literary text, we are left at the end of this chapter with a far more dynamic and even comical image. Just as children enjoy playing with a partly filled balloon, squeezing it hard so that it will squirt out in unexpected shapes and contours, so readers in Iser's model keep grasping tightly for meaning as they read, only to be startled by the lively and unexpected ways the literary work's meaning reemerges in new and unpredictable configurations.

Reading and Responding to Literature in a Primary Classroom

Iser's theory of aesthetic response helps make sense of the attraction for beginning readers of narratives such as Beverly Cleary's Ramona books. The strong overlap between the principal character's concerns and experiences and those of the reader help the elementary child initially enter deeply and engagingly into Ramona's perspective. But the narrator's "outside" perspective, as she observes and records the goings on in Ramona's world, invites readers to step outside Ramona's perspective, seeing her through others' eyes. By nudging the beginning reader in and out of Ramona's own way of viewing her world, Cleary's narratives promote the very "consistency building" among multiple perspectives that Iser describes as the hallmark of literary response. Artfully written books like *Ramona the Brave* can therefore give even the youngest beginning readers the absorbing and engaging reading experience we generally associate primarily with well-known works of literature read by experienced adult readers.

How can teachers maintain the excitement and involvement generated by such simply but elegantly structured chapter books when their students move beyond this initial encounter with longer works of fiction? What concerns should primary teachers have at this point for balancing the rewards of reading increasingly challenging and lengthy works of narrative fiction against the sense of frustration their students might feel if their attempts at comprehension are too consistently defeated? How can teachers select books that continue to foster the dynamic interaction with a text that gives the act of reading its sense of animated aliveness without intimidating all but their most able primary year readers?

In order to begin to answer these questions, Diane Barone, a primary teacher, and I worked over a three-year period with the students in her mixed-grade demonstration classroom of first, second, and third graders. As we followed these students year by year in their development as readers, we began to introduce increasingly lengthy and challenging works of fiction to those second and third graders who had moved beyond Cleary's chapter books, monitoring their responses to these works as they read them. In what follows I will explore the written responses of three students from this group as they read Roald Dahl's *Danny the Champion of the World*[6] and wrote responses to this work in dialogue journals, which each of them kept from the beginning to the end of the school year (see Diane Barone, " 'That Reminds Me Of': Using Dialogue Journals with Young Students," in this volume).

The group of nine second and third grade students who read *Danny the Champion of the World* (hereafter *Danny*) were introduced to this novel in January of the third year of our study and were given twenty-one class days (from the end of January to the middle of March) to read the novel's twenty-two chapters. *Danny* was the third of four lengthy children's novels the group as a whole read during the year, following Beverly Cleary's *Dear Mr. Henshaw* and Robert C. O'Brien's *The Secret of NIMH* and preceding Zilpha Keatley Snyder's *The Egypt Game*. All four of these longer works of fiction were experimental in the sense that they were being tried out for the first time with this top reading group, although two of the students in this group had already experienced such an enriched language arts curriculum the prior year (reading E.L. Koningsburg's *From the Mixed-Up Files of Mrs. Basil E. Frankweiler*) as second grade members of the most advanced reading group.

What makes the students' responses to *Danny* so valuable as a window on literary responses of elementary students in general is that this novel was the first work of longer fiction that the group as a whole responded to with the enthusiasm they had previously shown only for the Ramona books. Mary Martha, one of the three second graders in the group, expressed this general opinion in her final journal entry on the novel: "I liked the whole book because it was never boring. And it was always exiting and always explaind but the rats of nhim didn't." It was exactly this delicate and difficult balance between "excitement" and "explanation" that Diane and I were attempting to strike in the longer works of fiction selected for this top reading group. With *Danny*, we seem to have succeeded. Might the success of this novel with this group of nine readers be understood in terms of reception theory? Further, might it be explained in such a way to provide a guide for others interested in providing an enriching and appropriately challenging literature curriculum for their elementary students?

To gain an understanding of how this group of second and third graders successfully made their way through this long and demanding children's novel, I will focus on their responses to three separate moments in the story: Danny's description of the caravan in which he and his father lived (Chapter 1), Danny's discovery of his father's "most private and secret habit" of poaching pheasants from a rich neighbor's woods (Chapter 4), and Danny's own invention of a new way to poach pheasants by putting sleeping powder in raisins that his father stealthily fed to the birds (Chapter 11). In each of these sections of the novel, students were asked either to respond directly to what they had read or to create a cluster of associations around the chapter heading in anticipation of what they were going to read. It is therefore possible, in a rough and exploratory way, to compare the different ways that individual students in the group were making sense of the text of this narrative at these specific points in the story.

Danny's Caravan

Like the Ramona books, *Danny* focuses on the experiences and perceptions of a young person who is close in age—nine years old—to its readers. Unlike Cleary's better known narratives of Ramona's exploits, however, Dahl uses Danny to narrate his own story, thereby inviting his young readers to assume the perspective of his principal character from the novel's opening pages. Danny begins by telling his readers that his mother died when he was four months old, that his father thereafter looked after him "all by himself," and that he "had no brothers or sisters." In these respects readers in Diane's class might have recalled Leigh Botts from Beverly Cleary's *Dear Mr. Henshaw*: also nine, also a single child with a single parent. Third grader Nicole seemed to be preparing herself for just such a story, in fact, when she responded to the book's cover illustration of Danny and his father walking together in the woods with the words, "It looks like his parnts are dyvorst."

Contrary to the expectation of a difficult and perhaps lonely home life that these opening sentences suggest, however, Danny goes on to describe a "house and home" whose intimate scale and exotic appearance convey a protective sense of security mixed with a suggestion of "outlaw" excitement:

> We lived in an old gypsy caravan behind [my father's] filling station . . . The caravan was our house and our home. It was a real old gypsy wagon with big wheels and fine patterns painted all over it in yellow and red and blue. My father said that it was at least one hundred and fifty years old . . . There was only one room in the caravan, and it wasn't much bigger than a fair-sized modern bathroom. It was a narrow room, the shape of the caravan itself, and against the back wall were two bunk beds, one above the other. The top one was my father's, the bottom one mine. . . There was a wood-burning stove with a chimney that went up through the roof, and this kept us warm in winter. There was a kerosene burner on which to boil a kettle or cook a stew, and there was a kerosene lamp hanging from the ceiling. . . . For furniture, we had two chairs and a small table, and those, apart from a tiny chest of drawers, were all the home comforts we possessed.[7]

Since Diane's students were reading these words on the first day (January 26) that *Danny* had been assigned to them, they might have been expected to be primarily concerned with what this story was going to be about rather than with the picture created by these initial details. It is instructive to see, however, just what their different illustrations captured and what they left out when they were asked by Diane to "take one page [of your dialogue journals] and draw the inside of the caravan" in response to this first day's reading.

Mary Martha's depiction was the most carefully attentive to the narrative's details, as her responses in her dialogue journal tended to be throughout the school year. Here is what she drew as her rendering of the inside of Danny's caravan-home (Figure 2-1).

Figure 2-1.

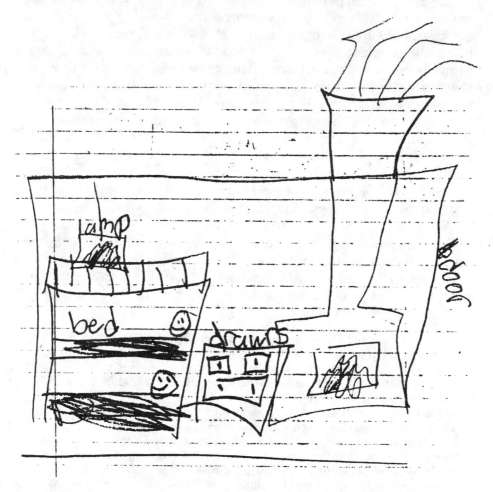

For a second grade reader beginning quite a demanding story, her illustration rendered the bunk beds, wood-burning stove, and "tiny chest of drawers" with remarkable accuracy. The lamp, as one might expect, looked more like a modern electric appliance than the kerosene lamp Danny's description intended, but Mary Martha had it appropriately "hanging from the ceiling" and cleverly placed it over by the beds to provide a second light source to balance the firelight from the wood-burning stove. Even more impressive, however, Mary Martha's illustration adhered quite precisely to the characteristic features of the scene that Danny describes in the concluding sentences of his opening chapter. "I really loved living in that gypsy caravan," Danny explains.

"I loved it especially in the evenings when I was tucked up in my bunk and my father was telling me stories. The kerosene lamp was turned low, and I could see lumps of wood glowing red-hot in the old stove, and wonderful it was to by lying there snug and warm in my bunk in that little room. Most wonderful of all was the feeling that when I went to sleep, my father would still be there, very close to me. . .lying in the bunk above my own."[8]

Turning from Mary Martha's response to third grader Michael's illustration (Figure 2-2), one might be justified in asking whether or not these two readers were responding to the same words from the same opening chapter. To make such a statement, however, would be to overlook some fascinating ways that Michael's drawing suggested that he was going about his own very different version of "consistency building." While Michael's illustration was certainly less responsive than Mary Martha's to the particulars of Danny's description of his caravan home, it was equally triggered, in a more general way, by elements from the novel's opening chapter.

Figure 2-2.

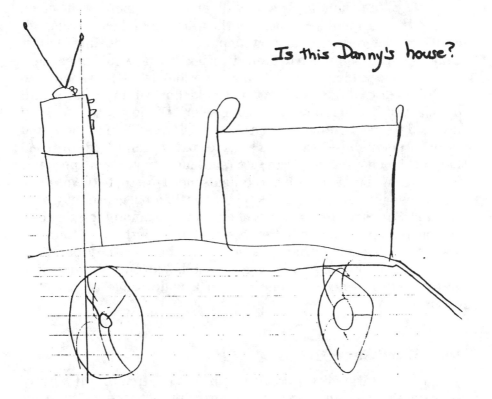

Diane's question in response to Michael's drawing—''Is this Danny's house?''—was certainly the appropriate one, since his illustration initially appeared so little related to the text. It is helpful to notice, however, that Michael's drawing captured at least one aspect of Danny's description that Mary Martha's illustration left out: its past history as a gypsy caravan. To represent this element Michael leaned rather heavily on the illustration of the caravan that appears in the first chapter, but he peered imaginatively ''inside'' the caravan walls of this illustration to discover a bed (with headboard, footboard, and pillow), a stand of some sort, and a television set! The presentation of Danny's caravan in the first chapter's text and illustration triggered for Michael the creation of an image that combined the security of his own home, with his much beloved bedside television set, and the adventure of gypsy travel. While he had not internalized the narrator's perspective as Mary Martha had done, he had at least begun the process of matching the new information in Danny's description against his own prior knowledge and experience. This process, as we shall see, eventually drew him successively further away from the television-oriented world with which he was familiar and toward the somewhat fantastical story-oriented world that Danny inhabits and describes.

The way Diane handled the wide diversity of responses she often received to the opening chapters of these longer and more demanding narratives reflected her own commitment to an interactive, reader-centered approach to literary response. She would raise questions for her students in their dialogue journals—in response to Nicole's claim that Danny's home had a ''kichin, a living room, a bath room, a desk, 2 bed rooms and a wine seler,'' Diane wrote,'' Are you sure? Did you read the description of Danny's house?''—and she would ask her students when they met as a group if anything had confused them in the chapter they had just read. Most important, perhaps, Diane was quite patient with her students' need to situate themselves, each in his or her own way, in relation to the fictional world they were entering. She established a basis of consistency among the group as a whole by writing down in her lesson plan book three or four key events for each chapter that could serve as a check on the group's collective understanding, but beyond these key events she not only allowed but also actively encouraged a wide range of personal responses.

Deep Dark Secrets

The most dramatic shift from the picture of an intimate and warmly secure world that Danny presents in the opening chapters of his story occurs in the fourth chapter, entitled "My Father's Deep Dark Secret." It is in this chapter that Danny learns about the "outlaw" side of his father's personality—his fascination with illegally poaching the pheasants from rich Mr. Hazell's nearby wood.

Diane prepared her students for reading this chapter by asking them to create clusters in their journals on the topic of secrets. "Ones [once] me and Jessice snuck cocklet cookies," wrote Nicole in one of her cluster's "bubbles," while Mary Martha wrote, "you don't want anyone to hear" and "I tell Sarah my secrets." Although these students were not being asked at this point to make any explicit connections to the narrative they had been reading, their prior knowledge was already helping them anticipate this chapter's focus on sharing new knowledge with an intimate friend and having this knowledge connected in some way with "outlaw" activities.

What neither Nicole's nor Mary Martha's clusters could have anticipated, however, is the abrupt and, for a child Danny's age, quite frightening way that this new knowledge is introduced. The "telegraphic-style" journal entry that Michael wrote after finishing this chapter—a style of writing he used frequently in response to the opening chapters of longer narratives—captured quite poignantly the drama of Danny's discovery. "Here I am at the age of nine," Michael's entry began, exactly repeating the opening sentence of the chapter, "and I din't have a worry in the woled." He next repeated the opening phrase of the next paragraph—"you will learn as you get older"—and then jumped immediately to the chapter's dramatic center: "Dad I shoted [shouted] Dad I don't know how long I sat there then a figer aperd it was him. He was up in Hazlis [Hazell's] wood he said that's six miles away."

Michael's summarizing journal entry recounted quite effectively the frightening experience Danny relates in this chapter of waking up in the middle of the night to discover his father is gone, absent from his familiar place in the bunk above him in their caravan home. While Dahl uses this incident to provide a motive for Danny's father to tell his son, after he has returned home later that evening, about his poaching expeditions, it is clear that the description (and accompanying illustration) of Danny sitting alone in "deathly" silence, waiting on the caravan steps with his blanket wrapped around him (25–26), profoundly affected all three of the readers we have been following. Both Mary Martha and Nicole chose the line "I don't know how long I sat there" as a point of departure for their double-entry draft responses to this chapter, recording these words from the chapter on the left side of their divided journal page and writing what recollections these words prompted for them on the right. As we have seen,

Michael also included these same lines as the center of the telegraphic-style, summarizing entry he wrote after finishing his reading of this fourth chapter.

What makes these similar choices significant is that they correspond to the first point in the narrative where readers are explicitly invited to go beyond what they have been told, reconfiguring what they thought they understood about Danny's relationship to his father. This invitation to resee the story from a new and larger perspective is provided by Danny himself in an aside that he includes in the chapter's second paragraph (referred to briefly above in reference to Michael's telegraphic-style journal response).

> You will learn as you get older, just as I learned that autumn, that no father is perfect. Grown-ups are complicated creatures, full of quirks and secrets. Some have quirkier quirks and deeper secrets than others, but all of them, including one's own parents, have two or three private habits hidden up their sleeves that would probably make you gasp if you knew about them.[9]

The import of this aside, as we learn later in the chapter, is that Danny's own father is willing to risk his own life, so it seems to Danny, as well as the security he has provided for his son, in order to satisfy his passion for pheasant poaching. While Danny does not say so directly, he clearly cannot absorb this new information without changing his understanding of his relationship to his father. What he does, appropriately enough, is ask to join his father in his poaching expeditions, establishing a new bond between them that is based on their shared sense of risk and outlaw ingenuity. What is equally interesting, however, is how the reading of Danny's account of this crucial episode prompted recollections by Nicole and Mary Martha that are themselves tentative and explorative forays into moments in their lives where they were beginning to define an identity separate from their parents.

Danny's ''I don't know how long I sat there'' passage prompted Nicole to recollect those moments when she was at her friend's house and her mother came ''to[o] erly,'' just as she was ''getting something out'' to play with, while Mary Martha recalled when she was four and rode her ''trycicle'' around the driveway, then would ''sit on the porch for a half an hour'' and play with her dolls. Each in her own way signaled in these responses that she has begun to think about her own emerging ''grown-up'' identity. In Mary Martha's response there was even the further suggestion that she was tentatively reconfiguring her own past, seeing her four-year-old moments of play-acting adult roles as part of a life-story narrative leading toward actual adulthood.

Although such interpretations of Nicole's and Mary Martha's responses are necessarily quite speculative, the choice that both these readers made to respond to the content of this chapter in double-entry draft form, and to use the "that reminds me of" format for their responses, shows that the novel was triggering for both of them the "stepping back and reflecting" function that Iser describes as so essential if the process of reading is to "animate" a literary text.

The Sleeping Beauty

It is difficult to argue for the power and value of the successive acts of immersion and distancing that characterize young readers' deepening sense of engagement with an extended narrative text if these individual readers' responses are simply described and compared as they read and respond to occasional chapters. In this final section of my argument, therefore, I will focus more broadly on one student, Michael, and how his responses to a single chapter from the middle of the novel might be related to his earlier and later responses. Looking at this larger pattern of responses will provide a fuller picture of how this novel became "animate" for this one reader and will, perhaps, make the case more convincingly for the value of introducing readers in their primary years to longer children's novels such as Dahl's *Danny the Champion of the World*.

The chapter I will use as my point of departure for examining Michael's overall pattern of responses is called "The Sleeping Beauty." Coming halfway through the story, the eleventh of the novel's twenty-two chapters, this title is one of the cleverly teasing verbal jokes that Dahl frequently uses in his fictions. Rather than anticipating a focus on the well-known fairy tale, the title in fact refers to "a methend" (as Michael calls it) for catching "fesen'ts" by slitting open water-soaked raisins, pouring small amounts of sleeping powder into them, and then sewing them back up. Danny, who invents and explains this method to his father in the chapter's first two pages, reasons that these "doctored" raisins could then be stealthily scattered on the floor of the well-guarded wood so that the pheasants would eat them before they flew up into their trees to roost for the night. Then Danny and his father could return to the wood at night, after the keepers have gone home, and there should be, as Michael puts it, "fesn'ts all over the place falling asleep to the ground." In admiration for his son's ingenuity, Danny's father names this method "The Sleeping Beauty," exclaiming that it will become "a landmark in the history of poaching!"[10]

The post-chapter journal entry Michael used to describe this complicated "methend" indicated quite clearly that by this point in his reading his level of comprehension had increased significantly beyond the tentative and confused perceptions his illustration of Danny's caravan-home suggested. This deepening sense of connection to the world of the novel is exactly what could have been predicted from Iser's model of how readers and texts become powerfully interanimate as the reading process unfolds. Michael's increasing confidence as a reader is still worth noting, however, given the focus that teacher-training in elementary level reading instruction has placed on not exceeding a young reader's "frustration level" in assigning texts for them to read. If a teacher were to have made such a determination while watching Michael read and respond to the initial chapters of Danny, it is not likely that he would have been encouraged to continue with the novel. In fact, it is not until the seventh chapter that Michael's confidence increased sufficiently for him to depart from his summarizing entries and begin the double entry draft form of response that Nicole and Mary Martha were writing by the end of their first week of reading (see Barone's "Using Dialogue Journals" in section two for the correlation between double entry draft writing and more assured modes of literary response among primary grade readers).

While it is heartening to see how quickly and confidently Michael at this point in his reading was able to "correct" the predictions he initially made about the content of this chapter, it is equally important to look carefully at what his initial predictions were and why he might have made them (Figure 2-3).

Michael's three short associations with the "Sleeping Buetey" chapter title—"prety," "gril asleep," and "nice"—all appear to have been referring to his recollections of the fairy tale. His fourth circled response—"mabe Danny's Dad is telling a story to Danny"—referred back to the novel's second chapter, where Danny had described what a "marvelous storyteller"[11] his father was and had recounted one extended bedtime story he told called "The Big Friendly Giant" (a story Dahl later wrote himself as a book, calling it *The BFG*). It is Michael's uncircled fifth and longest response, however, that stands out most strikingly from his cluster. With apparent confidence, Michael predicted that the eleventh chapter would describe how "Danny's Dad falls in love with a gril that is asleep."

Initially, this final prediction seems a bit like Michael's inclusion of the television set in Danny's caravan. It tells us a good deal more about Michael than it does about his interaction with this narrative. Yet as with Michael's unusual attention to the "gypsy" element in Danny's earlier description of his home, so in this seemingly quirky response to "The Sleeping Beauty" Michael once again brought out a dimension of Dahl's story that is only suggested at this point but which will figure more prominently in subsequent chapters.

Figure 2-3.

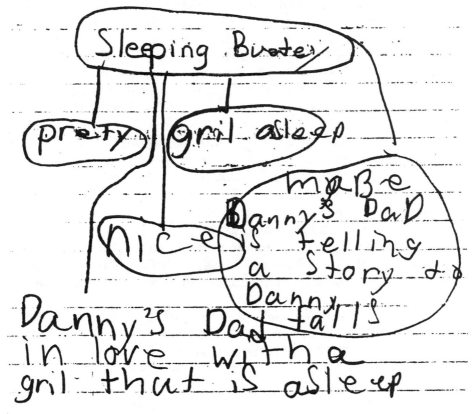

Bruno Bettelheim's *The Uses of Enchantment: The Meaning and Importance of Fairy Tales* provides the clearest insight into this dimension when he points out the connection between the sleep that the young girl of the fairy tales undergoes and the necessary periods of lethargy that adolescents go through—particularly female adolescents approaching menstruation—in their progress toward adulthood.[12] In this reading of the fairy tale, the adult prince who awakens the princess with a kiss signals her emergence from adolescent quiescence into sexual maturity. For Michael to imagine Danny's dad fulfilling this prince's role would suggest that he was reading *Danny* in part as a tale of sexual and social growth towards adulthood. Somewhat ominously, however, for Michael it seemed to be a growth for Danny's father only, leaving Danny himself entirely behind. If Danny's father were to fall in love with a "prety" girl "that is asleep," what role would be left for Danny? Since most readers are likely to expect Danny and his father to progress in some fashion beyond the almost womblike conditions of their caravan world, the only real question is how Michael might have arrived at this curiously ominous prediction as his own answer to this unresolved dimension of the narrative.

One can begin to answer this question by looking back at the cluster on "what you like about your dad" that Diane asked her students to create on the second day of their *Danny* reading. In addition to the somewhat predictable bubbles Michael created for his cluster on this topic—'my Dad takes me to the beach," "fun," "he tikels you," "he gives me toys"—he added two bubbles with the poignantly misspelled phrases "lost of work" and "do losts of work," and added the unusually expressed "he is going to have Baby." What Michael was referring to in this last bubble for his cluster was that his divorced father, having recently married a younger wife, was about to have a second child by this second wife. Is it any wonder that Michael, worried about the division that the arrival of this baby would be likely to create between himself and his father, would have been particularly aware of the possibilities for a similar separation between father and son in the narrative he was reading? Looking back at Michael's illustration of Danny's caravan-home, might the prominence that he gave to the wheels under this home be suggestive as well of his own doubts about the durability of the secure and intimate father-son world that Danny inhabits?

Such knowledge of Michael's personal background certainly helps make sense of his prediction that Danny's dad would fall in love with a "prety" girl, but how do the remaining chapters of this novel challenge Michael's conviction that, for one reason or another, there would come a separation between father and son? Consistent with what we have already noticed about Michael's journal responses, the answer to this question comes in terms of what he wrote in response to the second half of Danny about two of his favorite topics: toys and wheels. His responses to the latter chapters of Danny were written almost entirely in the form of double entry drafts using the "that reminds me of" form of response, but what he chose to write about in these entries, if read consecutively, constitutes a parallel story to the one he was reading—a personal story that makes an intriguing and sobering commentary on the *Danny* narrative.

If it makes sense to understand Michael's initial "he gives me toys" response in his "dad" cluster as holding out the possibility of future connectedness with his father against the separation suggested by "he is going to have [a] Baby," the double-entry draft response that Michael wrote one month later, after reading the novel's nineteenth chapter, takes on special significance. Responding to the point in the narrative where Danny's father is inviting Doc Spencer over to the filling station to share the "little surprise" of the poached pheasants, Michael wrote that this passage reminded him of when he went to his father's house and his dad said, "I have a sprise. It was a little car."

Yet by the very next entry Michael was recalling how a friend of his stood on his toy box and "broke all [his] toys," and in his last chapter-related entry he recalled (in response to the flying away of the reawakened pheasants) that he finally lost his "littel cars" and never recovered them.

So does Michael read the *Danny* story as a parable of the inevitable sundering of parents and children in general, and fathers and sons in particular? Certainly his responses to the final chapters of this novel suggest a rather somber view, not significantly modified by the novel's humorous and quite optimistic conclusion (i.e., Doc Spencer reveals six pheasants that were too overdosed with sleeping powder to fly away, and Danny and his father plan a pheasant dinner for the doctor and his wife). Yet if we look at Michael's final journal entry assessing what he liked best about the reading of *Danny*, we can detect a somewhat more interanimate relationship between this reader and the narrative that has been occupying his attention for the past twenty-two days. "I like the chapter goodby Mr Hazle [the best]," he wrote, "because [that was when] all the fesens got his car." Like a grown-up version of Michael in his love for his "littel cars," Mr. Hazell was inordinately fond of his "big shiny silver Rolls-Royce'—a "toy" that gave him the stature and prestige his actions could not come close to winning for him. When the reawakened pheasants that Danny and his father had poached "festooned" this elegant vehicle, "scratching and scrabbling and making their disgusting runny messes over the shiny silver paint,"[13] Mr. Hazell simply fumed at the birds and drove off, "the great Rolls [shooting] off down the road with clouds of pheasants rising up from it in all directions."[14] But then an extraordinary thing happened:

> The pheasants that had flown up off the car stayed up in the air. They didn't come flapping drunkenly down as we had expected them to. They stayed up and kept on flying. Over the top of the filling station they flew, and over the caravan, and over the field at the back where our little outdoor lavatory stood, and over the next field, and over the crest of the hill—until they disappeared from sight.[15]

The pheasants "got" Mr. Hazell's car, as Michael clearly delighted in recalling, but in another sense Mr. Hazell's car "got" the pheasants—woke them up to their unexpected "maturity" and their capacity to fly by themselves, above the secure and familiar world Danny describes in his narrative and on toward unknown horizons. Is it too much to assume that Michael was moving toward a similar higher perspective when he stepped back from his reading of this long and engrossing narrative and reflected on the comic picture of those seemingly clumsy, dumb, bumbling pheasants making a mess of proud

Mr. Hazell's elegant car, then discovering that, lo and behold, they can fly perfectly adequately all on their own?

Conclusion

Not only are readers in their primary years capable of reading fine children's novels—works that might be collectively referred to as the imaginative "sons and daughters" of E.B. White's *Charlotte's Web*— but they are also provided by their reading of such novels an opportunity to engage at a deep and significant level with the animateness we attribute to significant literature and to experience for themselves the reasons that our culture holds its greatest works of fiction in such high esteem.

To enter the imaginative worlds of such extended works of fiction requires time on the part of young readers and patience on the part of their teachers, however, since the routes that different readers take into these worlds will necessarily be quite different ones, as will the pace of their entry. As our reseeing of Michael's illustration of Danny's caravan-home has indicated, even the most seemingly arbitrary and divergent responses to literary narratives by young readers hold the possibility of being understood—sometimes in quite striking ways— when viewed in relationship to the totality of their responses to the literary work.

Iser's model of the reading process helps us see that the activity of immersion and distancing that characterizes the back and forth movement between a reader and a work of literature is best fostered by longer literary narratives, while Diane's practice of using dialogue journals as a complement to her whole group discussions, chapter by chapter, provides elementary teachers with a method of making the collective reading of such extended narratives accessible to a wide range of students with quite diverse ability levels.

Perhaps most important, however, the activity of following a young reader making his or her way through an engrossing literary narrative and working hard to understand how this young reader came up with the successive readings renews our own adult belief in the transforming and inspiriting power of story. Without such a belief, reconfirmed daily in our classrooms by the very differences we experience between ourselves and our students as co-readers, can we be truly said to be teaching in book-rich elementary classrooms?

End Notes

1. Wolfgang Iser, *The Act of Reading: A Theory of Aesthetic Response* (Baltimore: The Johns Hopkins University Press, 1978).

2. Iser, 108–118.
3. Iser, 118–123.
4. Iser, 125.
5. Iser, 129.
6. Roald Dahl, *Danny, the Champion of the World* (New York: Bantam Skylark, 1978).
7. Dahl, 3:5–7.
8. Dahl, 3:7.
9. Dahl, 3:23.
10. Dahl, 3:94.
11. Dahl, 3:9.
12. Bruno Bettelheim, *The Uses of Enchantment: The Meaning and Importance of Fairy Tales* (New York: Alfred Knopf, 1976), 225–236.
13. Dahl, 3:181.
14. Dahl, 3:182.
15. Dahl, 3:183.

3

Of Elephants and Savages
Ariel Dorfman

Ariel Dorfman is a novelist, playwright, and essayist who is also professor of International Studies at Duke University. A Chilean citizen, he was exiled from his country in 1973. He came to the United States in 1980. He has written about popular American and European literature, including children's literature, from a Third World perspective. In this chapter he lays bare the social and political messages in the first three books of the Babar the Elephant series—*The Story of Babar, Babar the King,* and *The Travels of Babar*—all by Jean de Brunhoff. We urge you to reread these books before reading Mr. Dorfman's brilliant chapter, taken from his book *The Empire's Old Clothes* (Pantheon, 1983).

Once upon a time, there were two children in a faraway land. One day their mother made up a story, as mothers sometimes do, about a little elephant.

This particular character, however, was not destined to be forgotten like so many other clumsy and adorable animals that inhabit the stories spun at the edge of the bed before the lights go out. This elephant would make a greater name for himself and attract a much more significant audience.

It just so happens that the elephant's father was a painter, and once he had baptized the elephant with the name Babar, he proceeded to illustrate his life in a series of children's books that would one day achieve worldwide acclaim.[1] Babar, owing to his peculiar education and ties to the world of men, would become king of the elephants and redeem and transform his country. On the other hand, even though the painter would not be crowned a king among men, he would, because of his tender, sensual, and simple style, come to be regarded as one of the princes of children's literature.

When the story is told like that—as the triumphant march of a character and his author—and recreated like a legend or a fairy tale, it could not seem more innocent and less worthy of critical analysis.

Babar is born like any average pachyderm. He grows up and plays in an idyllic world, along with the other little animals. Nonetheless, this primitive paradise must come to an end once a "wicked hunter" kills Babar's mother. Even though this initial contact with human adults and their civilization is negative—leaving Babar an orphan—the end result of such destructive activity turns out to be highly beneficial: Babar escapes to the bedazzling city, where fate rewards him with something even greater than what it had taken from him. He comes upon an "Old Lady," a female figure who takes his mother's place and eventually adopts him.

From that moment on, Babar is going to "progress." His initial desire is to be "well-dressed," and the Old Lady gives him all the money he needs. In the first few pictures he walks on four feet, but no sooner has he lost his horizontal nakedness and seen his clothed twin in a mirror than he becomes aware of his stature, his skin, his clothes. Babar rises up on two feet. He mimics men and begins to adopt biped mannerisms. That is when his education begins. Somehow, without losing his animal appearance, Babar will be transformed into a polite and decent human being. He uses a napkin, sleeps in a bed, does exercises, has his picture taken, bathes in a tub with a sponge, drives his own car, and dresses in the latest fashions. He's a pampered elephant, because the Old Lady "gives him whatever he wants." Babar responds by leaving behind the ignorance of his instincts, following the teachings and examples of the world that has given him refuge and learning how to behave in the proper manner. He also picks up some practical skills: A learned professor comes to teach him how to read and write, add and subtract, and interpret history and geography.

Could there be anything less pernicious?

Young readers are encouraged to conduct themselves in a similar manner: They should be obedient and intelligent, have good manners, get dressed by themselves, and eat with a knife and fork. Supposedly the child starts from the same point as Babar, free from social influences, and only gradually begins to lose his savage and ignorant ways in order to become a responsible member of society. He crawls on all fours and then, still babbling, begins to walk. One innocent identifies with another, and together they grow up. But be careful: There's more to this process than mere socialization. In a corner of the picture in which the learned professor teaches Babar 4 + 3, there is a map of the world where one can distinguish the continent known by its Greek name: Africa.

At this point in the story it is necessary to furnish the reader with a few uncomfortable historical facts. The year in which this charming tale was written was not once upon a time but 1931. It should be added that sixty years ago the countries of Africa, the supposed land of the elephants, had not yet achieved their independence. They were still colonies.

This is why Babar is something more than a child growing up. In contrast to his tiny admirers, he is dealing with a native country that has not evolved along with him and continues to be primitive, tribal, and naked. It is out of that reality—or, more precisely, out of those areas of his personality that can never be suppressed or erased, out of that ever present animality—that emissaries come to seek him out. There appear before him two totally naked little elephants. Although it may seem indecent in this childlike atmosphere, let us emphasize the word "naked."

That first contact between the now civilized (we might even say adult) Babar and the other elephants, who are like reflections of the way he once was, prophetically synthesizes the future of the country in which they all were born, for his cousins are immediately absorbed into the Old Lady's sphere of influence. She dresses them, and as a reward for having taken their first wobbly steps, they all go and have some cake. As Mary Poppins sings in the Walt Disney film, "Just a spoonful of sugar helps the medicine go down."

The time has now come for that medicine, with its domesticating sweetness, to be sent back to the jungle. There's no danger that Babar will revert to his primitive ways. As demonstrated by the rapid conversion of his cousins, this kind of education is contagious. From now on, every inferior place or person will either follow Babar's example or remain condemned to immobility, regression, and ridicule.

Such is the case when they leave Paris, all dressed up and perched victoriously with their suitcases on top of a car. Horns blaring and people cheering, they seem like tourists off to some out-of-the-way place. But who could that be behind them, running on all fours, choking on the dust churned up by the automobile? Could it be two big elephants?

Sure enough, it's the mothers of the two rascals who, it seems, had escaped from the jungle without asking permission. Their mothers have been looking for them. In a pedagogical book such as this, in which the virtues of submission and respect for one's elders are extolled, such disobedience cannot go unpunished. So, during their first confrontation with their unruly children (in a previous scene), the irate mothers scold the two little elephants, who show themselves to be repentant and contrite. However, once this elevated ethical function has been performed, things change. The youngsters are now fully clothed and upright, while the good ladies who supposedly brought them into the world still look at the horizon horizontally—and in the buff, to boot. They must run behind the vehicle that carries their progeny farther in the direction of progress.

This is the last time we shall see them. Whereas Babar's mother was eliminated by a depraved hunter, the mothers of Celeste and Arthur will be exterminated with more kindness and less trauma. They will be forgotten like so many others who did not know how to respond fast enough to the modern artifacts offered them by history. The painter's brush will simply omit them.

In contrast, the narrator tells us as Babar leaves that "he would never forget the Old Lady."

He's going to need her. For the king of the elephants has died accidentally. He's eaten a poisonous mushroom, proving himself stupid and ineffectual by doing something even the youngest readers would be careful not to do. The three oldest elephants get together to choose the new king. They are "extremely upset"; it is an "ill-fated day"; "what a calamity." Such are the circumstances of Babar's arrival like some kind of Messiah who will solve their problems.

Actually, the only difference between the previous king of the elephants and everyone else was the crown he wore on his head; but if he (presumably the very best of the elephants) behaves so irresponsibly, what are we to expect from the rest of them? The new ruler must come from the outside, a native instructed in the ways of men.

While the older elephants frantically deliberate, Babar has just left that prestigious town (complete with houses, a plaza, airplanes, a church, cars, monuments, and neatly planted fields in the background), bearing all the illustrious signs of his ties to that world. His reception in Elephantland is overwhelming. "What beautiful clothes you're wearing! What a lovely car!" Compared to the large, undifferentiated mass of gray that greets them, Babar, Celeste, and Arthur stand out because of their defined personalities. They've got color, movement, and savoir faire—the upright, external signs of their assimilation of the values, objects, and concepts of the fascinating and unknown universe of *Homo sapiens*. In a barbaric world such as this, where everyone is naive and defenseless, Babar's proximity to the Western cosmos (the adult cosmos), to the illustrious center, now and in future episodes will become the foundation of his investiture, the fount of his regency. And that's just how Cornelius, the oldest and wisest of the elephants, sees it when he suggests that they crown

Babar: "He's learned so much in the city." The other elephants agree because Cornelius has spoken like a book—in other words, like a cultural object laden with authority and wisdom, which men control and elephants do not.[2] At the outset, Cornelius is distinguished from his colleagues by a pair of spectacles. This small sign of urbanity singles him out for his function as interpreter or mediator, making him similar to the first blacks or Indians who had to learn the language of their conquerors.

Cornelius's reward isn't far behind. "You have good ideas," Babar tells him, even though the only one he's had was to proclaim the new arrival king. "I will therefore make you general, and when I get my crown, I will give you my hat." Whoever helps to place him in power is rewarded with the distinguishing features of civilization and the privileges that pertain to it. Babar imitates men. Cornelius imitates Babar. Eventually everyone will imitate Cornelius. The entire country will have to elevate itself. So the first thing Babar does to legitimize his pretension to the throne isn't surprising. He tells "the dromedary to go to the town and buy some beautiful wedding clothes." During the celebration that follows—which is also a wedding reception, since Babar is marrying the only female to equal him in hierarchy or status, his cousin Celeste—all the invited animals (mouse, lizard, hippopotamus, leopard, lion, rhinoceros, giraffe, and, naturally, the elephants) get up on two legs for the first time and dance. Although they are still naked, they are already transfigured. They are already beginning to raise their condition, seeking the elevation that is Babar's obsession. Gradually, they will shed their animal condition.

And on this dancing note, the first book of Babar ends.[3]

One might think that we are confronted with a structure that has its antecedents in children's literature and folklore; one which, from the dawn of time, has nourished the incessant dream of running away from home, on the condition that the prodigal or reluctant son not forget his homeland. One day he must return, having matured and acquired some device or special magic that aids him in saving his family or country.[4]

But this child's dream—the need to imagine alternatives to desertion, to explore the adult world, and to externalize the life of the psyche—does not take shape in a vacuum. It is nourished by history. In an age such as ours, in which there exists so much inequality between opposing societies and nations (not to mention individuals) and in which, of the two poles presented—city and jungle—one possesses the technological might and cultural prestige to absorb and subordinate the other, the return of Babar must not be understood as a mere staging of the mental and emotional forces that battle for a stake in the life of the child. As Bruno Bettelheim has suggested, the child's fear of being abandoned, his need to anticipate his future role and compensate for his immediate vulnerability, are certainly authentic and inevitable concerns.[5] But de Brunhoff's stories show that these dilemmas that every child must face are not just worked out according to abstract, ever repeating, metaphysical images that dwell in the psyche; they are grounded in concrete historical circumstances. That is where de Brunhoff got his characters, ideas, and actors. In addition to a pedagogical theory of how youngsters (elephants) are integrated into a benevolent adult world (the land of men), de Brunhoff also presented his children with a theory of history, an unconscious method for interpreting the contemporary economic and political world.

As he grows older, the admirer of Babar will find palpable evidence that there are developed countries and others that do not exhibit the characteristics of progress or modernity, and are therefore perceived as "backward," and that there is a set of solutions to such an abnormal predicament. Even before he can read, however, the child has come into contact with an implicit history situation in which some countries have everything and other countries almost nothing. The child may also be overcoming his infantile traumas, or, again, he may not. Such a process is difficult to verify. But what is definitely happening is that the reader is being handed an easy-to-grasp, easy-to-swallow historical version of the incorporation of Africa (and, by analogy, that of other out-of-the-mainstream continents, namely Latin America and Asia) into the contemporary world.

For this reason, geographical disguise is essential. Instead of Europe, there is a town; instead of Africa, a jungle. Although we can guess that the town is Paris, we haven't a clue as to where the jungle might be located. The land of the elephants stands for Africa without overtly representing it, without actually using the name, which might precipitate an overly painful identification. Jean de Brunhoff had the good sense not to mockingly deform the countries where these adventures take place. Or maybe it was something deeper: the self-assurance that goes with being a member of a colonizing nation with several centuries of experience in the field. De Brunhoff had in mind a *mission civilisatrice*, a civilizing mission. He probably felt that his stories had to pulse with a historic dimension; that they implicitly had to clear the past if they were to be successful lessons in how to grow, under the gaze and approving smile of a benevolent parent or mother country, into polite maturity.

In de Brunhoff's books the magical disappearance of the semantic link (Africa) can be attributed to a sense of history, a feeling that he was compelled to communicate in a world where he could not ignore his nation's responsibility for whatever had happened, for whatever would come to pass. He must have sensed the need to substitute for real history, full of accusations and contradictions, the colonial history that in 1931 was still going on right before his eyes, a parallel, ideal history,[6] a version of the westernization of those barbaric territories as he hoped his children would one day see it. His books contained a prophecy of what the author was certain would be Africa colonized.

That history then, Babar's history, is none other than the fulfillment of the dominant countries' colonial dream. It is not something new. From the sixteenth century onward, expanding capitalism would justify its intervention in other zones through visions and literature, with the utopian hope of being able to construct a perfect mythic space where conflicts such as those afflicting Europe (at that time undergoing the tumultuous transition from feudalism) would have no place. A nation would be created where nature and civilization could live side by side, where technical advances would not corrupt but bring contentment, where feudal and bourgeois qualities would be synthesized without antagonisms.

The result, as we all know, was disastrous. Nevertheless, four centuries later Babar succeeded where the conquistadors had failed. Babar slips progress into the jungle without upsetting the ecological balance, because de Brunhoff omits all the plundering, racism, underdevelopment, and misery from his story of the relationship between the two worlds.

So, for children then and now, the land of the elephants resolves the great contradictions in the history of capitalism. Not only is the way in which Europe handled the natives justified, but contemporary politics are cleaned up, too, as we shall presently see.

One has to be careful not to declare such fabrications and lies. In the Babar books, history is neither eliminated nor ignored. It is sweetened up, its meaning changed; it is reduced and inverted, but real history is there. It can be sought after, tracked down. De Brunhoff has taken the most conspicuous aspects of African history, abstracted and removed them from their immediate framework and problematical resonances, and rearranged them to form a subconscious set of identifications. Each stage in Babar's life formally corresponds (or will eventually correspond, as the child is able to locate and recognize it) to a stage in real life, a stage in real history. Certain historical elements, picked out and isolated, are allowed to function in a different context. Having lost their real links to history, unable to accuse their perpetrators or denounce their origins, they are absorbed by the dominant interpretations, sterilized, and made neutral.

This replacement of the true by the deformed (as in a fairy tale where some usurper takes the place of the princess) succeeds because these kinds of narrations don't pretend to teach a thing; they present themselves as guileless, make-believe, nonpartisan, and far from didactic. But if the truth were not inserted into Babar the Elephant's evolution, albeit hidden and bastardized, the child would not be able to correlate the fictional process settling in his brain with the real process pleading to be understood. In the future, subconscious comparisons will be made, and contradictions will be waved away as if by magic. Such an identification can operate, however, only if the child is able to equate and interchange the stages he has read with those that, in effect, exist in the world as it has been built. The guises under which these stages are introduced have been changed and their consequences substantially modified, but the framework and underlying order of history are there. The false system becomes the representative of reality in its entirety, which it is able to do because it includes the concealed problems of the world as it is presented to the child while he grows up. "Writing," suggests Roland Barthes, "being the spectacularly powerful form of the word, contains at one and the same time, thanks to a lovely ambiguity, the being and appearance of power, what it is and what it would like you to believe it is."[7]

The subjection of the barbaric Africans by the Europeanized Africans anticipates the fact that there remain sectors of the land of the elephants that might resort to force to oppose the changes that have taken place. Sure enough, in Babar's kingdom the rhinos are a long way from accepting the foreign customs of the Old Lady. While she rescues her friends from the circus to which they've been given (the first thing she does is dress her protégés and make them rest in separate beds, watched over by her benevolent and chaste portrait) Arthur (Babar's young cousin) has played a bad joke on Rataxes, the sleeping chief of the rhinoceroses, tying a firecracker to his tail. Cornelius, ever the polite European, begs forgiveness and promises to punish the child. The rhinoceros, however, will have nothing of it and becomes threatening.

The war that follows, in which Babar consolidates his leadership, once and for all establishing the superiority of his way of life over the law of the jungle, seems to originate in an insignificant act, in the eccentric personality of one of the rhino rulers, in fact in his lack of courtesy. There is no way to explain the belligerence of these animals, except by resorting to the savagery of their basic state. They are "lunatics" who distort the facts. No other evidence is offered us, a technique not exclusive to children's literature. Just as the rhinos want to "tweak the ears of this young King Babar and punish that rascal

Arthur,'' so thirty years later the news agencies would report that the war between El Salvador and Honduras began because of something as childish as a soccer match, conveniently omitting any reference to the multinational rivalries in the area or the migratory problems caused by an overexploitation of the land that goes hand in hand with a policy based on the production of crops mainly for export.

In such explanations, something basic to our understanding is always omitted. For instance, the war between the elephants and the rhinos (much like our familiar descriptions of the real fratricidal wars in Africa that the European way of life provoked) is not brought on by foreign powers seeking to establish the frontiers of their empires nor by the attempt to control valuable raw materials; rather, it is the acceptance of civilized, international models that both permits the avoidance of the ''barbaric'' state of war and brings on this particular one. If only the rhinos, too, could become eminently reasonable, ''Western,'' and mature, this nasty event would never happen.

Spiritual wealth in mass market literature is distributed by the same criteria that prevail in the not-so-literary world of economics. Faced with armed rhinos, Babar seizes on his ingenuity and strategic ability to outwit brute force and cruelty. With paint and wigs, he disguises the elephants' enormous rumps with eyes, noses, and multicolored hair. At a crucial moment, as the rhinos charge, those rumps rise up from behind a hill. ''The rhinoceroses thought they were monsters, and, terrified, they retreated in great disorder.''

It is the economic backwardness of the savages that has been the decisive element. They did not know how to close the technical gap that separated them from the elephants, which, with sophisticated weapons, demonstrated the importance of their link to the Western world; the adult world, too. For the rhinos are actually running from themselves: The backsides of their rivals are none other than great African masks. Those stupid animals can't even tell the difference between reality and its representation!

Small readers, therefore, can choose between two versions of childhood: They can be rhinoceroses threatened by the darkness of their own nightmares, their own faces deformed in a dream, or elephants that have advanced so rapidly they are even capable of using their own bottoms as instruments for controlling reality. Between the abyss of childhood and the heaven of adulthood, there doesn't seem to be much of a choice.

This identification of forms of evil with aspects of childhood is fundamental to the Babar stories because, as frequently happens in contemporary children's literature, it closes the juvenile imagination and its rebellious tendencies off from alternative routes. It does not leave much room for young minds to maneuver or go about choosing their own solutions. The roads that lead out of childhood (and poverty, as we shall see) are exclusively those that have been paved in advance by foreign bulldozers.

All insubordination must be left by the wayside. If it has its origins in a plausible misunderstanding, then we are in the presence of noble savages who will have no choice but to see the light of Rousseau and climb into the sheepfold of progress. If the savages are ornery, they will have to be exterminated or caged up. This is what happens to the rhinos, in whose characterization are mixed both the primitive (the taboo of anthropology that they share with the cannibals on the desert island) and the simply puerile (the superstitious). What condemns them most, however, is their destruction of nature without any reason. Because of their aggressiveness, "nothing was left of the great forest. There were no flowers, no birds. Everyone was sad."

Babar appears after the battle mounted on an elephant, one of his own subjects, his hands raised in a signal of victory. The goodness of the system has now been adequately tested by its military efficiency, and the time has come to put its prestige to work in constructing a new civilized order. After the war, they inaugurate a peaceful civilization identical to that of Europe. The time has come to build the first city of the elephants. Babar's travels and his second book close with the beginnings of the next step toward colonization, not only of a continent but of a mind.

Bruno Bettelheim has observed in his book *The Uses of Enchantment* that when fairy tales end with the protagonist as the king of a country (as ruler of his emotions and in control of his destiny), the monarch is never seen reigning. After a successful adventure, the character once again becomes an ordinary person in order to enjoy the normalcy of a satisfying life. This helps the child recognize himself.[8] Babar is not permitted such a respite. The power he has must be exercised, because he is enmeshed in both a historical reality and a dream projected onto that reality by the colonizers.

In the next book, *Babar the King,* "the dromedaries were bringing Babar the things he had bought on his honeymoon." Magically, all of civilization fits into these bundles. Babar gives a speech: "I have in these trunks gifts for all of you. I will give them out after we build our city." The elephants react favorably and get right to work. "They cut down trees, moved stones, sawed wood, and dug holes. The Old Lady played the phonograph for them, and Babar played the trumpet. The elephants opened their ears wide to hear." Babar, standing in their midst without moving a muscle, directs the harmonious division of labor, the smooth, luscious fruits of which will belong to everyone.

They all will have their own bungalows, while up on a hill (higher! higher!) behind them sit a two-story house for Babar and another identical house for the Old Lady.

"Then Babar kept his promise. He gave a gift to each elephant and also sturdy clothes for workdays and rich, beautiful clothes for holidays."

The drawing is noteworthy: Dozens of elephants entering a door, on all fours, wait in line to receive their gifts. Once they exit, the gray, amorphous mass disappears. Through the other door they emerge, dancing (like children? like blacks?) on two feet, half-dressed, presents in hand.

This is the end of an era in their utopian and idyllic history. Without a hitch, having easily beaten the rhinoceroses, they have created a city on the fringes of time, far removed from money and exploitation. They will dance until the centuries have ended.

Of course, civilization brings certain implacable laws along with it. For one thing, the elephants' day seems to have been split in half, which is further emphasized by their two kinds of outfits—one for leisure time and one for work. There will be a party on Sunday. But first they must work hard all week long to prepare for the occasion.

Clothing brings the elephants' fragmentation. The young ones go to school and "all the elephants who were too old to attend classes chose a trade." It is something that is voluntary, something that implicitly carries an immeasurable pleasure with it. The division of labor appears necessary, but it benefits everyone equally in this society based on the exchange of services. "If Capoulosse has broken shoes, he takes them to Tapitor, and if Tapitor is sick, Capoulosse takes care of him. If Barbacol wants to put a new statue on top of his chimney, he asks Podular for one and when Podular's jacket is worn out, Barbacol makes him a new one. Justinen paints a portrait of Pilophage, who in turn protects him from his enemies. Hatchibombatar sweeps the streets, Olur fixes cars, and when they're tired, Doulamor makes music." (The reader is asked to ignore the fact that Babar plays tennis with Pilophage and his wife—that is to say, with the military hierarchy).

The arcadian myth has been made concrete. The saintly and natural life of the savages, which incorporates the conveniences of technical process, combines both morality and civilization. This is not a welfare state in the jungle, as Bettina Hürlimann proposes.[9] This privileged space condenses Europe and its nostalgias; it eliminates the friction between developed and underdeveloped countries, between exploiter and exploited. The model that Babar proposed and put into practice has given prosperity and happiness to his people. Urban values have not ruined nature, they have perfected it. The barbarians have been integrated painlessly into the dominant economic structure, just as imperial myths have always said they would be.

European intervention has been a complete success. The shot that killed Babar's mother, the stupid war started by those savage rhinos, the cages in which they were imprisoned—they're all in the past. Ahead there is only a miraculous and excellent present of well-being and harmony for the elephants.

Thus, just below the surface of Babar, there lurks, half unconsciously, a whole theory of development. There exist backward countries that, once they imitate the more "advanced" (grown-up) countries, once they import technological know-how and begin working like they're supposed to, once they invite foreign professors and technicians to assist them, will succeed in improving their lot. There's no need to occupy these countries militarily, to exercise direct political control. It's enough to maintain economic, technological, and cultural control. It's enough if you've got internal, national collaborators. In Babar's case, the experiment is successful exactly because the elephants have accomplished it on their own.

In imagining the independence of the land of the elephants, Jean de Brunhoff anticipates, more than a decade before history forced Europe to put it into practice, the theory of neocolonialism.

First you must create a middle class that will facilitate the step from savagery to civilization but whose true function is to ensure that the ex-colonies' economic system will continue to be a fragment of the worldwide capitalistic system.

Babar develops his country in accordance with this dominant dream. He educates it according to modern and ultimately technocratic models, thereby demonstrating that only proximity to Europe (or the United States) guarantees success, and that when it comes to the weak and the dispossessed, you must adopt a loving, patient, and paternal attitude.

Such attitudes are possible because the poverty of some nations and the overaccumulation of wealth in others are not seen as part of the same phenomenon. It is not proclaimed that some are midgets because others are giants. Instead, the problems, hardships, and miseries of those countries that haven't yet reached a satisfactory standard of living are ethnocentrically likened to the turbulent aspects of Europe's transition from feudalism to capitalism or America's expansion *ab ovo*. Underdevelopment is no more than a "normal" stage in a "normal growth pattern" for any country that wishes to "stand on its own two feet."[10] In his classic description, W.W. Rostow outlined five successive plateaus for the countries of the Third

World in his book *The Stages of Economic Growth: A Non-Communist Manifesto:* "traditional society; the preconditions for takeoff; takeoff; the drive to maturity; the age of high mass consumption."[11] All these countries need to do is "get rolling" and "take off" and their growing pains will subside.

This superimposition of the individual on the social, of the biological on the historical, is at the heart of the way that books like Babar educate children. Not only do we find out how civilization has beneficently elevated Africa (or any other savage, strange, and alien zone), but we are simultaneously shown how playful, ignorant, adorable, and innocent beings—in short, children; in short, elephants—are ushered into and take their rightful place in the world of grown-ups. The psychosocial message is indistinguishable from the historical blueprint: The elephants have grown up and adapted to the world; that's what the child should do, too. While he's making this unsettling, almost unimaginable transition, he can feel reassured. It's okay to act both like a responsible adult and like a silly kid; just as in Babar's utopia you can be both African and European, man and animal, developed and underdeveloped. He can even work without being exploited and exchange goods without being contaminated by money.

The Old Lady tells her friends, "Let's work hard and cheerfully and we'll continue to be happy." If nature can enter the European world without losing its purity, there's no reason why children should have to deny their own distinctive traits as they get older, while those already adult are allowed the distinctly nostalgic pleasure of consoling themselves on the irreparable loss of past innocence. It is innocence, the basic substratum upon which this space is constructed, that allows fantasy and reality to be reconciled without doubts or schisms. The child is not suspicious of the animal, nor is the adult. The confidence one feels about these cuddly walking-talking dolls is transferred into the account in which these animals have deposited their hopes. The little one finds himself at just the right distance— neither too near nor too far—from his models to be able to intuit that they are and are not human beings.

This first fusion of nature with society, of the animal with the historical, is the introductory step to the creation of a utopia. In this state one lives tribally, in the midst of a landscape void of artificial constructions, one that combines contemporary architecture with splendid, unpolluted lakes. Relationships between people are simple and Edenic. In this Golden Age, this uterine scenario, this maternal paradise that the myths of all human societies have retained and perpetuated, it is easy for the child to identify with both the animal and the civilized forms that he internalizes simply by being human. Elephants and children, both small savages, begin life in a supportive environment, crawl on all fours, learn how to get dressed, and finally reach a point at which they must assume greater responsibilities. In Babar's case, this learning process, which is part and parcel of all growing up, contains a pseudohistorical vision of how he got where he was and at the same time, stacks the deck in favor of a world construct that the child does not fully comprehend but of which he does possess—like commercials for products that haven't come out on the market yet—an image.

The stages of colonial penetration, the stages in which the native assumes the Western norms as his models, are felt by the reader to be the stages of his own socialization. The adult world can hang on to all its dominant formulas and pass them on to the child without creating negative antibodies as long as the formulas are permeated with simplicity. To the extent that the child prepares himself to become an adult, to become Babar, he understands that colonization (that of his parents as well as that of the more powerful nations) is highly beneficial to those who receive it, and any kind of dependence and submission is the inevitable price you pay to be admitted into grown-up ranks, to gloriously and uninterruptedly continue the labor begun by your ancestors, the Old Lady, grandmother, schoolmarm, mother church.

This confusion of individual psychological life with national historical life enhances the dominating dimensions of both. You get treated like a child for your own good, and that's how the indigenous and backward must be treated, too. Those who are underdeveloped are so because of their childlike natures, not as the result of the international economic system, and all those little people need is education and technology in order to gain access to the Western, Christian, adult world.[12] By biologizing social stages and socializing bodily growth, the familial system (and colonial and neocolonial systems, too) creates a certainty that, as far as peoples-who-are-the-same-as-children are concerned, there is only one river flowing to success: namely, established values.

We've reached the end of human history. Just as elephants are men and men are countries, so are the tensions between city and country, development and underdevelopment, Europe and Africa, order and freedom, work and play, brains and brawn nonexistent, and it's possible to go on simplifying and reconciling as long as you live. Babar's utopia resolves the antagonisms that history, like a wicked step-mother, refuses to deal with. He whispers in our ear that there's no need to work them out through a daily struggle that could end up transforming our circumstances as well as our own personalities, because the contradictions (between city and country, etc.) are not irremediable.

All this is reinforced by the incredible ease of transitions in such stories. The movement from one moment to the next, one stage to the next, one historical period to the next is deceptively instantaneous. Birth and maturity, past and present, are contiguous. Erased are not only intermediate centuries connecting one moment to the next but also the immense effort and even greater suffering that such a passage of time implies. It is a magical process. The civilized world conquers and elevates the barbarian spirit with the same speed that the natural world regenerates the pure, tired souls of tourists. There is no point of contact between these two dimensions of contemporary humanity, for they are conceived as juxtaposed spaces, between which it is possible to leap back and forth without any problem. Mass market literature represents historical change, as if historical epochs were static blocks frozen next to one another, like products on an assembly line, frames in a comic strip, cans on the shelf in the supermarket, houses in the suburbs, or cars on the highway.

Such instantaneousness has nothing to do with imagination. Whoever thinks that fantasy consists of leaps and pirouettes is a prisoner of a notion that opposes imagination to the everyday, workaday world; that supposes it to be a form of entertainment. In commercial entertainment, and certainly in commercial children's literature, everything has been predigested and defined in advance; everything has been imagined by another's mind. The spectator sits back, consumes, and is entertained, without realizing that true imagination is hard work. It is a siege to bring into being that which had previously existed only in a no-man's land. True imagination implicitly criticizes the prevailing version of reality and invites us to make our own substitutions.

Jean de Brunhoff died in 1937, leaving the next book *Father Christmas* nearly finished. It's impossible to know what new adventures he would have offered us had he lived. Perhaps he would have succeeded in avoiding the temptations of industrialization and assembly lines to which his son fell prey ten years later, after the Second World War, when he resumed his father's series of books. Jean de Brunhoff wrought every volume with splendor (although he was inspired by the values we have revealed), and he also plumbed certain underwater fears and chasms that neither the child nor the adult who projected his anxieties onto that child knew how to express. He did it with exceptional graphic talent, constructing gigantic natural panoramas and pictorial movements that, for the first time in the history of children's literature, were on the young reader's scale, achieving an almost physical involvement in their ambience of drama and joy.[13]

In any event, de Brunhoff left his son with a character at a point in his evolution where he could afford to walk away from his past and retrace it, as if it had never existed. Up to this point Babar's case has been especially interesting. He is prototypical because he has traveled a road seldom taken by other cartoon creatures. Usually they are atemporal and asexual; their countries neither advance nor regress; they were never born; they have no fathers, mothers, or permanent jobs. Yet, in the end, Jean de Brunhoff left Babar in a situation hardly different from that of other run-of-the-mill cartoon beings. By ignoring his historical origins, the stages of his genesis, he now stood poised, ready to be assimilated into the mainstream of contemporary children's mass literature. Babar, together with his family and kingdom, is ready to enter the secure territory of superficial change within an eternally stable framework, and it's hard to imagine that Jean could have taken a different path than the one adopted by Laurent.[14]

From the moment Babar's country became equal to the metropolis, Babar acquired the same freedoms that are the privilege of any little animal born in Europe or the United States. He can now step into many roles, and he can be molded to fit all the standard versions of mass market literature.[15] Each successive incident will structurally resemble the last, and become just another in a chain of basically similar situations. This is how characters can be transformed (as has happened to Babar himself in France) into dolls, pillows, toothpaste, a monthly magazine, and a television series, although, in all fairness, not on the Madison Avenue scale we have come to expect in mass-media products. From now on, his family will be standardized, practically homogenized, resembling any other family in the media, dividing their time between adventures in other spaces and incidental, everyday domestic calamities. This ''Americanization'' even encroaches on the original scriptlike writing, which is converted into regular print. The child can now come directly into contact with the written word, without the parental figure as a reading intermediary. But some of the magic has also gone.

Such a movement, from inferior to superior, from primitive to urban, from poverty to progress, coincides with the aesthetic experience of reading that the reader has of that world, the way that he vicariously consumes the life of its characters. The reader begins these cartoons as if he were in an underdeveloped territory, with no control over events, and ends up having acquiesced to illumination, revelation, and success—thereby resolving his tensions and ignorance.

The worlds of these animals are sheltered from all criticism. It's not just that it's impossible to infiltrate the Old Lady's social class and raise a hand to display a photograph of a hungry child, an illiterate person, a military coup taking place, or a violation of human rights. It's that the reader himself has already accepted a formulation about children's literature—it's all harmless fun—that leaves no room for any alternatives. Facing an already predefined genre, everything in the reader's daily experiences—certainly the way work and play, competition and relaxation, the interrelation of the individual and the group are structured—reinforces the notion that when it comes to children's books and comics everything should be ''just entertainment.'' Politics, being part of a serious and solemn, not to say boring or even painful, other universe, can't conceivably be part of this. Taste, tradition, habit disallow it. Even those hallowed American values—plurality, debate, and freedom to criticize—are forbidden in that universe.

In the end, the reader himself stands at the door to his kingdom like a guardian demon, forbidding entrance to anyone who wants to ask impertinent questions; and by using that defense mechanism known as ''Oh, that's weird,'' he is ready to repel any intruder who instigates a rebellion.

When the door shuts behind him, leaving him supposedly secure in that magical, saintly space called children's literature, he won't see the blind alley into which he's stumbled, the blind alley that is his past without history and his future without history. He doesn't see it because someone—the Old Lady; Babar; or the reader himself when he becomes an adult and must raise his own children—is painting the four infinite walls, the floor and ceiling, someone is painting on a very hard and very real wall—a horizon that does not exist.

End Notes

1. See Maurice Sendak's Introduction to *Babar's Anniversay Album*, by Jean and Laurent de Brunhoff (New York: Random House, 1981). The back cover also has a short introductory note by A.A. Milne.
2. A view of the world as having been written, as a sort of scripture, in Michel Foucault, *The Order of Things* (New York: Pantheon Books, 1971). The impact of books (and other means of communication) on nations and tribes that still live in an oral stage of history, in—among others—the section ''The World Turned Upside Down,'' in Edmund Carpenter's *Oh, What a Blow that Phantom Gave Me!* (New York: Holt, Rinehart & Winston, 1972).

3. All the quotations, up till now, have been taken from that first, book, *Babar the Elephant* (New York: Random House, 1937). I have preferred this form of reference in order not to burden the text with notes. I'll use the same method for each book.
4. Stith Thompson, *Motif Index of Folk Literature* (Bloomington: Indiana University Press, 1955), 6 vols., and Marc Soriano, *Les Contes de Perrault: culture savante et traditions populaires* (Paris: Gallimard, 1968).
5. Bruno Bettelheim, *The Uses of Enchantment: The Meaning and Importance of Fairy Tales* (New York: Vintage Books, 1977), especially the introduction, "The Struggle for Meaning," 3–19.
6. "The myth, therefore, does not give meaning to an object which before the myth lacked it; on the contrary, it takes as its point of departure the signs which compose social reality and superimposes upon them a second meaning. . . . This second, 'superimposed' meaning is presented in the myth as the only one and makes the other disappear or, if you will, 'hides' it." Eliseo Verón, *Conducta, estructura y communicación* (Buenos Aires: Jorge Alvárez, 1967) 26.
7. Roland Barthes, *Writing Degree Zero* (New York: Hill & Wang, 1977).
8. Bettelheim 57.
9. Bettina Hürliman, *Three Centuries of Children's Books in Europe* (Cleveland: World Publishing Col, 1968) 181.
10. "From the newly constituted League of Nations they accepted the duty of governing them [the African countries] as a 'sacred trust of civilization' until such time as they were able to stand on their own feet in the arduous conditions of the modern world." Roland Oliver and J.D. Fage, eds., *A Short History of Africa* (New York: Penguin Books, 1962) 210.
11. W.W. Rostow, *The Stages of Economic Growth: A Non-Communist Manifesto* (London: Cambridge University Press, 1960).
12. See Paulo Freire's *Pedagogy of the Oppressed* (New York: Herder & Herder, 1972).
13. Alec Ellis, *A History of Children's Reading and Literature.* (Elmsford, NY: Pergamon Press, 1968).
14. In condensing this essay for publiction, space demanded that I leave out the examination of the concrete ways in which mass-media literature for children works. See the original essay in *The Empire's Old Clothes* (New York: Pantheon, 1983) as well as the essays in that book on the Lone Ranger and The Reader's Digest. Also, with Armand Mattelhart, *How To Read Donald Duck* (International General, fourth printing, 1990).
15. Dallas Smythe, "Time, Market and Space Factors in Communication Economics," *Journalism Quarterly* (Winter 1962).

4

Psychological Interpretations of Stories: On Catching Mice

Stephen Simmer

Stephen Simmer is a professional storyteller and a professor of religious studies. He works with children as a clinical social worker. He is a healer, who takes the power of stories seriously. The power of stories is very old: The same stories, motifs, and images can be seen at work over and over again in ancient forms. It is also very much alive in the present: Stories not only delight and inform us, but they can also be used to bring understanding to the spirit. In this chapter, Simmer explores the psychological power of stories.

In Hungary a storyteller would often begin a performance by saying, "I see it before me, as if it were happening now."[1] We can imagine her saying these words as she scanned the assembled villagers in the audience, as if to say: "You are the story I shall tell." Although the story might have seemed to be set in a distant land, long ago, this was merely a rhetorical device. Its true place of occurrence was in the lives of the people before her. The story touched living tissue. It articulated specific concerns of the villagers, and it was the sense that the story was rooted deeply and immediately in life that accounted for its bewitching power. Symbolically portrayed in the tales were the dilemmas, magic resources, trials, and resolutions that the villagers would encounter in the course of their lives, individually or together. Stories were a psychological resource, mapping paths through the wilderness of human dilemmas.

In Italo Calvino's *Castle of Crossed Destinies*,[2] several individuals have crossed a large forest and have met at a castle. Each has had various adventures and is anxious to relate them to the others. They assemble around a large table but discover with mortification that they have all lost the power of speech. One of the travellers sees in front of him a pack of Tarot cards, the deck comprised of the great symbolic images that emerged in medieval Europe: the Hangman, the Castle, the Lovers, Temperance, the Fool, the Magician. He takes cards of the pack and begins to lay them face up on the table. The others watch in fascination and realize finally that he is attempting to use these images to tell of his experiences in the forest. After he has completed the tale, the others do the same until all the stories are told.

When we try to communicate small things to each other, our difficulties are not great: "Pass the butter." "When is the next bus to Geneva?" "Have you seen my watch?" Our language, honed as it has become into a system of definite technical meanings, seems adequate for the job. But when we wish to communicate great mysteries—of love, death, time, despair, joy—our language fails us as it did the adventurers in Calvino's castle. Then we need to communicate with images like those of the Tarot pack—or like those found for untold generations in stories.

One of the most widespread types of tales is that commonly referred to as "The Animal Spouse."[3] A popular example of this is the opening story in the Grimm collection, "The Frog-Prince." In these tales, a witch or wizard has typically cursed a princess or prince, changing him or her into the inferior form of an animal: a mouse, bear, pig, frog, or (in our popular tale "Beauty and the Beast") into an amalgamation of various creatures. The challenge to the hero is to move into the animal realm, live with it there, and eventually learn to love it. Then a miracle may occur, and the animal may change into its true, royal form.

Our work with fairy tales is similar to the work of the hero or heroine in the animal spouse tales. The Wicked Witch of the West—Western culture, that is—has transformed stories into an inferior, alien form—children's entertainment or primitive folklore. It is difficult for us to perceive these stories as containing profound psychological intuitions. But if we live patiently with the stories, brush our lips lightly over them and kiss them to life in retelling them, and learn to love them, even in their ugliness, a change occurs. Like the mouse who changes into a princess, the stories themselves are transformed. Our gaze is returned by the gaze of a lover with nobility, grace, and animal wisdom, and they may revitalize us like nothing else can.

Stories as Food for Thought

It has frequently been noted that many traditional stories end with the storyteller mentioning food. Often the happy ending of a tale involves a great feast. An Irish tale, for example, ends this way:

> They went then to the castle of the king of Leinster, and if ever anybody saw a feast of pride and rejoicing, it was there he saw it. The feast lasted for seven days and seven nights in honor of Art and his people, and when it was over, everybody made off to his own home. That's the end of my story.[4]

At times the ending indicates that the storyteller and the audience are invited to partake in the feast. An Arabian tale, for example, urges the audience to prepare for the banquet:

> Now trim your nails, if they are long;
> Wear fine robes and costly gowns.
> For seven days and seven nights
> All food and drink and gay delights
> Will cost us nothing—not you, not me—
> But all will come from the king's treasury![5]

In a Russian tale the teller announces, "There's a tale for you, and a crock of butter for me,"[6] indicating an exchange of tales for food. At other times, however, the storyteller adds lines that contrast his situation with that of the fortunate fairy tale characters: While the characters gorge themselves, he goes hungry. A common Russian ending runs,

> From that time forth he lived with his wife in kingly style, drove around in a carriage, and gave great feasts. I too was present at these feasts; I drank wine and mead, but howevermuch I drank, only my mustache got wet![7]

Why are there these constant references to food in stories, even in situations where they do not seem to be an intrinsic part of the action? Some have suggested that these endings are requests for payment, the ring of the cash register after a sale. Another suggestion[8] is that these lines mark the necessary transition points between the fairy-tale world, where all things end happily, and the everyday world, where misery and hunger are part of the human condition. Without denying the validity of these suggestions, I offer a third possibility: These typical lines are indications to the audience of how the story is to be treated. The work of story telling is not completed when the performance is over. According to a Russian ending, "They made a fire, put the pot of gruel on a tripod, and began to cook. When the gruel is ready, the tale will continue; for the time being it is ended."[9] Unless the story is cooked by the audience, it cannot continue. Without this extra work it only wets the mustache but does not enter the mouth.

In Transylvania the tellers in the logging camps often told stories in the dark and could not depend on the normal eye contact with the audience to determine whether the people wanted to hear. Before he began a tale, the storyteller would ask, "Bones, people?" If the audience didn't want a story, they said nothing. But if they wished to hear it, they would respond, "Soup!"[10] This exchange implies that the story presented by the teller is only bones—by itself inedible, a mere skeleton. It only becomes a succulent story when the members of the audience heat the tale with their attention, add chopped and diced ingredients from their own lives, and boil out its intrinsic flavors. With listening of this kind, the audience may eat the teller's words, drink in what he says, and not merely wet the mustache. Digested, the story becomes meaning, food for thought, and is transmuted into themselves.

There's an Echo in Here

What is interpretation? One potential danger in our understanding of interpretation is that we might assume that there is a single answer, that stories are like math problems that can be summed up in one "bottom line." When we talk about "the moral to the story" we fall victim to the monolithic idea of interpretation, by assuming that there is a single lesson that has been disguised in the images of the tale. Charles Perrault, for example, in his famous early collection of fairy tales, affixed a verse to each tale explaining the moral. That for the story "Bluebeard," for example, is given in this verse:

> Ladies, you should never pry,—
> You'll repent it by and by!
> 'Tis the silliest of sins;
> Trouble in a trice begins.
> There are, surely—more's the woe!—
> Lots of things you need not know.
> Come, foreswear it now and here—
> Joy so brief, that costs so dear![11]

But a story is more than a moral and is lessened by being reduced to a lesson. The psychologist C.G. Jung preferred the term *amplification* to the term *interpretation*. *Amplification* means making the image more ample: fattening it, nurturing it, giving it weight. For Jung this was done through searching for parallels to a particular motif in world mythology, esoteric science, or religious history. For example, when I read a story about a bear, I might think of all kinds of other stories about bears: of the Greek story of the nymph Callisto, who was changed with her son Arcas into a bear—the two of them preserved eternally in the constellations Ursa Major and Ursa Minor; of the bear sacrifice in prehistoric Japan; of the sport of bear-baiting in Renaissance England; of the Scandinavian fairy tale "East of the Sun and West of the Moon," where a young girl is married to a bear, who eventually turns into a prince. In sifting through these stories, certain parallels may emerge that, for Jung, could suggest something universal in the way bears are imagined. This Jung would call an *archetype*.

In discussing dreams, Aristotle remarked that the best interpreter was one who could think in terms of analogies. In the interpretation of fairy tales the same principle holds. I would ask, "What in my life is parallel to the image in the story?" In spite of Jung's theories, which suggest that the parallels are found through wide knowledge of cultural history, the parallels I reach in the process of amplification aren't necessarily the results of extensive research. They require instead that I become aware of the places in my experience where the story echoes. For instance, in reading about Hansel and Gretel, I might ask, "What in my life is like the witch's house—all sweet and kind on the outside, but treacherous on the inside?[11] I might think of people I've known who present a sweet and inviting facade but who are insidious beneath the surface, like certain deceitful neighbors, two-faced co-workers. I might think of similar characters I have met in literature: Uriah Heep in *David Copperfield*, Iago in Shakespeare's *Othello*, for example. I might think of myself when I am all nice and sugary to others while inside I am ready to pounce. When I begin to list these parallels, the single image of the sweet house with the witch inside becomes much more complex. I can hear many sounds, there is resonance there, because now when I hear this motif I am aware of many memories that are touched at the same time. There's an echo in here, in my experience.

The interpretation process is like replaying the motif through a stereo system: Amplification is analogous to the operation performed by a stereo amplifier. When I first hear the story of Hansel and Gretel and haven't thought of parallels, the sound of the image is monophonic: It's only the story of the witch and the house. But as I become aware of the parallels, the ripples that move outward from this image, my hearing becomes more complex. Through amplification I play the image through many parallel speakers, and the sound of the story motif is polyphonic. Interpretation gives the image volume—not just in the sense of loudness but in the sense that its sound envelops me, seems to have space and dimension. No longer does the motif blare from just the story, like sound from a cheap portable sound system. The effect is more like that of live music, where

I am in the midst of a music that surrounds me completely, and I hear not just with my ears but with my bones and my eyes and the pores of my skin.

Donald Davis tells a delightful story about an apocryphal family of North Carolina called the Jollies, who had lived in a particular cove for several generations. Davis's Uncle Frank used to claim that this cove was a perfect echo chamber and that all the Jollies' conversations of the past several centuries were still reverberating there. But recently, his uncle claimed, scientists had developed an ''electron microphone,'' analogous to the well-known electron microscope, which was able to separate each sound in the extraordinarily complex echo contained in Jolly Cove. As a result, they were able to record each individual conversation between members of the Jolly family for the past several centuries.

The audience of a story—the thousands or millions of individuals who have heard or read a tale over the centuries—is an echo chamber like Jolly Cove. As an individual member of an audience, a story's images has echoes in my experience. In my relationship with any story, motif, symbol, or image, I am like the Jolly Cove in Donald Davis's story—an echo chamber, with many complex resonances to each thing I hear or read. Other readers and listeners are likewise echo chambers, though their particular echoes are different from mine. Interpretation is like Uncle Frank's fanciful electron microphone. It seeks to hear the subtlest reverberations of the story in my experience and in the experience of others. Interpretation is the development of a differentiated ear, that can hear the many resonances separately.

When I hear of Little Red Riding Hood's trip to Grandma's, numerous associated thoughts spring spontaneously to mind. One train of thought that occurs to me is that of my own grandmother on her deathbed, how she wavered between her normal state and senility. As she rambled on it was no longer her. The Wolf of Death had dressed in her clothes, a death I had never seen before. This wolf is like the Fenris Wolf of Eddic mythology, whose howl signalled the end of time and who in the final battle with the gods swallowed the highest God, Odin. But in standing next to my grandmother's bed in my first encounter with it, death did not come from outside—like the Fenris Wolf from the lowest depths of the earth. I was left to discern its features as it emerged from my grandmother, this most gentle, most familiar of beings. This makes death even more insidious and ineluctable— something not alien but appearing, feature by feature, from within. Like the wolf in the tale, death hears and sees me better, hugs me closer than those who love me most. Even now it leaps into the present out of this bed of memory and threatens to devour me.

But when I hear this tale at other times, I see a different path through the woods of the story. I hear echoes of sexual awakening, the wolf being that wolf-whistling, seductive, animalistic sexuality that lures me off the straight-and-narrow path of life, tempts me with the sweet sensuality of flowers. In some versions the girl carries the basket with food—symbolic of the fecund womb, the biological heritage that Red Riding Hood bears, the link between herself, her mother and grandmother.[12] The connection with the womb is indicated in Grimms' version by the fact that she carries the bottle and the cake in her apron. The associations with sexuality seems indicated again in the French version of the tale, where the disguised wolf invites Red Riding Hood into bed with him. Eventually she is eaten by the wolf, as I myself was devoured by the overwhelming sexual power that emerged during adolescence. But the ending in the Grimm version is not my own. Emerging from that belly has been no miraculous event: No woodcutter was wandering through the forest to hear the cries of my lost innocence. Sexuality was not severed suddenly by adult insight. My own problem with the story's ending is not unique: Storytellers have offered several possible endings over the centuries. Sometimes the story ends tragically with the wolf devouring Red Riding Hood, at other times the wolf is killed by a woodsman or Red Riding Hood's father.[13]

These are two alternate paths through the woods: The story leads me to thoughts about death on the one hand, sexual awakening on the other. Further reflection may reveal many other paths through the story: One may hear in the story something about the treachery of male domination in Western culture, another the economic seduction by the wolf of capitalism. In each case the story might be seen to yield a coherent answer. How can there be so many possible interpretations? Perhaps the story is like the Sibyl of the *Aeneid,* who prophesies from a cave with 100 openings and whose voice sounds different from each entrance.[14] A story is not an inert object but is rather a sibylline voice emerging in multiple ways, an oracle whose enigmatic answer depends on the location of the listener. The particular answers we receive in the process of interpretation depends on the question asked. The story itself, however, is not exhausted; it is like the magic tablecloth that produces food anew each time it is spread—the only difference being that the menu perpetually adjusts according to the dietary needs of its owner.

The Only Story

If a story reflects something about my experience, precisely what does it disclose about my experience? Perhaps we can stand before the mirror of a story and ask this question, acknowledging in advance that the language of the answer may be baffling and ambiguous like the replies given by the ancient oracle at Delphi.

In an Irish tale, a young prince is sent on a quest to find "the only story." This mysterious tale, he is told, is in the possession of a wizard. The prince undergoes several trials and at last corners the wizard and forces him to divulge the story. The tale the wizard tells is of his own youth. He once lived with an aunt who was a powerful sorceress. Whenever he made her angry, she would take a magic rod and tap him on the head, turning him into an animal. When she forgave him she would return him to human form, using the same rod. The young wizard soon grew weary of these dizzying changes so on the day his peevish aunt had changed him into a dog he observed her secretly while she hid the rod beneath her pillow. She left for an errand several days later, and the wizard-dog pulled the rod from her bed and into the street. A young boy was walking by the house, and the wizard-dog dropped the rod at his feet and began to growl and gnash his teeth. In terror, the boy picked up the rod and tried to ward the dog away with it. In the process he hit the dog on the head, and the wizard returned to his human form. Taking the rod from the boy, he then hid it in a place where his old aunt would never find it—precisely where we are not told.[15]

It is curious that this humorous tale is called "the only story"—the story that represents the quintessence of all stories, particularly in a land as rich in tales as Ireland. We might have expected that "the only story" would be a great epic with Fin MacCumhail, Cucúlin, or the Druids, with great quests and horrible sufferings and great boons to be won. Instead, we have a comic tale of conflict between an adolescent wizard and his petulant aunt. The story is unresolved at the end, because we are never told where the wizard hid the wand. In calling this "the only story," however, perhaps the Irish storyteller was trying to say that the transformations between one form and another—so central to this tale—embody the essence of stories in general. And the wand that holds the power to change: where could the wizard have buried it? Perhaps this mysterious device is imbedded in the story itself. To a listener stories have always had this magic—the power to transport and transform. In imagination we enter other worlds, other lives, and then at a story's end we reenter our human selves enriched.

Catching Mice

At the end of Grimm's "Hansel and Gretel" are the lines, "My tale is done, there runs a mouse, whosoever catches it, may make himself a big fur cap out of it."[16] These lines are like the tail of the tale and tease us with some hidden insight about stories in general. The story itself, it suggests, is a mouse. If we can capture this elusive small thing, we can make a huge cap from it: This means a change in our heads, our thinking. So the purpose of working with a story is not to change it into our rational, civilized style of thought but to change our thinking into the wild, elusive, mysterious style of the story. This suggestion is reinforced by a similar ending of a tale from the Languedoc region of France: "I passed through a mouse hole. And my story is whole."[17] For the story to be whole, the teller must pass through a mouse hole—must become mouselike. Once again the story's power is linked to the mouse.

The human psyche was often thought to take the form of a mouse, according to European folklore. The mouse was frequently held to reside within the human body. The etymology of our word muscle is from *L. musculus,* "little mouse": the twitching of the muscles was thought to be due to the movements of mice beneath the skin.[18] According to a widespread European belief, the mouse was a form of the soul that left the body at death and during other states when an individual was unconscious.[19] In Eastern Europe, it was believed that a mouse departed through the mouth of a person at night and wandered and that the sleeper experienced this wandering as dreams. If the mouse did not return in the morning the sleeper would die, so it was considered bad luck to wake a sleeper.[20] Mice infesting fields were thought to be the souls of unbaptized children.[21] Ancestral spirits in early Europe were believed to take the form of a mouse as well.[22]

Ironically, we still associate mice with the psyche. The classical experiments for behavioristic psychology have always used mice as their primary subjects. The assumption that we can learn something regarding human behavior through observing mice is perhaps based unconsciously on the ancient belief that humans and mice are symbolically connected. But the mice of the experiments have been changed—albinoed, caged, disinfected, all the darkness taken away. This difference in the mice represents the difference between the cleaned-up, quantified, rationalized view of psyche presented by the behaviorists and the psyche of our dreams: elusive, nocturnal, associated with magic and disease, uncaged.

The etymology of the word *mouse* suggests numerous connections with *mystery,* particularly the mystery of speech. The word *mouse* comes from the L. *mus* and the Gr. *mus.* Perhaps because of the traditional association of mice and filth, *musos* meant anything dirty or tainted. *Mus* is closely related to Gr. *muo,* "to close or shut," which is the root for our terms *mystery* and *mysticism.*[23] Perhaps the Greeks may have observed that mice seem at home in closed, dark, mysterious places. Curiously, this linguistic complex of *mus/muo* is also connected with language. The word *mu* in Greek meant "muttering," the sound made through closed lips, and *muao* meant "to bite or compress the lips."[24] The word *muthos* was anything told by words, the auditory connection with *muo* suggesting that mythological speech is mysterious and obscure.[25] So mouse and the mouth are connected in this linguistic skein:[26] Words crawl out of human darkness like a mouse emerging from his hole. The mouse is at home where things are closed, in the obscure places—is at home in the mystery. And our mythological speech—our story language—is dark, nocturnal, and elusive like the mouse.

For the prologue to his *African Folktales* Paul Radin used an epigram from an Ekoi legend of a mouse:

> Mouse goes everywhere. Through rich men's houses she creeps, and she visits even the poorest. At night, with her bright little eyes, she watches the doing of secret things, and no treasure chamber is so safe but she can tunnel and see what is hidden there.
>
> In olden days she wove a story child from all that she saw, and to each of these she gave a gown of a different color—white, red, blue, or black. The stories became her children and lived in her house and served her because she had no children of her own.[27]

The Ekoi legend weaves together several strands of the connection we have noted between mice and stories. Like the mouse, the story itself goes everywhere: It is able to penetrate into the secret places, has eyes that can see into the darkness, and has access to hidden treasures. The story presents a nocturnal vision, like the dream-wanderings of the mouse in folklore. Like the mouse the story is the awareness that can move behind the walls, underneath the floor-boards, in the dark corners. It is precisely this mouse-vision that gets woven into the many-colored story-children.

When stories are wild and untamed we react hysterically—we need distance, like those who stand on a chair. So long as stories are in cages, marked *Children's Literature* or *Folklore*, they are safe for us to have as pets. Outside these intellectual cages, we are terrified that they might crawl inside us, but it is inside us that they belong. Like the mice of European folklore that represent the dreaming self, the stories are our lost psyches, and they yearn to return to their home within. Just as mice know our homes—beneath the stove, between the walls— better than we do ourselves, stories know our innerness more deeply and thoroughly than we do. The stories are about what gnaws at our insides in the night, in the dark corners of our lives.[28]

End Notes

1. Linda Dégh, *Folktales and Society: Story-telling in a Hungarian Peasant Community* trans. by Emily M. Schossberger (Bloomington: Indiana U. Press, 1969) 87.

2. Italo Calvino, *The Castle of Crossed Destinies* (New York: Harcourt, Brace, Jonanovich, 1977).

3. Many examples of these tales are to be found in European folklore. In the Scandinavian tale "East of the Sun and West of the Moon" a young girl is married to a bear. In "The Three Feathers" of the Grimm collection—very similar to the story named "The Frog Princess" in Aleksandr Afanas'ev's Russian collection—a hero marries a frog who turns out to be a princess. This type of tale is also quite common among the American Indians, several examples of which are discussed by Stith Thompson, *The Folktale* (Berkeley: U. of California, 1977) 353–358. In general, the American Indian tales differ in that the animal does not change into a human at the end. Either the animal is betrayed and abandons the human spouse forever, or the human chooses to leave the human world and follow the animal spouse.

4. Sean O'Sullivan, *Folktales of Ireland* (Chicago: University Press, 1966) 117.

5. Inea Bushnaq, *Arab Folktales* (New York: Pantheon, 1986) 114.

6. Aleksandr Afanas'ev, *Russian Fairy Tales*, trans. by Norbert Guterman (New York: Pantheon, 1973) 192.

7. Afanas'ev 541. A similar ending is found in Ireland: "So the king's son married Auburn Mary and the wedding lasted long and all were happy. But all I got was butter on a live coal, porridge in a basket, and they sent me for water to the stream, and the paper shoes came to an end." Joseph Jacobs, *Irish Fairy Tales* (Secaucus, N.J.: Castle, 1984) 242. An Italian ending of this type is "They lived happily ever after, While we sit here picking our teeth." Italo Calvino, *Italian Folktales* trans. by George Martin (New York: Harcourt Brace Jovanovich, 1980) 656.

8. Von Franz 28-29.

9. Afanas'ev 348.

10. Linda Dégh 84.

11. Charles Perrault, *Fairy Tales* trans. by A. E. Johnson (New York: Dover, 1969) 43.

12. In the Grimm version the girl carries a bottle of wine, which her mother warns her not to break by falling off the path. This caution about breakage may symbolize an admonition over breakage of the hymen.

13. Various versions of the story's ending are summarized by Iona and Peter Opie, *The Classic Fairy Tales* (London: Oxford University Press, 1974) 94.

14. Virgil Aeneid 6.41-4.

15. Myles Dillon, collector and translator, *There was a King in Ireland* (Austin: University of Texas, 1971), "The Knowledge of the only story and Dudanis sword, 77–96.

16. *The Complete Grimm's Fairy Tales* (New York: Pantheon,1972) 94.

17. Geneviéve Massignon, *Folktales of France* (Chicago: University Press, 1968) 142. In Mexico a story ending is "I enter through a broken pipe and leave through another/And now I want you to tell me another." [Howard Wheeler, *Tales from Jalisco Mexico* cited in Pellowski, op. cit., p. 154.] There is no explicit animal here, but again the reference might be to the mouse, who is naturally at home in broken pipes.

18. It was believed in Finland that the twitching of the eye or muscle was caused by the "life-mouse," whose attendance sustained life. Jan Bremmer, *The Early Greek Concept of the Soul* (Princeton: University Press, 1985) 65.

19. The view was expressed by A. Hultkrantz that these various animals represented the free soul, which migrates during death, trance, or dreams. [Conceptions of the Soul Among North American Indians (Stockholm: n.p., 1953), p. 64]. It should be noted that Jan Bremmer suggests that the mouse—indigenous to the body—was not an example of the free soul, but of the bodily soul. [The *Early Greek Concept of the Soul* (Princeton: University Press, 1953) 65]. This view seems too hasty a categorization, given the evidence that the mouse wanders outside the body, like other animal forms that exemplify the free soul.

20. Beryl Rowland, *Animals with Human Faces* (Knoxville: University of Tennessee Press, 1973) 128.

21. Rowland 128-9.

22. Julius von Negelein, cited in Leo Kanner, *Folklore of Teeth* (New York: Macmillan, 1928) 48.

23. Liddell-Scott-Jones, *Greek Lexikon, mus, muo.* Of the word mysterion the Theological Dictionary of the New Testament concludes, "The etymology of the word itself is a mystery." [Gerhard Kitteel, editor. Translated by Geoffrey W. Bromiley. Vol. 4 (Grand Rapids, Mich.: Wm. B. Eerdmans, 1967) 803]. Athenodorus 3.98d very early suggested a relationship between musterion and mus terei, "mouse-hole." Though this connection has been discounted as spurious, there certainly was an auditory connection between mus and musterion, mouse and mystery, to the Greeks, which would have connected these terms intimately in the Greek imagination.

24. Liddell-Scott-Jones, mu, muao.

25. There has been a longstanding debate about whether mythos is connected etymologically to muo, "to close." Much recent opinion discounts a direct link, but Walther Prellwitz, [*Etymologisches Wörterbuch der Griechischen Sprache* (Göttingen: Vendenhoeck and Ruprecht, 1905)] suggests that both mythos, "saying," and muo "silence" are rooted in mú, the word for muttering, so that speech and silence ironically have the same root. Gerhard Kittel, ed., *Theological Dictionary of the New Testament,* trans. by Geoffrey W. Brimiley, vol. 4 (Grand Rapids: Wm. B. Eerdmans, 1967) 765.

26. Leo Kanner in *The Folklore of Teeth* points out that there is an inexplicably wide-spread tradition in folklore of a "tooth mouse," which exchanges the soft milk-teeth for a harder "mouse-tooth" which can gnaw through hard things, like mice can. This connection underlines the connection in etymology between the mouse and the mouth.

27. Paul Radin, editor, *African Folktales* (New York: Schocken, 1970) 21.

28. Marie-Louise Von Franz says the mouse symbolizes "an obsessive nocturnal thought or fantasy which bites you whenever you want to sleep." *Interpretation of Fairytales* (Irving, Texas: Spring Publications, 1978) 63-4.

PART II

Using Literature in the Elementary Classroom

Introduction: What to Do on Monday Morning

So what? So what does all this talk about structuralism, reader response, sociopolitical contexts, and psychoanalytic interpretation have to do with what teachers do when they walk into their classrooms on Monday morning? What are the pedagogical implications of putting stories at the center of the curriculum? How should literature be taught to children in the elementary school?

While the four authors presented in the first section of this book each develop a different perspective on how stories work, there are at least three points that emerge from these discussions that need to be taken seriously by teachers. First, there is widespread agreement that, as Temple, Lovell, and Simmer suggest, reading stories involves the negotiation of meaning between reader, author, and text on the one hand and among readers on the other. Reading is an interpretive act; it requires making meaning rather than just taking it from a text. Second, these authors suggest that stories work in systematic ways. Despite the fact that reading involves individual response (Lovell), teachers need to search for the basic structures that underlie stories and thereby help children recognize these structure (Temple). Finally, Ariel Dorfman reminds teachers about the social, political, and historical implications of the stories they share with children.

All three of these themes are developed further in this second section, in which a number of teachers share some of the ways they have most effectively integrated stories into their classrooms. The first of these themes—that reading requires negotiation—is explored in three different, but complimentary, ways in the first three chapters of this section (by Susan Hepler, Diana Barone, and James Plecha).

Susan Hepler begins by describing the type of classroom atmosphere necessary for the serious exploration of literature with children.

Hepler makes the case that in order to become literate a child must be a member of a ''community of readers;'' that learning to read is essentially a social activity. She shows how oral interaction (real talk) among students and teachers is a necessary condition for learning how to select, read, respond to, reflect upon, and negotiate the meaning of stories. In making her case Hepler shares a plethora of methods for helping children ''pick their way to literacy.''

Diane Barone continues this exploration of how to help children negotiate meaning by providing a description of how she has used dialogue journals with first, second, and third graders. Barone has worked extensively with Jonathan Lovell in using dialogue journals to explore how children respond to stories. Here she provides a detailed analysis (complete with examples from her students' journals) of how her students used journals to respond to the stories they were reading. She concludes that while the responses of first graders generally mirrored their oral responses to literature, the written responses of her second and third graders were often richer than their oral responses. Barone provides an example of how writing can be an effective means of helping even young children respond to stories.

James Plecha, senior editor for Junior Great Books, provides an overview of the ''shared inquiry'' approach to teaching literature that has been developed by The Great Books Foundation. In reading Plecha's description of the Great Books approach to everything from selecting stories to designing interpretive questions and conducting meaningful discussions, one is immediately made aware of the fact that teaching literature in an open-minded way requires an extraordinary amount of thoughtful planning by teachers. Recognizing the interpretive and negotiated dimensions of reading stories with children does not mean that anything goes: Plecha provides teachers with a means of thinking through stories so that they (teachers) will be better able to help children realize that interpretation is a disciplined activity that involves justification of one's interpretation.

Hepler, Barone, and Plecha all focus on ways of helping children come to terms with the meaning of what they read. In the next chapter Joy Moss describes how literature played a key role in a ''focus unit'' on the sea that she developed with a group of fourth graders. She illustrates how careful selections of stories based on common themes and structures can help teachers integrate literature into other areas of the curriculum such as art, science, and math in exploring a topic (the sea) that knows no disciplinary boundaries. She also shows us how stories can be integrated into the everyday classroom life of children.

Frances Temple shows us why we must integrate good stories into everyday lives of children. Temple is concerned, as are many parents and teachers, with the effect of the mass media (in particular television and video) upon children. She views effective exposure to good literature as an essential "counterbalance" to the culture of the mass media. She shows us how we can use reading, writing, talking, and acting about stories as a means of recreating a more balanced classroom culture for the children with whom we work. In reading Temple's examination of the effects of mass media on children, one immediately recalls Ariel Dorfmen's analysis of the Babar stories. Dorfman and Temple both remind us that as teachers we need to be sensitive to the value-laden nature of the stories we read to children.

In "Before, During, and After: Using Drama to Read Deeply," Pat Collins provides us with an overview of various ways in which classroom drama may be used to help children approach the stories they read. In doing so he illustrates how drama can be used to do more than just act out stories. Classroom drama also provides a meaningful context in which children can negotiate meanings while discovering the basic structure of the stories.

In the penultimate chapter in this section Paul Wilson asks the question, "What kinds of readers should the schools be producing, and how can the use of literature contribute?" Wilson answers these questions by examining the relationship between voluntary reading and reading achievement. He maintains that, despite the fact that it has been shown that there is a positive relationship between voluntary book reading and measures of reading achievement, the "amount of voluntary book reading that children actually do is distressingly low." Wilson then describes a variety a ways in which teachers can provide students with skills, attitudes, and values they need to become voluntary readers. In reading this chapter one cannot avoid being struck by the fact that, as Dorfman suggests, it is not only the content of stories that may send subliminal messages to children but also how we teach the stories to children that has a subtle but long-lasting effect on the kinds of readers they become.

In the final chapter of this section Kieran Egan turns the table on us. Egan does not describe methods and techniques of teaching stories to children; rather, he proposes that story telling itself may serve as a powerful paradigm for thinking about teaching. Egan suggests that teachers may benefit from thinking of teaching as an act of story telling; he suggests that teachers view themselves as storytellers. He outlines the general contours of how we may reconceptualize teaching as an act of sharing.

This sampler of ideas for sharing stories with children is hardly exhaustive, but our hope is that the ideas shared here will provide teachers with a starting point for reconceptualizing their own work with children. We suggest that you read these descriptions of classroom practice in a most imaginative fashion—looking not so much for ideas to implement in your own teaching but searching for sparks that might ignite it.

5

Picking Our Way to Literacy
in the Classroom Community
Susan Hepler

Susan Hepler received her doctoral degree at
The Ohio State University. She is coauthor of
Children's Literature in the Elementary School,
a successful text on using children's literature,
and is an influential consultant in the field of
children's literature and education. Here she sets
out guidelines for establishing in the classroom
a climate and procedures that encourage children to collaborate in exploring, talking about,
understanding, and appreciating literature.
These ideas are informed from her own ethnographic studies of children's book reading in
elementary classrooms.

All classrooms are social settings, ''communities of readers,'' in which
children may help each other become readers. The degree to which
this happens easily is largely a result of what the teacher does—and
purposefully does not do—in the way of intervention. Margaret Meek
concluded *Learning to Read* by saying that ''for all the research we
have financed, we are certain only that good readers pick their own
way to literacy in the company of friends who encourage and sustain
them and that . . . the enthusiasm of a trusted adult can make the
difference.''[1]

Suppose we teachers acted on these assumptions:

- Children learn to read by reading, talking, and writing about real
  books;
- Children discover, process, modify, and amplify their understandings about stories by talking about their reading;

• Children think by doing as well as talking; "doing things with books" makes a book memorable to the individual reader and visible to the reading community.

If these assumptions were true of classroom learning, what kinds of teacher practices might proceed directly from them? What would happen if a teacher manipulated times, settings, and expectations in certain ways over the year to help readers develop to their full potential? What could teachers learn about the social nature of classrooms that would help them let lifelong readers create themselves?

Real Books in the Classroom

When asked when he learned to read, Tolstoy said that he was always learning to read. In this sense, the real challenge to teachers is to carry the reading child along so that this process of refinement unfolds naturally. When children build background with memorable books, they often make important discoveries about the patterns in literature. Kindergartners can talk easily of being nervous about receiving a big dog's affection after hearing Hilleary's *Fletcher and the Big Dog*. They may, as first graders, ache for Christopher when his dog Bodger is killed in Carrick's *The Accident* and understand the boy's difficulty in considering a new puppy in *The Foundling*. Trailing threads of experience such as these, third graders are better prepared to understand Daniel's angry love, following the death of his beloved old dog Captain, of a near-dead dog he discovers in a drainage ditch in Thomas's *The Comeback Dog*. All four of these books are superficially related by content: "a boy and his dog," but they are truly related by the theme of the rewards and difficulties of loving and wishing to be loved in return. While no first grader is going to be able to see that, many third graders are and will articulate this thematic pattern if given the chance to work it out on the road to becoming readers.

When middle graders study the patterns in "Cinderella" stories, they are delighted to see cultural variations and varied qualities of the heroine in such stories as Ai-Ling Louie's Chinese *Yeh Shen*, Climo's *The Egyptian Cinderella*, or Huck's *Princess Furball*. Comparing the versions brings out the passive versus the active heroine and the role of magical objects or helpful mentors. A sixth grader with some knowledge of this literary pattern might be delighted to discover how another scullery maid and a prince in an imaginary kingdom come to love each other as they strive against the roles society has prescribed in Cynthia Voigt's *On Fortune's Wheel*. Readers with background like this keep becoming readers, circling around in reading to deepen and broaden their experiences and understandings with books. Most teachers probably already know what *Becoming a Nation of Readers*[2] told us about the importance of real texts, literature-rich classrooms, and time during the day when trade books are read as essential to the development of readers.

Basal texts with their simplified words and stories, removal of character motivation, and the deletion of idiosyncratic features of "real" text do not provide enough upon which readers may hand their natural expectations concerning text.[3] Readers taught with basals begin to separate "reading" from the pleasurable act of messing around in books. Rasinski and Deford[4] examined three first grade classrooms, each with a different approach to the teaching of reading. While good readers in all three classrooms had a much richer definition of reading than did poor readers, the number of readers who saw reading as meaning related was highest in the literature-based reading classroom. In each of the other classrooms—one a mastery learning classroom, the other a basal reading one—children were more likely to define reading as converting symbols to sounds. In response to this, publishers have packaged "literature-based reading programs" in which stories lifted from real books are presented in basal text form. One need only examine the acknowledgments in most of these series to see the many "abridged from" citations, further evidence that these programs are more of the same basalization of real books.

Tunnell and Jacobs examined research findings on literature-based instruction and concluded that for a variety of children—older and stalled poor readers, ESL readers, minority readers, and regular readers—"the affectivity of literature based, Whole Language programs gives meaning and pleasure to the process. . . [I]t is safe to say the basal reader is not the only way to successfully teach children to read."[5] It would seem that, even if many systems teach children to read, the systems that are best foster or, at the very least, leave intact these things: the child's love of reading, the child's willingness to go on reading, the child's understanding that real reading is getting meaning from text, and the child's developing sense of how literature works. The following discussion of the social nature of classrooms assumes that real books are present in book corners, in displays, in children's desks, and in readers' hands as part of informal discussion and planned inquiry.

The Information Network in the Community of Readers

In the past, talk in the classroom has frequently been regarded as "cheating," as "not doing your own work," or, as one teacher put it, "If your mouth is engaged, your brain is not.'' In recent years, however, we have come to see how important talk is to thinking, to writing, and to developing a social structure in the classroom that supports learning. Several years ago I spent ten months observing a combined classroom of fifth and sixth graders in which reading was taught with trade books. In this classroom permeated by books, children talked about, shared, argued over, handled, and reread trade books. I was struck by how much and in what ways they used each other as they developed their reading abilities.[6]

The amount of information exchanged between children about reading, as they talked informally and in more structured situations, was overwhelming. A ten-minute segment of conversation could be interpreted as densely packed information for the community. After each daily silent reading period, for instance, the teacher asked readers to talk about what they were reading. As Tammy talked about Mazer's *I, Trissy*, others listened, chimed in if they had read the book, or helped the sharer.

> *Tammy:* ''You can read it really fast because the girl 'types' it.''
> *Margie:* ''I read it in one day.''
> *Tammy* [showing illustrations of the main character]: ''She wears red, white, and blue to school as a protest—red for anger, blue for innocence, and white for. . .for. . .''
> *Barb:* ''Peace.''

In this informal kind of talk about reading, children gained information about what to read next. (Tammy had heard Mitty talk about *I, Trissy* the week before.) They taught each other how to talk about books, how to pick out important plot elements, how to categorize characters, and ''what was good.'' Readers also clarified the plot and meanings for themselves in this sharing. The nature of ''sharing'' was such that when Tammy forgot what white stood for, another student could help without teacher comment. Less able readers gleaned enough information from these discussions to risk taking on a more difficult book such as Byars' *The Pinballs* (a title eventually read by eighteen of the twenty-four children in the class).

But the teacher also used the time to help children build a framework for their self-selected reading. She asked children to pick ''an especially good book from your November reading list;'' to share ''a new book, something no one else has read yet,'' ''another funny book,'' or ''a good historical fiction title;'' or to recall ''other books by this author.'' After one child had recapped Sauer's mysterious time-slip fantasy *Fog Magic*, the teacher commented, ''So it's one of those books that opens up into another time. Does that remind you of any other books?'' In the ensuing discussion, several boys talked about other characters' entry into a fantasy world, citing three other titles. The teacher had said very little during this exchange of patterns in fantasy but had provided the opportunity to let children roam around in their own reading history. With repeated discussion experiences such as this, children were building a repertoire of what to read, what to notice, how to reflect upon, and how to talk about books.

Over the school year, children who were "key recommenders" of books changed. Initially, the articulate readers of realistic fiction, who were almost exclusively female, dominated the sharing time. In winter, however, when the class became a more cohesive community, children who were previously lone readers (readers whose choices did not reflect much influence from other children) became key recommenders. The unique reader's contributions became more valued while the unique reader's essential nonconformity continued. ("I'm not going to read *The Pinballs* because everyone else has read it," said Nathan, one rugged individualist, toward the year's end.) Once children even applauded a lone reader who finally volunteered to talk about her reading—a recognition of this unique act (no other book talker had ever been applauded).

Younger children rely, too, on the classroom community for information as to what to read and how to talk about books. The adult readers in the classroom dignify titles by their attention and actually help readers develop a wider literary scope. A teacher detailing her first graders' work with Zolotow's *Say It!*[7] showed how repeated readings of this evocative story of a mother and daughter's walk on a windy autumn day helped children overcome their initial indifference to the book. The teacher liked the book so much that she planned activities that related to and extended the book's content, such as taking a fall walk; making watercolors in the style of the book's illustrator, James Stevenson; small group discussions; observations of the words the author used; and four rereadings. The teacher commented on the quality of writing, discussion, debate, and language enrichment as children discovered how much there was to enjoy about this book. The teacher also learned much about the insightful comments six- and seven-year olds can make about their reading. Talk in the classroom makes reading and readers highly visible.

Talking to Make Meaning

Children recall or rehearse content and explain, clarify, or define meanings for themselves; in other words, they practice comprehension skills if we provide the time for talk to occur. Children think aloud about what they read if teachers take time and listen. One teacher followed a child's lead in discussing Carle's *The Very Hungry Caterpillar*.[8] She had asked him if he thought this story could really happen.

> *Child:* Hmmmmm. It might and it might not.
> *Teacher:* Why do you think it might happen?
> *Child:* Because that caterpillar ate a hole in something every day so I think it might be able to happen because he only ate one hole in it.
> *Teacher:* Um hummm.
> *Child:* He didn't eat the whole thing; he only ate one hole. And he ate it day by day; he didn't eat it all in one day. So I think it could happen.
> *Teacher:* Why did you think maybe it couldn't happen?
> *Child:* On the other chance, 'cause caterpillars might not be that hungry.

By holding this boy's "might and might not" structure, the teacher was able to listen, to inject the second question, and to help the child work out his own meanings for the story. The rest of the discussion, with the teacher offering very little, was the boy's proposal for how he could test whether caterpillars truly eat little holes in things, hence, whether this story could really happen. Discussions of this sort, sustained at length on one key idea, don't happen unless a teacher is prepared to listen and, in this case, to ask the key question.

In a fascinating discussion of classroom discourse Cazden[9] points out that many "lessons" in a typical classroom follow an Initiation/Response/Evaluation (IRE) structure. That is, the teacher asks a question ("Is this story true?"), the child responds ("No"), and the teacher evaluates it ("Right. It's just a story.") before asking the next question. In this way, the teacher controls the sequence, the amount of wait time between talkers, and the content of talk. In this way, a teacher doesn't have to be prepared for any conversational surprises. However, children then practice producing what the teacher wants rather than what they truly think about what they have read. Is it any wonder then that one teacher says of her fourth graders who have had little chance for focused talk in the classroom: "They stumble around with their words and don't know how to say what they think?"

In the caterpillar example, the teacher initiated the topic and continued to follow the boy's lead. In the following example, Cazden quotes a sequence from Vivian Paley's kindergarten class[10] in which children are discussing Lionni's *Tico and the Golden Wings*. Notice how closely the discussion resembles a real conversation with five-year-olds reacting to each other while the teacher refrains from nominating the next speaker, acknowledging comments, or rephrasing the previous speaker's comments. The teacher sees Tico as a nonconformist while the children see him as a threat to the community:

> *Teacher:* I don't think it's fair that Tico has to give up his golden wings.
> *Lisa:* It is fair. See, he was nicer when he didn't have any wings. They didn't like him when he had gold.

Wally: He thinks he's better if he has golden wings.

Eddie: He is better.

Jill: But he's not supposed to be better. The wishing bird was wrong to give him those wings.

Deanna: She has to give him his wish. He's the one who shouldn't have asked for golden wings.

Wally: He could put black wings on top of the golden wings and try to trick them.

Deanna: They'd sneak up and see the gold. He should just give every bird one golden feather and keep one for himself.

Teacher: Why can't he decide for himself what kind of wings he wants?

Wally: He has to decide to have black wings.

It is evident that, when we slow down the discussions, pose the opportunities, and wait, children will talk about what they read in some depth.

Discussing Books in Small Groups

Groups formed for the purpose of discussion help a teacher focus on one text, aspects of several texts, or aspects several readers may have raised in response journals (see below). These groups have the advantage of giving child readers a chance to react to a book in the company of other readers. The teacher provides the setting and, in some cases, the direction, and children talk their way through books. Often teachers assign parts of a book, a frustration to the reader who wants to finish it overnight, but children may certainly reread or at least reperuse the part assigned for discussion. This gives readers an agreed-upon pool from which to give evidence. Many questions prepared for commercial guides are organized into chapter chunks for this reason.

What do we know about literature discussion groups? Watson and Davis[11] observed one fifth grade classroom shift into literary discussion groups as part of their reading program. The teacher allowed readers to select their own book, which produced across-ability groupings. The teacher used the students' leads to follow fruitful discussion topics, which ranged from the author's use of parentheses and how to handle unpronounceable words in a story to personal reactions and varying interpretations of passages. All readers, not just the privileged few, benefitted from these discussions. Dorothy Stephens, a primary grade teacher, demonstrated how she used discussion groups to focus first graders' attention on good leads as a way to influence their own written stories.[12] Children's written work improved as they focused on their own leads and edited their stories for greater effect on the reader/audience. Four teachers provided evidence from their own classrooms of how children in literary response groups demonstrated that they were using comprehension strategies such as recalling facts and details, identifying cause-effect relationships, predicting probable outcomes, and monitoring their own cognition.[13] Each of these specifically formed groups make use of children's natural inclination for sharing what interests them in the classroom context. They give a teacher a way to influence readers (and writers) in ways that do not violate what we know about how readers make meanings.

How can teachers influence more positively what happens in group discussions? Cazden has some suggestions, based on the work of researchers such as Mary Budd Rowe, Shirley Brice Heath, Susan Philips and others, for helping teachers approach significant conversation in the classroom. Increasing the amount of wait time from one to three seconds, for instance, seems to produce longer student utterances, a more cohesive discussion, better and fewer questions from the teacher, more articulate students, and greater visibility on the part of invisible students. Rearranging chairs from facing the teacher to facing a circle seems to encourage more child participation. Allowing small groups of children to discuss something among themselves as a kind of practice session before presenting their ideas to the group produces higher quality discussions that involve less of the teacher's time. Children from minority cultures benefit from the teacher's understanding of that culture's communication patterns. For example, one teacher of Polynesians noted that allowing children to overlap comments rather than taking structured turns produced better discussions; another teacher of Native Americans observed that when children talked at great length, others listened and that while a conversation may have seemed disjointed, on further observation it had a fine cohesion to the ideas under discussion. While this discussion by no means exhausts the ways teachers can manipulate classrooms, it does suggest that if we fault children for their lack of discussion abilities we are blaming the wrong part of the classroom community.

Focusing Children's Talk: Good Questions

In the examples of teacher questioning above, we have seen how one teacher gradually built into the curriculum a set of questions that focused on various aspects of literature following children's self-selected reading. We saw another teacher hold the child's question in mind to help him extend his discussion of *The Hungry Caterpillar*. We witnessed a third teacher stand back after raising the question of the responsibility of the individual to the community in *Tico and the Golden Wings*. But what determines a good question?

Questioning strategists often differentiate between closed and open questions, higher level and lower level questions, in-the-book and out-of-the-book questions, and chains of questions or hierarchies that lead to "the big questions." While structures such as these may be helpful to us as we discuss questions, they are often less helpful to the teacher who is searching for the question that will kindle children's talk. Any questioning strategy when rigidly adhered to sacrifices children's responses and the power of the book to the design of the curriculum; a cart drives the horse. In *Questioning: A Path to Critical Thinking*, Christenbury and Kelly[14] suggest four things to consider:

1. Use a questioning schema, but don't let it use you. Use it as a guideline, not as a rule, when you write out questions.
2. Follow your students' lead. The discussion is more fruitful if students are first allowed, within limits, to talk about what interests them before proceeding to the teacher's questions.
3. Be flexible with your questions. Be prepared to jettison the order of the questions if the discussion is fruitfully proceeding in another direction.
4. Don't always play it safe. While convergent questions are more easily graded, the open questions pose more complex tasks for the students. Interestingly, some research shows lower ability students benefit most from open questions but teachers tend to ask more closed questions with this kind of reader.

Good questions should improve the quality of the reader's experience with the book. Topics for questions might include why people in stories did what they did, the consequences of those actions, and what that implies for the reader. Julia Redfern, in Eleanor Cameron's *Julia and the Hand of God*, is destined to become a writer. Readers don't know this, however, until well into the book. Asking children, "What qualities might a good writer possess?" before they read the book would allow many children to contribute from their own experiences. Asking what writerly qualities Julia possessed after children have read the story would allow them to recall key incidents about Julia's particular talents for observation, sensitivity, creative mischief, and brooding over history as important to her development as a writer. They would return to their **first** discussion with new insight into the challenges all writers **face**.

What happens in a story to change a character? Often children discover a theme statement after discussing this. In *The Comeback Dog*, Daniel realizes that he can't make the stray dog love him by beating love into him. What does this say about the nature of love? Children who often have difficulty talking about themes succinctly nonetheless need the practice. A teacher asked her ten- and eleven-year-olds, ''What messages did Jean Craighead George have in mind when she wrote *The Cry of the Crow*?'' in which a teenager finally must kill her pet crow rather than risk it blinding her younger brother.

> *Linda:* I think the book was the kind of book for people that like crows and maybe for people that don't like crows. I feel that I don't like crows because I wouldn't be allowed.
>
> *Tom:* I think the author wanted to teach us to be kind to animals and to take responsibility like feeding and taking care of that animal or whatever.
>
> *Margie:* I guess what the author was trying to say was that to be sure what you're getting into or doing before you tame a wild animal) because it could get people into trouble. It's really kind of hard to explain.[15]

None of these three children could say succinctly that if you try to tame a wild animal, you must always be prepared for its eventual adulthood and the problems this brings. However, each struggled with the larger ideas and gained some practice in articulating them.

In group situations unguided by a teacher's presence, children often make surprising headway. Douglas Barnes shows how four girls discussing a poem, ''The Bully Asleep,'' use ''exploratory talk'' to arrive at a thematic statement. ''One puts forward a view, another takes it up and modifies it, another finds evidence, and another sums it up. Group discussion is not always as neat as this, as every teacher knows, but it is by such collaboration that a group will achieve whatever success it does achieve.''[16]

Other profitable strains of questions center around how a reader feels about the story and what in the story causes those feelings. Middle-grade readers often decide *The Great Gilly Hopkins* by Paterson is not a ''good book'' because it doesn't end ''happily.'' But Gilly gets what she wants, and real life often takes strange turns. By helping children talk through their feelings, a teacher can help children make important leaps in understanding. Frequently, commercial guides for the discussion of novels overuse this kind of question assuming that children will rush to identify with the characters if we but ask, ''How would you feel if?. . .,'' ''What would you do if. . .?'' and ''When have you ever felt like. . .'' Direct inquiry of this sort not only runs the risk of violating a reader's privacy in the community of readers but can also lead the discussion away from the book, never to return again.

Since a picture book derives its definition from how the text and pictures work to create a story, good questions necessarily help readers focus on both the visual and the textual. What do readers notice about how the illustrator works (media, use of humor, use of line and color, page arrangement)? For instance, when comparing versions of "The Three Bears," kindergartners are fascinated by the contrasting print sizes in Paul Galdone's depiction; they notice that James Marshall's version presents Goldilocks in a persona entirely different from Galdone's; and they notice Marshall's droll telling as well as Goldilocks's repeated use of "I don't mind if I do" and adopt it as their own.[17] Good questions may be as simple as "What do you notice about the words?" and "What things are funny about the pictures?" Good questions follow up with "How can you tell?" or "What evidence in the book made you think this?" as a way of letting readers in on their own metacognitive skills. A good question doesn't need to be complex to help children discover complexity in how literature works.

Many commercial guides exist that can help a teacher plan good questions. However, teachers might examine the questions first to see what assumptions lie behind the guides. Those that reduce literature study to a series of fill-ins, vocabulary and dictionary drills, word searches, and gimmicks unrelated to the book violate our knowledge of reading as a meaning-related, highly personal act. Those guides that ask for factual recall above all else suggest that reading is educating the memory rather than the heart or the imagination. Teachers who design their own questions and guides often discover how much they learn in the process and how much easier it becomes to plan the good questions that help children get to the essence of a book.[18]

Graphic Organizers as Ways of Focusing Talk

There is no doubt that the right visual tool unlocks children's abilities and helps them concentrate longer on a task. Thus, teachers often ask children to make a list or chart as a way of encouraging and saving talk. Then, these charts and lists can be returned to in light of new information, as in the discussion of what qualities make a strong writer before and after children have read *Julia and the Hand of God*. A fourth grade teacher asks children to list and talk about clues to the mysterious Finn Learson's identity as she read aloud Mollie Hunter's fantasy, *A Stranger Came Ashore*. It is a way of mapping the story with children, but she is also helping them look at the author's craft.

Teachers find that comparison charts allow children to examine a variety of aspects as represented in a collection of similar titles. Betsy Byar's popular novels all seem to have no parents on the scene, humorous figurative language, difficult situations a child has to handle on his or her own, a helpful adult figure, and a small character change. A comparison chart with titles listed down the side and categories to be compared allows children to focus on and compare the works by this author. The chart then becomes a catalyst to which other readers may add their titles or discover new similarities, a double benefit to charts.

Currently, there is much enthusiasm for graphic organizers or story maps that call attention to the relationships among parts of a story such as plot structure, character development, settings, and so forth. These structural models seem tidy: Circles are tied together with lines, arrows point to squares, and terms such as "setting, problem, goal, events, reactions and outcomes" appear to guide readers reading. While some researchers[19] suggest that these help children grasp the essentials of the story, it is easy to see how confused children may become about their own personal responses to a story when it is reduced to a series of problems and solutions that arrive at a grand final "outcome." Certainly graphic organizers have their place. A comparison of the structure of Calmenson's *The Principal's New Clothes* and Scieszka's *The True Story of the 3 Little Pigs by A. Wolf* with the folktales from which they are derived would call children's attention to the ways authors manipulate well-known stories. Exercises such as this help children prepare for writing their own folktale parodies. But graphic organizers, like anything else overused in the teaching to reading, tend to obscure the personal uses to which children put reading. They tend to become ends in themselves rather than means to enhance reader response.

Collaboration on Good Activities

Good activities help children stand back from their reading even as they are returning to it for a deeper look. Two readers at work on a diary that the title character of Steig's *Dr. DeSoto* might have kept would have to discuss what happens on a typical mouse dentist's day and plan a format before they began to write. In talking about the mouse's point of view, they would work through and rehearse what they wanted to write before the pencil touched the paper. A side benefit to the community of readers would be the publicity this book received when the two children read aloud their created diary for the enjoyment of others.

There are obviously many activities centered around books which invite children to collaborate. In fact, nearly any book extension activity may be advantageously turned into a collaborative project—a game made from Van Allsburg's *Jumanji* benefits from several designers and lingers in the classroom to interest readers; a puppet show or other dramatic retellings, of course, need multiple players;

art projects such as murals depicting the setting arena of a story or the seasonal changes in a book such as Hall's *Ox-Cart Man* become enriched by discussion before and during the making.

Journals as Collaboration

Collaboration with the teacher is another form of social interaction in the classroom, but most teachers don't have the time to meet daily with each individual child. The response journal, book log, or dialogue journal has become a valuable tool in which children record their thoughts about what they are reading (see Barone in this book). Teachers can then write back when they have some reflection time. In her middle school classroom, Nancie Atwell instituted this writing "as a way of extending and enriching reflection through collaboration. I suspected kids' written responses would go deeper than their talk."[20]

When invited to write about their reading, children often follow certain patterns, retelling the story, questioning particular words and meanings, reacting with like or dislike to a particular part of the story, relating some part of the story to their own lives, or otherwise reflecting on their own reading. Working with a group of third graders, Barone[21] modeled both the response journal (child writes or comments, teacher responds) and the double-draft entry (on left of paper child copies or paraphrases quote from book and on right side interprets or comments on the quote). Barone showed how one perceptive boy worked on correlating information in Snyder's mystery *The Egypt Game* with what he knew of the world. He frequently commented on how he would have behaved if he were a character, speculated on the motives of characters, predicted what might happen next, and generally made specific to himself and the teacher what he was doing as a reader. Barone makes the point that if she had merely seen his last entry, which is typical of the traditional book report format ("I liked *The Egypt Game*. The professor was being weird 'til the end. And I liked it. And I think the book was real weird."), she would certainly be suspicious of a child's basic comprehension. But with the continuing dialogue, it was obvious that he had understood the story very well.

Teachers who worry about the amount of time focused discussion takes might introduce response journal writing following their individual reading time or reading aloud period as a way of "talking," but in writing, with each reader. Teachers may be tempted to impose more structure on these response journals with assigned topics such as writing "about a time when you felt like the main characer feels" or "as if you were the main character," but the primary power of the journals, say those teachers who use them, is that the child owns the ideas, the child is the director of the reading and the response, and the child reflects on what interests him or her. One teacher of fourth graders writes, "The thoughtfulness and engagement engendered by the journals resulted in richer, more complete, elaborate responses that I had received when I assigned questions. . .The most striking development facilitated by the journals was students' growth in confidence and motivation to read."[22] This doesn't imply that the teacher merely follows and does not lead. It just suggests that tightly focused questions, the noticing of literary techniques, or the discussion of patterns in literature become part of the classroom arena during some other time.

Some primary teachers have found a "story journal" a useful idea in inviting children to react to what they read. These are more product-oriented and less encouraging of whatever the child has to offer in terms of personal insight. In this, children draw pictures or write about the story they have just heard read to them. Sometimes the story suggests certain possibilities such as new adventures for the characters, alternative endings, or particular formats. These book-related story journals are shared publicly as a way of making both the reader and the book more visible in the classroom.[23]

Planning Widely for Language Use

Another way teachers can make use of children's desire to talk and work together is to plan for literature-reading across the curriculum. When teachers plan chains of reading experiences, such as the kindergarten comparison of several versions of "The Three Bears" or the first graders' revisiting of *Say It!*, children consider literature over time and in the light of new discoveries. Many articles and guides exist that help teachers plan for various and repeated experiences with a book or a theme.[24] All of these assume that the teacher is setting up small groups of inquiries so that pairs and groups work with each other, with the teacher, with the whole class, and alone. In this way, children satisfy their need to work together, and the teacher gains valuable time as she does not have to monitor each work spoken in class and can spend time on settling larger issues. Goubeaux[25] details a lengthy discussion her fifth graders held with her as they decided on a usable scale to create their model city during a thematic study beginning with Cesarani and Ventura's *Grand Constructions*. This fifth grade teacher planned the thematic study to involve many collaborative projects and then spent her time choreographing inquiry, troubleshooting, procuring books, asking the right questions to facilitate children's work, and rejoicing over what children were learning.

Teaching, as the many teachers mentioned in this chapter show us, takes planning and the optimistic knowledge that out of all this literature-filled richness, readers are indeed "picking their way to literacy." We have the evidence now that letting children talk and collaborate on their way to becoming readers not only facilitates the process but, indeed, is essential to the making of readers.

End Notes

1. Margaret Meek, *Learning to Read* (London: The Bodley Head, 1982) 183.
2. Richard C. Anderson, et al., *Becoming a Nation of Readers: The Report of the Commission on Reading* (Washington, D.C.: National Institute of Education, 1985).
3. Kenneth Goodman, "Look What They've Done to Judy Blume: The 'Basalization' of Children's Literature." *The New Advocate* 1, no. 1 (Winter, 1988): 29–41. See also Kenneth Goodman, S. Murphy, and P. Shannon. *Report Card on Reading* (Urbana, Illinois: National Council of Teachers of English, 1987).
4. Timothy V. Rasinski, and Diane Deford, "Learning Within a Classroom Context: First Graders' Conceptions of Literacy," ED 262 393. Arlington, Virginia: ERIC Document Reproducing Service, 1985.
5. Michael O. Tunnell, and James J. Jacobs, "Using 'Real' Books: Research Findings on Literature Based Reading Instruction," *The Reading Teacher* 42.6 (March 1989): 470–477.
6. Susan Hepler, *Patterns of Response to Literature: A One-Year Study of a Fifth and Sixth Grade Classroom* Ph.D. diss., The Ohio State University, 1982. See also Susan Hepler and Janet Hickman. " 'The Book Was OK. I Love You.:' Social Aspects of Response to Literature." *Theory into Practice* 21, no. 4 (Autumn, 1982): 278–83.
7. Joetta Beaver, "SAY IT! Over and Over." *Language Arts* 9, no. 2 (February, 1982): 143–148.
8. Celia Genishi, Andrea McCarrier, and Nancy Ryan Nussbaum. "Research Currents: Dialogue as a Context for Teaching and Learning," *Language Arts* 62, no. 2 (February, 1988): 187.
9. Courtney B. Cazden, *Classroom Discourse: The Language of Teaching and Learning* (Portsmouth, New Hampshire: Heinemann, 1988).
10. Vivian Paley, *Wally's Stories* (Cambridge, Massachusetts: Harvard University Press, 1981).
11. Dorothy J. Watson, and Suzanne C. Davis. "Readers and Texts in a Fifth-Grade Classroom." In *Literature in the Classroom: Readers, Texts, and Contexts* ed. Ben Nelms (Urbana, Illinois: National Council of Teachers of English, 1988).

12. Dorothy Stephens, "First Graders Taking the Head: Building Bridges between Literature and Writing," *The New Advocate 2*, no. 4 (Fall, 1989): 249–258.

13. Dorothy Strickland, Rose Marie Dillon, Leslie Funkhouser, Mary Glick, and Corrine Rogers. "Research Currents: Classroom Dialogue During Literature Response Groups," *Language Arts* 66, no. 2 (February, 1989): 192–200.

14. Leila Christenbury and Patricia Kelly, *Questioning: A Path to Critical Thinking* (Urbana, Illinois: National Council of Teachers of English, 1983) 8.

15. Hepler 1982, 88–89.

16. Douglas Barnes, *From Communication to Curriculum* (London: Penguin, 1976) 28.

17. Sharon Stutzman and Susan Hepler, "The Three Bears Go to Kindergarten." (In press.)

18. Susan Hepler, "A Guide for the Teacher Guides: Doing It Yourself," *The New Advocate* 1.3 (Summer, 1988): 186–195.

19. Zephaniah T. Davis and Michael D. McPherson, "Story Map Instruction: A Road Map for Reading Comprehension," *The Reading Teacher* 43.1 (December, 1989): 232–240.

20. Nancie Atwell, *In the Middle: Writing, Reading, and Learning with Adolescents* (Upper Montclair, New Jersey: Boynton/Cook, 1987) 165.

21. Diane Barone, "The Written Responses of Young Children: Beyond Comprehension to Story Understanding," *The New Advocate* 3.1 (Winter, 1990): 49–56.

22. Julie E. Wollman-Bonilla, "Reading Journals: Invitations to Participate in Literature," *The Reading Teacher* 43.2 (November, 1989): 119.

23. Pamela J. Farris, "Story Time and Story Journals: Linking Literature and Writing," *The New Advocate* 2.3 (Summer, 1989): 179–185.

24. See Joy Moss, *Focus Units in Literature: A Handbook for Elementary School Teachers* (Urbana, Illinois: National Council of Teachers of English, 1984). See also Joy Moss, *Focus on Literature: A Context for Literacy Learning* (Katonah, New York: Richard C. Owen Publishers, Inc., 1990). See also Barbara Peterson, *The Web* (Columbus, Ohio: The Ohio State University, 1990). See also Sonia Landes, and Molly Flender, *Book Wise Curriculum Guides* (Needham, Massachusetts: Christopher Gordon Publishers, Inc., 1987).

25. Sherry Goubeaux, "Teacher Feature: Grand Constructions," *The Web* 14.1 (Fall, 1989).

Children's Books Cited

Byars, Betsy. *The Pinballs.* New York: Harper, 1977.

Calmenson, Stephanie. *The Principal's New Clothes.* Illustrated by Denise Brunkus. New York: Scholastic Hardcover, 1989.

Cameron, Eleanor. *Julia and the Hand of God.* Illustrated by Gail Owen. New York: Dutton, 1977.

Carle, Eric. *The Very Hungry Caterpillar.* New York: World, 1968.

Carrick, Carol. *The Accident.* Illustrated by Donald Carrick. New York: Clarion, 1977.

Carrick, Carol. *The Foundling.* Illustrated by Donald Carrick. New York: Clarion, 1977.

Cesarani, Gian Paolo and Piero Ventura. *Grand Constructions.* New York: G.P. Putnam's, 1983.

Climo, Shirley. *The Egyptian Cinderella.* Illustrated by Ruth Heller. New York: Crowell, 1989.

Galdone, Paul. *The Three Bears.* New York: Clarion, 1972.

George, Jean Craighead. *The Cry of the Crow.* New York: Harper, 1980.

Hall, Donald. *Ox-Cart Man.* Illustrated by Barbara Cooney. Viking, 1979.

Hilleary, Jane Kopper. *Fletcher and the Big Dog.* Illustrated by Rick Brown. Boston: Houghton Mifflin, 1988.

Huck, Charlotte S. *Princess Furball.* Illustrated by Anita Lobel. New York: Greenwillow, 1989.

Hunter, Mollie. *A Stranger Came Ashore.* New York: Harper, 1975.

Lionni, Leo. *Tico and the Golden Wings.* New York: Pantheon, 1964.

Louis, Ai-Ling. *Yeh Shen: A Cinderella Story from China.* Illustrated by Ed Young. New York: Philomel, 1982.

Marshall, James. *Goldilocks and the Three Bears.* New York: Dial, 1988.

Mazer, Norma Fox. *I, Trissy.* New York: Delacorte, 1971.

Paterson, Katherine. *The Great Gilly Hopkins.* New York: Crowell, 1978.

Sauer, Julia. *Fog Magic.* Illustrated by Lynd Ward. New York: Viking, 1943.

Scieszka, Jon. *The True Story of the 3 Little Pigs by A. Wolf.* Illustrated by Lane Smith. New York: Viking Kestrel, 1989.

Steig, William. *Dr. DeSoto.* New York: Farrar Straus Giroux, 1982.

Thomas, Jane Resh. *The Comeback Dog.* Illustrated by Troy Howell. Boston: Houghton Mifflin, 1981.

Van Allsburg, Chris. *Jumanji.* Boston: Houghton Mifflin, 1981.

Voigt, Cynthia. *On Fortune's Wheel.* New York: Atheneum, 1990.

Zolotow, Charlotte. *Say It!* Illustrated by James Stevenson. New York: Greenwillow, 1980.

6

"That Reminds me of":
Using Dialogue Journals with
Young Students
Diane Barone

Diane Barone teaches literacy education at the
University of Nevada, Las Vegas. For many years
she served as head teacher in the laboratory
school at the University of Nevada-Reno, where
she began a collaboration with Jonathan Lovell.
Alone and with Lovell, Barone has written extensively about children's written responses to
literature. Here she illustrates the use of written
response journals with primary grade students.

Wanted: a natural way to engage students in reading and writing. Must
require no commercial materials, diagnostic tests, or teacher training. Must work equally well with first and second language learners,
from kindergarten through adult years.[1]

As a teacher who was implementing process writing and a literature
based reading curriculum with young students, I was particularly interested in finding a way to combine reading and writing informally.
I was searching for a special practice, not bound by commercial
materials, exactly as Staton described.

At the beginning of my search, I investigated the literature on
response, particularly the responses to stories of elementary children.
Most of these response studies focused on oral response by individuals
(student to teacher/researcher) or by discussion groups. Applebee[2]
and Hickman,[3] two researchers working in this area, described the
changes in children's oral responding as they became older. Applebee
noted four classifications of response: retelling, summary, analysis

85

or understanding through analogy, and generalization about the work or theme. Hickman summarized the strategies that students might use in reacting to a story. Her response strategies included, but were not limited to, summary, classification, and theme statements.

More recently, Eeds and Wells[4] explored the discussions between fifth and sixth grade students and their novice group leaders (students enrolled in undergraduate reading classes). When the discussions were analyzed, Eeds and Wells discovered patterns of retelling, inference support including confirmation or rejection of hypotheses, personal responses, and critiques related to the author's craft.

While the literature details children's oral response patterns, the written responses of young students to independently read texts has not been extensively studied. My search, therefore, moved away from investigations of the oral responses of younger students to the work of researchers investigating the written responses of older students. These studies provided an awareness of the role of dialogue journals in fostering communication about literature through writing.

Staton[1] defines dialogue journals as "a responsive form of writing in which the student and teacher carry on a conversation over time, sharing ideas, feelings, and concerns in writing" (p. 47). She describes how these journals had been used for several years in Leslie Reed's sixth grade classroom in Los Angeles. One conclusion Staton reached after observation and analyses of the students' journals was that, through written dialogue, "the teacher supports the student's emerging reading and writing competencies and acquisition of more complex reasoning skills" (p. 199).

Atwell[5] deliberately attempted to discover a way to replicate with her students the discussions about books that she and her friends had around her dining room table. She experimented with dialogue journals with her eighth grade students for two reasons: There was not enough time to engage in these extensive discussions with each student in her large classes, and the students' talk about text rarely developed beyond retelling the story.

During the sharing of her thoughts and feelings about creating these reading/writing relationships, Atwell discussed the potential importance of writing about narrative texts.

> I suspected that a written exchange between two readers, student and adult expert, would take readers even deeper inside written texts. As a teacher of writing I'd learned how writing conferences—the dialogue between writer and teacher—helped students to consider and develop their thoughts. As a teacher of reading I welcomed another opportunity to engage my kids in what Vygotsky termed "mediated learning," cooperating with them as an experienced reader in this special context. Finally, I believed this special context—a teacher initiating and inviting first-draft chat—would provide a way for me to be responsive to every reader as well as a specific occasion for them to write and reflect.[6]

Berthoff[7] provided an adaptation to a dialogue journal called a double-entry draft, which she routinely used with college students. The double-entry draft adds another dimension to the dialogue journal for now the student reflects upon his or her own writing and the teacher then comments on both of these responses. In other words, the student has a written conversation with himself or herself before the teacher enters into the dialogue.

When using the double-entry draft response, the student divides his or her notebook page in half. On one side the student copies any sentence, phrase, list, or other interesting information from the text, and on the other side of the paper the student writes thoughts about what he or she has copied from the text. By using this technique, Berthoff reminds us "that students, in whatever they write and with whatever they read, are interpreting and composing: They are making meaning" (p. 46).

Introducing Dialogue Journals

Based on Atwell's, Berthoff's, and Staton's ideas about dialogue journals, I decided to experiment with the young students in my classroom. Before looking at the responses written by the children, a brief explanation about the children and the literacy environment in the classroom might be beneficial. The organization of the children was unusual in many ways. The classroom consisted of first, second, and third grade students. When the students entered in first grade, they usually remained for three years. The children were as different from one another as they could possibly be. Academically the range was from gifted students to special education students. The majority of the students were enrolled from a nearby city public school, and the remaining students came from the outlying area. As a result, there were large socioeconomic differences among the children. Children in the class were also culturally and linguistically different. At least one child at each grade level was learning English as a second language.

Children's literature was the core for all learning in the classroom. Reading events occurred several times during the day. The children shared stories in literature groups. These small groups of children read, discussed, and wrote about the same story. The children often read next to each other, in a cozy part of the classroom, and they would giggle or gasp in response to the stories that they were reading. Each afternoon the children read self-selected books using a sustained silent reading (SSR) format. Following SSR, I read to the children for approximately thirty minutes. These reading sessions included poetry, a picture book, and a chapter from a longer novel. The reading and writing activities were truly the center of this classroom. As much as possible, all subject matter was themed around children's literature.

The reading of children's literature was balanced with children's writing. The students in the room wrote from the very first day of first grade. Each morning a journal awaited them at their desks. Several of the first graders and the children learning English as a second language drew pictures in their journal and gradually invented spelling began to accompany their drawings. After a brief whole group sharing time, the children moved into process writing during writing workshop. Each day the students spent forty five minutes writing to their own topic and occasionally writing to a teacher directed topic. The students routinely conferenced with each other, and before their stories were published they would conference with me. At the end of each workshop, one or two children would share their books, and the students would comment on the part they liked or ask a question about a confusing part of the story. The children were always supported in their writing attempts, and my oral and written comments were focused on content, not form. Because of the frequency of writing and the acceptance by the children that writing was just a routine part of the curriculum, the expectation was that when the children were asked to write in dialogue journals they would not consider this activity unusual. This easy acceptance of dialogue journals might not be the case in classrooms where writing was not an ordinary occurrence.

During the first week of school, a dialogue in the form of a letter and double-entry draft were modeled for all of the students in the class. *Superfudge*[8] served as the stimulus for the modeling of the letter. I wrote on an overhead transparency about a chapter of the book in which Fudge and Peter have a new baby sister and shared it with the children. They asked questions or commented in general about what I had written. They wanted to know what Fudge might do to his baby sister and were determined to get me to give away several of the episodes. I then suggested that after they read their books they might also write a letter about their story and I would write comments in return.

On the following day, I modeled the double-entry draft response. In the book *Ramona the Brave*,[9] Mrs. Quimby decides to return to work. Ramona's first concern about this change in her home environment is reflected in her question, ''Who will bake cookies?'' This sentence and a part of the following dialogue were copied onto a transparency and served as the stimulus for a double-entry draft (D.E.D.) response. Here are the results of the demonstration.

D.E.D.

"Who will bake the cookies?" she asked. "Oh, cookies." Mrs. Quimby dismissed the cookies as unimportant. "We can buy them at the store, or you can bake them from a mix. You're old enought now." (pp. 40–41)	I bought tons of TV dinners for my kids when I started going to school every night. I thought that they would love picking out whatever they wanted for dinner. They thought they were GROSS, not like home cooked dinners. So now on some nights they cook dinner for me.

These were the only forms of response modeled for the children. The students were never given specific directions about the kind of response that they might write. I did not give specific directions because I was curious as to what students would write without this guidance. The only expectations were that they would write something each time they independently read a story and that I would respond to the content of their responses.

Each day the literature groups met, and any child who felt comfortable would share his or her written response. This initial sharing provided the impetus for the group's discussion. The discussions were chiefly centered on the plot of the story. The children often used each other to make sure that they understood all the events that had occurred in a chapter. For example, while one group was reading *The Egypt Game*, the children asked each other about the fingernails or fingers that had been used in the ceremony. They were anxious to discover exactly what the kids were doing during their pretend ceremony.

I had several questions that I hoped would be answered through analysis of the students' written responses. Would the students mirror their oral discussions about stories, most often retelling or summarizing the plot, in their writing? Would the writing limit their responding? Would the cognitive load of the writing task limit the ideas that they would be able to represent? Would the writing move the children to consideration of other, less literal facets of their reading, similar to the findings of Atwell? These questions were constantly considered as I began a year-long investigation into the patterns of response that would be produced by the twenty seven children in my classroom.

Response Writing Throughout the Year

First Grade Responders

We will begin by looking at the writing of a group of first graders at three points during the year. These observations provide a glimpse into the development of written response over a few short months. I will then focus on a group of second and third graders as they read *The Egypt Game*.[10] The responses provided by these students will allow us to consider the similarities and differences among responses to the same book and to note the continuing development in response writing.

The first grade group was made up of six first graders. These children began first grade as beginning readers and writers. Most of their reading instruction during the fall consisted of language experience activities and the sharing of predictable text. The children often created "Big Books" that followed the pattern of a book that had been read to them. They might have chorally read a predictable text and then performed a play based on the story or created a mural. As the children moved beyond these supportive reading activities and were able to read independently, dialogue journals were introduced.

The first responses that they wrote after reading independently were in January to the book *More Spaghetti I Say*.[11] The children each drew a picture to accompany their writing. Annie's and Heather's responses in Figure 6-1 illustrate this combination of writing with drawing. Interestingly, the writing was produced first and the illustration second, so in this case the children were using the illustration to extend and support their writing, the primary form of communication. We might have expected, because of the age of these students, to see the reverse of this situation in which the writing occurs after the illustration. These children demonstrated by their writing priority that they were competent and confident with this form of communication.

The responses of all the children were very similar. Each child moved beyond the literal content of the story to include what they, personally, would do with all that spaghetti. Here are the responses of several of the children.

> *Heather:* I would eat it with sauce.
> *Annie:* I would eat with sauce and bread and mushrooms and lettuce and milk and sometimes chocolate milk and for dessert chocolate cake but I don't like it too much that I'd throw it around like the monkey in the book.
> *Dylan:* I wish everything was made out of spaghetti and we could eat the whole wide world.
> *Aamir:* I wish everything was made out of spaghetti, and we could eat the whole world up.

The children definitely had experience eating spaghetti. Most of the comments indicated that they would eat spaghetti as part of a larger meal that included chocolate cake. Annie was the only child who considered the behavior of the monkey. While she enjoyed eating

spaghetti, she said that she wouldn't be as excited as the monkey—
"I don't like it too much that I'd throw it around like the monkey in
the book." Dylan's and Aamir's responses were almost exact duplications. While this might be a concern to some teachers in some situations, I was pleased to see that Dylan and Aamir were reading and
writing together. Aamir was a student who was learning English as
a second language. His partnership with Dylan allowed him to practice English through the shared reading and discussion of the story.
They wrote as a team, each adding an idea of their own to the response. As Dylan's and Aamir's later responses were observed, Aamir's
growing independence as a reader and writer would be noted.

Our next visit to this group comes one month later during the early
part of February. The children have just read *Caps for Sale*.[12] Here are
their responses to this story.

> *Aamir:* A guy had 17 caps and he can't sell them. He was sad; very, very
> sad. So he slept on a tree and 17 monkeys took the hats.
> *Dylan:* A guy had 17 caps and he could not sell any caps. He napped. So these
> monkeys took his caps and he woke up. He saw the monkeys and they copied
> him.
> *Annie:* A man walked down the dirt road and he sold caps. And one day
> nobody wanted a hat and he went to a tree and he fell asleep. And the monkeys
> took his hat and he found out. And he got them back and went back to his place.
> And he started again, selling his hats again.

> *Kirstin:* It is funny and I like it. It is a blue ribbon book. It is good. I love it.
> *Heather:* It is funny and I like it.

When comparing these responses to the first written responses, the
most obvious difference is length. These children have become able
to process a considerable amount of written text. With the exception
of Heather's response, all the responses were longer. The extra mental processing required of writing when compared to oral discussion
did not seem to be interfering with their ability to communicate
through writing alone. Although it is not evident in the listing of the
responses, none of these responses were accompanied by an illustration. The children were relying on writing alone to communicate, a
significant change from their previous responses and again supporting the observation that writing was not limiting their communication capabilities.

These responses tended to be closer to the story than the first
responses. The students were not talking about how it would be for
them to sell hats; with the exception of Heather and Kirstin, they were
mainly summarizing the story. They deleted several of the story's
events and focused on the monkeys taking the hats. Perhaps selling
hats was more distant in their personal experience than eating

Figure 6-1. Annie's Response

I woud eat it  wiht
saos and brad and
mushrums and lituc and
milk and somtimes coklit
milk and for disirt coklit
cake but I dont Like it to
muce tahr I troit aroond
like the monkey in the
book.

Annie

Figure 6-1 (continued). Heather's Response

spaghetti was, so they did not place themselves in this experience. The story could also have been more difficult to read and the children might have been limited to comprehending the story literally rather than sharing related personal experiences.

Aamir's and Dylan's responses were again similar. They certainly began the same, ''A guy had 17 caps,'' but this is where the similarity ended. Aamir moved beyond the literal story and concluded that the man is sad because he has not sold any hats. Dylan stayed with the literal events of the story and related that the man naps. Again, this change in Aamir's writing is interesting. His writing demonstrates his growth as a reader and writer in his second language. While he had certainly read and discussed the story with Dylan, he now added his own ideas about the story. In this case, he had considered the feelings of the character and demonstrated his understanding of the more abstract qualities of the story, ideas not yet written about by Dylan.

Heather and Kirstin's responses to this story were different from the other children's. Neither of them wrote about the literal events of the story. They seemed to assume that because we were all reading the same story in this group and knew what has happened, they could just share their feelings about it. Kirstin had discovered that the book had been awarded a blue ribbon and concluded, therefore, it must be good. She was using this award to support her decision that the book is good. Heather and Kirstin both shared their feelings that the book is funny. What neither of them did, however, was attempt to support these feelings with examples from the book.

The stories to which this group usually responded were short stories, ones that could be read in one sitting. At the end of the year, this group made the transition to longer stories or chapter books. The shift to these longer narratives was gradual. They began by reading the Hobans' Frances books and Lobel's Frog and Toad books.[13] Generally the children read one chapter a day.

Our next observation will be of the children's responses to one chapter in *Days with Frog and Toad*. The chapters in this book each tell a different tale about Frog and Toad. In the chapter called ''The Kite,'' Frog tries to fly a kite with the help of Toad. The responses to the kite flying chapter are shared below.

> *Kirstin:* I love flying kites. OK. Let's get to the real thing now. Frog and Toad tried to fly their kite but the kite would not fly. They tried and tried and tried and the kite flew.
> *Aamir:* Frog wanted to fly a kite but it didn't fly. He tried and tried and tried but no it wouldn't fly. Then it did fly.
> *Dylan:* The kite got lost and they could not find it. Then they found it and flew it.

> *Annie:* Frog and Toad were trying to fly a kite and it wouldn't fly. And he tried again and again and finally they got it to work. And it went higher than the birds.
>
> *Jeff:* Frog wanted to fly a kite. And Toad had to run with the kite. And tried and tried to but the robins laughed at him. And then the kite flew.

In a comparison of these responses and those written previously, length is the dominant characteristic. These responses are all longer than earlier responses. As with the *Caps for Sale* responses, they are summaries of the literal events of the chapter. Each child has commented on the difficulties that Frog and Toad had in getting the kite to fly and then the final success of getting the kite launched. Kirstin's response was the only one to include her personal love of flying kites. She carefully separated her personal response from the summary of the chapter though with the words—''OK. Let's get to the real thing now.''

All of the children's responses to the chapters of this book followed a summary format. None of them shared the writer's feelings about the characters or events in each chapter. Perhaps these young responders chose the summary form for these chapters because each chapter is in fact a short story. They appeared to be reading each chapter as if it were a separate book. A second observation is that very few of the responses were extended with illustrations. Of the twenty four responses to this book, only seven were accompanied by illustrations, an indication that these young children were favoring writing to communicate their ideas about their reading.

This group of six children wrote 274 responses to stories between January and June. The majority of their responses (75%) were either retelling or summary responses. The children preferred to write about the more literal aspects of the stories that they were reading. The above examples illustrate the summary type of response that they most often used. While they infrequently chose the letter format in their responses, they never chose the double-entry draft. As we will see with the group reading *The Egypt Game*, the double-entry draft strategy often resulted in interpretive responses. Perhaps because these children were beginning readers and writers, they were limited to writing about the more literal aspects of a story. Cognitively, they may not yet have been able to include inferential, more abstract qualities about the story in their writing on any routine basis. As a result of the added complexity of communicating through writing, they may have been limited to writing about the surface elements of the story.

The kind of story that the first graders were generally reading may also have influenced the form of their responses. They were most often reading short stories or chapter books that were really a collection of short stories; this kind of narrative may have caused the children to respond more literally. Squire[14] discovered that students' responses changed as they read a longer story. They often began with literal responses, and then as they progressed in the story they considered the more abstract issues. The kind of book that these students were independently reading may have narrowed their response patterns.

While these young students were predominantly responding to the more obvious elements of the stories that they were reading, we can certainly see through the sharing of their responses that they were capable of writing about their reading. These responses indicate that they comprehended these independently read stories very well. Their summaries supported each child's ability to pare down the story to its most crucial elements.

Second and Third Grade Responders

The second and third graders wrote over 1,000 responses during this school year. They began writing in a dialogue notebook in September and continued through June. Their responses showed more variety than those produced by the first graders. Fifty-four percent of the responses were literal responses (summaries and retellings) and 56 percent were inferential (most often analogies to personal experiences). They often chose to write using the technique of the double-entry draft. When this form was used, the children's responses moved beyond the literal aspects of the text. They often started their response with the words, "That reminds me of," which directly led to a personal analogy of an event in the story.

To better understand the responses produced by this group of children, we'll focus on the notebooks of nine second and third graders as they read Snyder's *The Egypt Game*. This book is about a group of inner-city children who pretend they are in Egypt. They play their imaginary game in the lot behind an antique shop owned by a mysterious professor. A murder mystery plot is also interwoven throughout the story. The children were reading sections of this book daily during May and June. The routine for reading began with the students meeting in a group, during which time they shared thoughts about the story triggered from the responses written in their notebooks. The conversations were student led, and I was a participating member of the group. The children infrequently talked about the personal connections that they were making with the characters or events within the story. The children tacitly considered these connections personal, and they were almost always only shared through writing. The notebooks served as a way to remember what had been read yesterday and as an entry to the literature group's discussion. Following a retelling of the important events, I would guide the conversation to today's reading. This preparation often included predictions for the upcoming chapter based on past reading. The students would then move to a comfortable place in the classroom for silent reading and writing in their notebooks.

Here are their first responses to the story.

Elder—	**D.E.D.**
The discovery of Egypt	That reminds me of when we wrote the cluster. That was fun. I think King Tut was a very fineman. I wish I was there when he was alive. That would have been really fun. He would have given me lots of money.

Lucas—	**D.E.D.**
The discovery of Egypt	That reminds me of when I found out that could clean my room and I did it— the best.

*Mary Martha:*Dear Mrs. Barone,
Two girls pretended they were in Egypt. They took Egypt statues and pretended that they were real people. They used weeds for flowers and gave them to one of the statues that was supposed to be the god.

Anti: When I read the book, it was weird because the strange guy owned a department store and on the top it said A–Z. And no one really knew the strange guy's name or what A–Z standed for. That's why it was weird.

Eldon—	**D.E.D.**
Marshall, Marshall don't get stuck.	If Marshall is five and the girls are old, how could they get through the fence easier?

These responses illustrate the variety of response forms freely chosen and the diversity of the ideas expressed. Three children chose to write letters. Mary Martha's letter summarized the chapter through her discussion of the characteristics of the Egypt game. Elder and Lucas wrote double-entry draft pieces, which clearly show how this form lends itself to personal connections. Elder shared his knowledge about King Tut and the idea of going back to that period of time, particularly to enjoy all that money. Lucas appeared to be making connections to the word *discovery.* He realized that he could clean his room, perhaps a surprising discovery to an eight-year old boy. The remaining responses group together because of their differences. Eldon questioned the logic of an event in the story, and Anti decided that this story was weird and was supporting this opinion. Overall, the responses centered on the literal happenings in the story. As in Squire's study[14] of students' responses throughout a book, the children preferred literal responses at the beginning of stories. They used these retellings and summaries as a way into a long book. The responses helped them to get a sense of the plot and were necessary before they were able to move into freer interpretations.

The next responses are taken from various points during the reading of the middle of the book. The frequent use of the double-entry draft is obvious in these responses.

Mary Martha—	**D.E.D.**
Me? Scared?	This reminds me of when I was three years old and I left my doll outside and I finally remembered and I asked my brother if he would get it for me. But he said, ''you are too scared'' and I said, ''I am not too scared but will you go with me?''

Eldon—	**D.E.D.**
Do you still play with paper dolls?	Why would a girl 11 play with paper dolls? Where do you get them?

Michael—	**D.E.D.**
Bury the bird	That reminds me of when I went to my friend's house. He said, ''Let me take you to the grave.'' I was afraid it might be a real grave. But he buried a bird and made a cross for it so it looked like one.

Sam—	**D.E.D.**
Melanie said that she had read about some people who cut off their fingers as sacrifices	Once upon a time Vincent Van Gogh cut off his ear. It probably wasn't pretty.

Elder—	**D.E.D.**
The Oracle of Thoth	That reminds me about Yoda. He is a character from the movies Star Wars and Return of the Jedi. He was really old. Yoda's age was about 400 years old. I think that is really old. But then he died. I feel really sorry for him, don't you? And so there you have it folks. So now I leave you. Bye Mrs. Barone and have a happy day.

These double-draft entries demonstrate how this form facilitates the building of personal connections with the story. The children were using key words or phrases to trigger their memories of similar experiences in their own lives. The words "that reminds me of" were the convention that they often used to record these memories. It is interesting that the children chose these words to lead them into their explanations of the phrases that they copied from text. They parallel the function of "once upon a time" in fairy tales.

Eldon's response was unique in these examples but was often chosen by students when they didn't understand a portion of the text. He did not have an enormous amount of background about paper dolls but what little he had puzzled him. Obviously, he felt that 11-year-old girls were too old to play with paper dolls. His response was a plea for his fellow readers to help him make sense of this situation. This kind of response would frequently be shared with the group of readers.

Our last look at the responses to this story comes at the end of the book. Mary Martha's entry is representative of these final responses.

> I really liked *The Egypt Game* even though it was easy to guess what was going to happen. It was full of mystery and excitement. Mysteries are my favorite kinds of books. I think the most mysterious part of the book was when the girl got kidnapped because it tricked you and made you think it was the professor. It did not give you any clues either like all the others so that you could tell who or what was doing it. I could figure it out, everything except that I have one question where did you buy the book? I would like to buy it so that I could take it home and read it to my mom. If I really liked it, I think she would really like it.

This entry illustrated the students' return to more literal responses at the conclusion of a book. The students summed up their favorite parts and offered their critical opinions of whether the book was liked or disliked and why. Again, this return to more literal responses at a book's ending replicates the findings of Squire

When all of the responses to this book are considered, it seems that the students preferred inferential responses. Of the 184 responses written about this book, 81 percent were inferential. They were often D.E.D. entries and generally followed the form of "that reminds me of" with a close tie to personal experience.

Closing Discussion

The children's responses provided answers to the questions that accompanied my inquiry about dialogue journals. The first graders' responses generally did mirror their oral discussions about books. They tended to retell or summarize the stories that they were reading. Their written retellings and summaries were briefer than their typical oral responses. In noting the differences in their responses over time, the most obvious change was in the length of each response. While their initial responses were brief, their subsequent responses became longer and better matched the richness of their oral responses. Perhaps the most interesting development of the written responses with the first graders was the diminishment of the accompanying illustration. The children's first responses used illustrations to extend the meaning of the written response, but the majority of their subsequent responses conveyed meaning solely through the use of words.

These results are similar to the findings of Applebee.[15] The young students who discussed their favorite stories often utilized the retelling or summary format. Typically, we would expect that children's written communication would lag behind their oral production. The writing task for beginning readers and writers requires an enormous amount of cognitive energy. Young children compose most words letter by letter and are often limited in the ideas that they can convey through writing alone because of this fatigue factor. Surprisingly, perhaps because these students were very comfortable expressing their ideas through writing they were able to produce responses that closely matched their oral discussions about stories.

The second and third graders' written responses were often more complex than their oral responses. During oral discussion, the children often retold the plot and commented on actions within the story. The double-entry draft provided a structure that allowed the children to share personal experiences that enriched their understanding of stories. Their responses matched the findings of Atwell[16] in that the written responses were more complex than oral discussion about a story. The written responses deviated from the findings of Applebee[17] and Hickman[18] in that they corresponded more closely to the oral responses of older students. The oral conversation examples of fifth and sixth grade students shared by Eeds and Wells[19] parallel the written response produced by these second and third graders. The dialogue journal format provided the vehicle for these young children to consider the more abstract qualities of stories. These findings address the second and third questions posed earlier. Writing did not limit the responding of these young children. Certainly the first graders did not express themselves as fully in writing as they did in talking, but their skill in communicating through writing quickly developed. This development in writing competency was especially evident when we consider the responses of the second and third graders. Initiating the use of the dialogue journal with these young children helped them develop personal understanding of the stories that they read.

Mikkelson[20] discussing the qualities of exceptional literature, says that:

> Some books keep us remembering, discovering, and sharing our discoveries long after we first encounter them. The power of the story to generate light. The power of the light to generate the story. And we ourselves may determine the worth of books by the stories we elicit in response to them, the stories we choose to tell ourselves, the stories we are given to remember. (p. 619)

Following from the logic of this discussion, we realize that quality literature includes those stories, plays, and poems that cause us to remember our own personal stories. They are written in such a way that we, because of our personal experiences, understand and empathize with the character's situation. This kind of reading involvement is usually reserved for our most sophisticated older students.

My experiment of having young children write in dialogue journals throughout the year supports the assertion that this type of reading involvement can begin much sooner. The double-entry draft technique provided the scaffolding that allowed these younger students to share their related personal experiences. As the teacher and responder to these entries, I found my understanding of each story was expanded. I doubt that I would have ever before compared the ''Oracle of Thoth'' to Yoda. Now, however, each time I return to this story, I will have that mental image of the Oracle. Sam's response about Van Gogh was also startling. Without the notebooks, I doubt that I would have ever discovered his knowledge about painters.

The response notebooks allowed the entire community of readers to build upon individual knowledge and to extend this personal knowledge through communication with an interested reader and writer. The readers, through the use of dialogue journals, each discovered more about themselves as they came to understand the stories that they were reading.

End Notes

1. Jana Staton, ''Dialogue journals: A new tool for teaching communication,'' *ERIC/CLL News Bulletin* 6.2 (1983) 1–2, 6, p. 1. See also Jana Staton, ''The Power of Responding in Dialogue Journals,'' ed. T. Fulwiler, *The Journal Book* (Portsmouth, NH: Heinemann, 1987) 47–63.
2. Arthur Applebee, *The Child's Concept of Story* (Chicago, IL: University of Chicago Press, 1978).
3. Janet Hickman, ''Everything Considered: Response to literature in an elementary school setting.'' *Journal of Research and Development in Education* 16 (1983): 8–13.

4. Maryann Eeds, & Dawn Wells, "Grand conversations: An exploration of meaning construction in literature study groups." *Research in the Teaching of English* 23.1 (1989): 4–29.
5. Nancie Atwell, "Building a Dining Room Table: Dialogue Journals about Reading, ed. T. Fulwiler, *The Journal Book* (Portsmouth, NH: Heinemann, 1987) 157–170.
6. Atwell, 158–159.
7. Ann Berthoff, *The Making of Meaning* (Upper Montclair, NJ: Boynton/Cook Publishers, Inc., 1981).
8. Judy Blume, *Superfudge* (New York: Dell Publishing Co., Inc., 1980).
9. Beverly Cleary, *Ramona the Brave* (New York: Dell Publishing Co., Inc., 1975).
10. Zilpha Keatley Snyder, *The Egypt Game* (New York: Scholastic, Inc., 1967).
11. Richard Gelman, *More Spaghetti I Say.* (New York: Scholastic Book Services, 1977).
12. E. Slobodkina, *Caps for Sale* (New York: Scholastic Book Services, 1976).
13. Arnold Lobel, *Days with Frog and Toad* (New York: Harper, 1979), Russell Hoban, *Bedtime for Frances* (New York: Harper, 1976).
14. James Squire, "The responses of adolescents to literature involving selected experiences of personal development," diss. University of California-Berkeley, 1956.
15. Applebee 1978.
16. Atwell 1987.
17. Applebee 1978.
18. Hickman 1983.
19. Eeds and Wells 1989.
20. N. Mikkelsen, "Remembering Ezra Jack Keats and The Snowy Day. What makes a children's book good." *Language Arts*, 66.6 (1989): 608–624.

7

Shared Inquiry: The Great Books Method of Interpretive Reading and Discussion

James Plecha

James Plecha is a senior editor at the Great Books Foundation, publishers of Junior Great Books, a program that for some thirty years has trained teachers and volunteers to discuss stories intelligently and deeply with children from kindergarten up. Here he explains the kinds of questions that are asked, how the discussions are run, how the stories are chosen, and more. These ideas will be useful to anyone wishing to discuss quality literature with children.

Shared inquiry is a method of approaching literature originally developed by the Great Books Foundation for use in its adult reading and discussion programs. The Great Books approach to continuing adult self-education was inspired by the idea that thoughtful readers, regardless of their educational backgrounds, could come together and, by pooling their differing perspectives and insights, help each other derive personal meaning from reading major works of literature and philosophy. The result was a nontraditional learning situation emphasizing the ability of each reader to interact successfully with an original text and promoting an unusual atmosphere of intellectual collaboration, openness to ideas, and reflection on one's life and outlook.

Since 1962, the Junior Great Books program has brought this unique method of cooperative learning to younger readers. The aim of Junior Great Books is to make substantial literature a regular part of classroom reading for all children, from kindergarten through high school. It is the Foundation's conviction that only by enjoying a positive experience with high-quality literature throughout their school years can students develop the coordination of skills, habits, and attitudes that characterize successful readers—readers who think for themselves and have the persistence of mind to reach for meaning.

By combining their resources through shared inquiry, students are able to read challenging literature with comprehension. The stories in the Junior Great Books program are selected from outstanding traditional and modern literature, including children's classics, folk and fairy tales, and modern short stories from cultures around the world. These stories are rich in ideas and have been carefully chosen for their ability to support the intensive interpretive work with a text that shared inquiry involves. They have not been rewritten for a particular grade level, nor is their vocabulary "controlled." When deciding in which series a selection belongs, the Foundation places primary emphasis on appropriateness for the age group rather than standard assessments of reading levels for each grade. This ensures that stories contain themes and characters that students feel motivated to reflect upon and investigate thoughtfully.

Because shared inquiry is a cooperative exploration of a story's ideas, less able readers can participate on an equal footing with advanced readers. The Great Books' focus on open-ended questions means that students always start from their own opinions, interests, and cultural perspectives; differences among students' learning styles and life experiences complement each other. The program's large oral component—the opportunity for reading aloud and sharing notes and questions—enables all students to participate in developing their thoughts and feelings about a work of literature.

Shared inquiry is also an opportunity for students to experience their teacher in a new role as an active and involved partner in open-ended inquiry. As a shared inquiry discussion leader, the teacher guides students' thinking only by careful questioning, focusing on questions to which he or she has no satisfactory answer. During discussion the teacher does not offer personal opinions or attempt to teach a single authoritative interpretation. Rather, the teacher's aim is to help students explore, support, and develop insights that originate with them. He or she is a model of a person whose mind has been stimulated by an intellectual problem and whose broad experience enables him or her to guide the group toward finding their own solutions.

Well-directed, thoughtful, interpretive discussion has great potential for opening up a work of literature for a reader. Too often children are asked to respond to a story in ways that an adult would find artificial and which ultimately cannot provide them with the guidance they need to appreciate and enjoy reading on their own. The Great Books Foundation believes that, as far as possible, children should be encouraged to find in their reading the same rewards and pleasures as adults—the same intellectual stimulation, imaginative challenge, and thoughtful enlarging of experience. By concentrating on interpretive reading and discussion, Junior Great Books provides a natural and consistent approach to literature in which children join forces in a search for meaning. Through shared inquiry, students are able to relate what happens in a story to their subjective experience in a heartfelt and intelligent way and so learn to incorporate what they have read into their understanding of life.

Interpretation: The Focus of Shared Inquiry

In shared inquiry, reading and discussion focus upon interpretive questions—fundamental questions of meaning in a story that present a challenge to the understanding both of children and adults. Good interpretive questions are not broad questions that can be asked equally well of any work—e.g., ''What is the theme of this story?'' or ''What is its main idea?'' or ''How are the main characters similar or dissimilar?'' Rather, interpretive questions reflect the students' and teacher's thoughtful responses to a story's particular characters and situations.

For example, in discussing ''Beauty and the Beast,'' students might develop answers to the questions: Why isn't being grateful to the Beast enough to make Beauty love him? Does Beauty love the Beast because of his fine qualities or because he needs her? Why does the Beast turn into a handsome prince only after Beauty realizes that she loves him as he is? For *The Strange Case of Dr. Jekyll and Mr. Hyde*, students might consider: Why is Mr. Hyde able to destroy Dr. Jekyll? Why does the author have Dr. Lanyon destroyed by his desire for knowledge?

Such questions lie at the heart of understanding the wisdom of these stories and are the kinds of questions that would involve an able adult reader in deep reflection. Making such questions the focus of discussion encourages students to look at the story from many perspectives and to turn frequently to the text to support their viewpoints. By sharing their initial, tentative opinions, students come to read more carefully and to see significance in details that might have escaped them at first. Repeated discussion experience develops students' ability to revise their ideas in the face of new evidence, build upon partial answers, and raise new questions in response to the differing opinions of their classmates.

For instance, in the tale "Jack and the Beanstalk" (as retold by Joseph Jacobs, *Junior Great Books Series 2*), discussion might focus upon the interpretive question, Why does Jack go up the beanstalk the third time? After all, Jack has already secured endless wealth by taking the hen that lays golden eggs, and he has only narrowly escaped being eaten by the ogre on previous visits. Why does he return—what more does he want? Has Jack become greedy? Has success made him desire finer things? Has he grown irrepressibly curious and adventurous, or is his third trip evidence that he still has a score to settle with the ogre?

Such questions cannot be answered simply by pointing to some portion of the text that either explicitly states or obviously reveals Jack's motives. The story does not say that Jack is driven by greed or youthful cockiness or inspired by newfound courage. It does state that Jack was "not content" even after securing the magic hen but leaves to readers the task of interpreting that phrase, of explaining the reasons for Jack's lack of contentment. The evidence of the text points in different directions and so requires students to read more closely and thoughtfully, to weigh and revise their initial partial answers if they are to achieve comprehensive insight.

This seemingly simple opening question can—in conjunction with the teacher's thoughtful follow-up questions—stimulate a substantial investigation into the story. Sustained discussion of such a question enables participants to develop their ideas about why Jack is able to secure wealth and happiness and to see new ideas that otherwise may have remained hidden. For instance, in discussion it may occur to participants for the first time that Jack's adventures have helped him grow up, that his return to the ogre's domain is a sign of his maturity, or that he now longs for something more than wealth to make life complete—the beauty of the singing harp. This insight may in turn lead to other questions about Jack and further insight; for instance, if the wealthy Jack is motivated by a mature longing for beauty, why does the story also tell us that he displays the harp for money?

Interpretive questions about "Jack and the Beanstalk" arise because the finely woven texture of ideas and depth of characterization make simple thinking about this story unsatisfactory. Although Jack's adventures are fantastic, as a literary character he is not shallow or simply amusing; rather, he is a reflection of fundamental human qualities and longings. While we do not literally trade cows for magic beans, climb beanstalks, or defeat ogres, we do take risks, undertake difficult tasks, and overcome huge manifestations of our fears. This is why the story has meaning for adults as well as for children—"meaning" in the sense of being relevant to us all and contributing to our understanding of our common human experience. Considering interpretive questions not only helps students appreciate how Jack's particular trials change him but also helps them understand their own struggles—to grow up and succeed and the equally difficult challenge of knowing when to be content. It is this empathetic response to such a tale—the sense that it is, in its way, true to experience—that initially draws children to the story and makes them want to discuss and interpret it.

Shared Inquiry Discussion

A teacher preparing to lead shared inquiry discussion reads the story carefully, searching for what he or she feels are the selection's important problems of meaning, and then prepares a basic interpretive question and several related questions that capture a personal doubt about how to understand the story. For instance, Why does Jack go up the beanstalk the third time?

1. Why isn't Jack content even though he has a limitless supply of gold from the magic hen?
2. Does Jack return a third time because he wants to acquire more things or because he wants to outsmart the ogre?
3. Why isn't Jack afraid of being eaten by the ogre, as the other boys were?
4. Why does Jack risk his life by taking the singing harp?
5. Why is Jack successful on his third trip even though this time he doesn't have the help of the ogre's wife?
6. Why does the author have Jack take the singing harp against its will?

The essential characteristic of these interpretive questions is that there are several plausible answers to each based upon the text. They can, then, serve as turning points in a reader's understanding of the story.

Shared inquiry discussion begins when the teacher poses a basic interpretive question about the story. As students begin to respond, the leader follows up by asking how their comments relate to the initial question, to other ideas put forward by the group, and to the text. In the course of discussion, the leader may ask some of the other prepared questions as they become appropriate. Because the leader has doubt about the answers to the prepared questions—that is, there is no one answer for any of them in mind—and does not offer personal opinions, participants are challenged to think for themselves. By trying out and exchanging ideas, they build their own answers and develop their own ways of understanding the work.

The leader's aim in discussion, however, is not merely to proliferate independent viewpoints but to examine how they can coexist and to help students weigh their merits against the text. Shared inquiry is not a case in which any answer will do. While there may be no single correct answer to an interpretive question—that is, students may justifiably disagree about the way to answer it—answers to it are not just matters of personal opinion or expressions of private feelings. While opinions that directly contradict the text may be quickly eliminated as false—for example, if someone should suggest that Jack returned for the singing harp at his mother's request—other answers may not be so easily eliminated. An initially plausible explanation of a character's actions might, upon further exploration, not jibe with all the details in the story and so need to be revised. By eliminating weak answers and improving on good beginnings, students move beyond a partial understanding of a story, perhaps to favor one way of looking at a character over another (e.g., to view Jack as greedy rather than adventurous) or to see how apparently conflicting elements can coexist in the same personality (e.g., Jack's eager pursuit of riches evolves into a longing for adventure and power).

Interpretive discussion, then, involves building a network of inferences and conclusions that encompass many elements in the story. In shared inquiry, understanding the relationship of events, the character's motives, and the author's overall intentions is a complex task requiring a progressive synthesis of ideas, a building upon initial thoughts and reactions in order to piece together a coherent understanding of the whole work. It requires students to generate original ideas about the meaning of a story and calls upon a wide range of their thinking skills—their insight, imagination, and judgment. In shared inquiry, skills such as reading closely, recalling details, seeing connections, and drawing inferences always have the overall purpose of working out an answer to a substantial question of interpretation.

Ultimately, satisfaction with a particular interpretation depends upon the unique experience of each group, upon which parts of the text seem to participants most striking or curious, or upon which personality traits they see most prominently displayed in the characters. It is this subjective element, mixed with the rich possibilities the text presents for showing us human experience, that enables stories such as "Jack and the Beanstalk" to remain continually fertile for interpretation.

The Students' Active Reading Routine: Reading Twice, Taking Notes, Asking Questions

Shared inquiry is a sustained process of working with literature that is built around two readings of a story, note taking, discussion, and, whenever possible, post-discussion writing. Fundamental to all these activities is an emphasis upon asking questions as a way of engaging with the text.

In Junior Great Books, good preparation means reading the story twice. The first time we read a story, we tend to concentrate on the action—on what characters think, do, or say. But in discussion students will be thinking more deeply about the story, not just about what happens but about why things happen the way they do. Reading a second time gives students more ideas about what the story means to them and can help lead to questions they might want to explore with the group. By noticing details that they may have missed on first reading or rethinking their initial reactions, students may change their opinions about why the characters behave as they do or even whether they like or dislike them.

In shared inquiry, students are encouraged to complete both readings with pencil in hand and are given guidance during each reading in taking notes and sharing their responses. Even very simple notations—marking with an exclamation point whatever they find puzzling or surprising—make students' reading a more personal, interactive process. It helps them understand that their subjective responses to a story are valuable and form the basis for the kinds of questions that will be the focus of discussion.

By sharing their notes with the class, students increase their awareness of a story's interpretive range and improve their ability to call up and use supporting evidence for their opinions. Even very young students, after having the story read to them, are encouraged to share their reactions and questions with the class. Older students learn to write specific questions about a story by reflecting upon their notes and turning them into questions.

During discussion, students soon learn that the leader is not the only one who may ask questions. As participants strive together to probe and resolve problems of meaning, they have a responsibility to listen carefully to each speaker and to request clarification from their peers should they need it; in this way, both the questioner and the student questioned benefit. The student asking the question receives information that perhaps is needed by others as well, and the student presenting the idea has time to think it through again, making it clear for himself or herself as well as for the group. Students soon come to recognize that questions are asked as a sign of respect for the ideas of others and from the awareness that incipient ideas are worth pursuing. By conversing directly with each other, students learn that changing one's viewpoint is a natural result of this kind of open exchange.

Shared inquiry emphasizes the connection between reading well and the careful development of ideas through writing. Beginning with students' note taking, writing becomes a natural part of the thinking process at all stages, not something reserved for finished essays. Through discussion, students experience an important stage of the prewriting process as they continually formulate, revise, and refine their ideas. They learn to draw inferences and reasoned conclusions and to order their thoughts effectively. When post-discussion essay topics are assigned, students have, in a sense, already composed several drafts of their thinking. Writing about literature thus ceases to be a mysterious or overwhelming task but becomes a natural means of communicating their developing ideas about a story.

The Role of the Teacher in Shared Inquiry: Balancing Structure and Openness

The teacher's unique role in Junior Great Books begins with preparation. The teacher does not rely on an instruction manual or look to an answer key but goes through the same kind of intensive engagement with the story that is to be encouraged in the students. The teacher reads the story several times, making notes of subjective responses—of what is puzzling or surprising him or her, what makes him or her think or provokes a strong reaction. These notes serve as the basis of the interpretive questions that will be developed—questions that reflect a personal search for meaning in the story and that he or she has not been able to resolve. Writing his or her own interpretive questions and pondering possible answers enables the teacher to become well enough versed in the work to spontaneously ask follow-up questions in response to students' comments.

Writing interpretive questions is an evolutionary process of generating, testing, and refining ideas. During several readings of a story, a leader drafts a list of rough questions and then tests them, ideally with a colleague, by trying out answers. The teacher looks for questions that endure—that remain questions even after thinking about the story; that lead to several interesting, reasonable answers and so present possibilities for taking the reader more deeply into the text.

If while testing a question a leader settles upon a satisfactory interpretation, the question must be dropped from the list since it would no longer be possible to maintain an open mind about how to approach and resolve it—there would be no ''doubt'' about the answer. During this testing process, the leader also drops from the list all questions that can have only one answer, known as ''factual'' questions in shared inquiry. Factual questions can be answered either directly from the text or by drawing a simple inference. They cannot serve as the basis for shared inquiry discussion because they generate no meaningful controversy and do not invite the reader to see the story in more than one way. For example, the answer to the factual question "What does Jack take the first time he goes up the beanstalk?" is stated explicitly in the story: a bag of gold. Similarly, the question "Does the author think that the ogre is mean?" has only one reasonable answer.

Factual questions deal only with a very literal level of comprehension of a story. While achieving such basic comprehension may be no small thing for a child, in shared inquiry this challenge is met through open discussion of broader, more thoughtful questions. In this way, children learn to think while they read and practice basic skills in a context for which they have a genuine purpose. Because it is a tenet of shared inquiry that teachers do not talk down to children and that the interpretive questions they ask the students are questions for themselves also, children do not feel tested or threatened by the leader's questions. When factual questions arise in discussion, they do so spontaneously, as they are needed to ground and substantiate adequately a student's opinion and further inquiry into the basic interpretive question.

The leader also drops from the list any "evaluative" questions— that is, questions that lead away from the text and bring up issues that are strictly a matter of personal opinion and are irrelevant to interpreting the story. For example, "Should you, like Jack, defy your mother if you think she is wrong?" is not an appropriate question for shared inquiry because children answering such a question would end up recounting a variety of situations that have no bearing on Jack's experience. While it is important to the success of Junior Great Books that children connect emotionally with a story, the focus of interpretive discussion is always upon characters and events in the story, not upon events in the child's life. Questions about what a child would do in situations similar to those in the story, while occasionally helpful in discussion, are generally discouraged as distracting students from the text and inviting digressions.

Finally the leader groups the questions, placing together those that seem to deal with the same issue in the story. From these "clusters" he or she selects or writes a basic interpretive question that seems to pose most comprehensively the problem they all address. The leader will begin discussion with this basic question and follow up with spontaneous questions in response to the students' comments. Even though a leader may not use all the prepared questions during discussion, they have served their purpose by helping him or her explore the story thoroughly, with a questioning frame of mind.

Only by engaging in this kind of personal and intellectually rigorous preparation can teachers ready themselves for the challenge of leading Junior Great Books shared inquiry discussion.

By maintaining an open mind about the answers to the interpretive questions asked in discussion, the teacher invites students to collaborate in the search for meaning. Leaders who have no doubt about the questions they ask reduce discussion to a pedagogical device that has lost its intrigue as a process of discovery. Pretense of open inquiry is quickly sensed. When the teacher already has an answer in mind, the child's motivation for learning becomes mixed with a natural desire to please and succeed. This situation make a student feel that he or she is "jumping through hoops," and then the price of education becomes the child's pride.

When the teacher's curiosity about a problem is genuine, however, and he or she has turned to the students for insight, he or she communicates a respect that is undisguised and draws students into inquiry in a way that is animated and whole-hearted. This openness prompts the child to believe, "I am needed in this search for answers," and every educator knows the enthusiasm with which children can express their ideas, once convinced that they are important. In shared inquiry students become dedicated in the pursuit of answers for their efforts have a purpose and they recognize that their "mistakes" and wrong turns can prompt in others valuable insights that, in turn, can progress their own thought.

Choosing Stories that Support Shared Inquiry

Successful shared inquiry is possible only with stories that are rich in ideas and present a special challenge to the individual reader. Such stories call upon both adults and children to be especially active in the effort to understand, to interpret. If a story's meaning or the author's intentions are transparent, it cannot support shared inquiry or be the focus of an interpretive discussion.

For instance, many modern versions of classic stories, while capturing the basic plot line, lack the richness of language and subtleties of character that make interpretation rewarding. To take an example, there are many retellings of Charles Perrault's "The Master Cat" (renamed "Puss in Boots" in most nursery collections) embodying varying degrees of respect for the author's original portrayal of the wily and somewhat unscrupulous cat that masterminds a plan to enrich a lowly miller's son. Versions that soften the sharp edge of the cat's personality or downplay its canniness can present a homogenized portrait of a magic, lovable pet—a far less complicated and intriguing figure than the original. In the effort to make things easier and more pleasant, children lose the opportunity to think about and learn from one of literature's enduring characters.

To some extent, every piece of literature requires interpretation; reading can never be wholly passive. With most children's stories, even very good ones, however, following the plot and the excitement of the action leaves little left to reflect upon. For instance, although several of Rudyard Kipling's stories are included in the Junior Great Books series, not all of his classic works support interpretive discussion. Our selections from *The Jungle Books* ("Mowgli's Brothers," "Tiger-Tiger," "Letting in the Jungle," and "The Spring Running") do; but the perennial favorite "Rikki-Tikki-Tavi," also from *The Jungle Books,* does not—despite the fact that all these stories touch upon many of the same themes, such as the love and loyalty owed to one's adopted family, the nature of courage and honor, taking pride in one's accomplishments, the inevitability of encountering evil and the self-sacrifice required to vanquish it.

"Rikki-Tikki-Tavi," which tells how a brave young mongoose protects a human household from two menacing cobras, is an inspiring tale of animal heroism and a clear model of devotion and courage. It is a suspenseful, compelling, and satisfying story in which evil is vanquished and Rikki's resourcefulness and courage are rewarded. Readers do not need the help of others to interpret this story for the motives of the characters are clear. Its happy outcome raises no particular questions or problems of understanding in the reader's mind. There is nothing paradoxical or curious about the story that invites further reflection or demands explanation. There are no "why's" for reflection.

The Mowgli stories, on the other hand, are problematic. Here we are led more deeply into themes of belonging and isolation and of uncertainty about finding one's proper place. The Junior Great Books selections tell how the boy Mowgli grows up a member of the Seeonee wolf-pack—known as the "free people"—only to be cast out by his "brothers" as he approaches adulthood. As we read these stories we wonder why Mowgli ends up belonging neither to the wolf pack nor to the man pack. Why does the wolf pack want to cast Mowgli out after he has lived and hunted with them for so long? Why does the young Mowgli have no desire to live among people, returning to them only reluctantly? Why must he then go back to the jungle to mature? Why can he return to human society only when he has become a man?

Because it is not clear why Mowgli must be cast out, both by the wolves whom he loved and by the people of the village that is presumably his proper home, the story presents interpretive problems that can be addressed in shared inquiry discussion: Why is Mowgli safe as long as the noble Akela has authority over the ''free people?'' Why does Mother Wolf love Mowgli more than her own cubs? Why do only Baloo, the bear, and Bagheera, the panther, speak for Mowgli at the council of wolves? Why do Mowgli's two sides—man and wolf—present a problem to both the men and the wolves but not to Mowgli himself?

Sixth graders reading *The Jungle Books*, aware of their own need to belong to a social group, readily empathize with Mowgli's plight and feel motivated to think about these interpretive questions. By focusing on such questions, students are able to go beyond reading the Mowgli stories merely as adventure. They are able to appreciate Kipling's subtle portrayal of profound human forces and concerns; to grow close to and gain insight from the character of Mowgli, who grows up noble and strong despite being isolated from his own kind, hunted by enemies, and confused by the dual worlds he inhabits.

Becoming a Junior Great Books Leader

For some children, the experience of shared inquiry may be the first time that an adult has looked to them for insight into an intellectual problem. With this example before them, they begin to take themselves and each other seriously as partners in a mutual endeavor. The intellectual respect shown by the leader for the student, beginning with the opening interpretive question, engenders the expectation in students that they can find answers within themselves and so take responsibility for their own learning.

To help prepare teachers and school volunteers to be effective discussion leaders, the Great Book Foundation provides an intensive two-day, in-service training course. The Basic Leader Training Course is required for all leaders of Junior Great Books programs and is conducted in any district or school that has decided to adopt Junior Great Books. The Great Books Foundation, based in Chicago, Illinois, was established in 1947, and is an independent, nonprofit educational organization.

8

Literature in the Elementary Classroom: Making Connections and Generating Meaning

Joy F. Moss

Joy Moss is literature specialist at the Harley School and Adjunct Associate Professor of Education at the University of Rochester. Her 1984 book, *Focus Units in Literature,* has been one of the most consistently recommended works on teaching with children's books. Grouping books to share with children quite naturally draws their attention to features of literature, from genre to theme to characterization to the style of a particular author or illustrator. In this chapter she illustrates the focus units idea with a selection of books on the sea.

"The boy in this story is like that guy who tried to ride Pegasus to Mount Olympus to visit the gods."

"He's like Icarus, too."

"And that other myth about the kid who rode too high in the sun chariot! I think this author probably read the Greek myths in fourth grade, like us!"

"Something else is the same. They were all warned not to do it. Like that goddess warned about getting the gods angry if he rode Pegasus too high. In the Zephyr story, the warning was hidden in that song the old sailor sang about Samuel Blue! You just knew that the boy would crash, too!"

"A lot of stories have warnings like 'Don't open that door' or 'Don't go into the forest' and you just know they're going to do it anyway."

"I just figured out something else. The place where the boat started to fall was at the church. That's God's house. So, it's like when Zeus made Pegasus fall to punish Bellerophon."

"The Zephyr story is sort of like a fable. Remember the ones we read last year about pride before the fall. That's what this story is about.

"But in this story he [the central character] didn't pay attention. He wasted his whole life searching for the magic sails."

"Yeah—some people never learn!"

The nine-year-old children who generated this dialogue after listening to Chris Van Allsburg's *The Wreck of the Zephyr*[1] have learned to enjoy literature and to stretch their minds and imaginations to construct meaning. The study of literature is an integral part of the curriculum in their classroom; constructing meaning is viewed as the essence of language and learning experiences.

An analysis of this dialogue reveals significant literary and literacy skills and understandings. The students' responses reflected their active involvement as learners: They generated predictions and hypotheses; they developed concepts; they connected past and present literary experiences; they identified literary patterns, allusions, and themes; they detected the author's literary techniques. They constructed meaning by bringing their own literary history and experience to the text. They made predictions based on their knowledge of traditional literary patterns and writers' craft. They seemed to have developed an awareness of the fundamental unity of world literature and the way modern writers have drawn from traditional literature to compose new stories.

The curriculum for this fourth grade classroom included a series of literature units designed to introduce the students to literature and to invite them to become thoughtful students of literature. This author has used the words Focus Unit to identify the literature units she has been developing for and with elementary school students for more than fifteen years. The Focus Unit is defined as a framework for enjoying and studying literature in the classroom. Each unit is structured around a central theme or focus: Related literary selections are introduced in a planned sequence so that responses to each new text are informed by prior literary experiences. A cumulative dialogue links the reading, writing, art, and drama that extend these literary experiences. Each Focus Unit is designed to foster literary awareness and appreciation and to provide a context for building literary, language, and thinking skills. Examples of Focus Units designed for diverse age groups can be found in two books: *Focus Units in Literature* and *Focus on Literature.*[2]

The Focus Unit that served as the context for *The Wreck of the Zephyr* dialogue featured sea tales and was developed as an integral part of a larger study of the sea. The study of literature need not be confined to the language arts program; it can be incorporated into learning experiences across the curriculum. Literary, literacy, and content learning are complementary and interrelated when fiction and non-fiction are integrated in content area learning. The exploration of a particular topic can begin with stories and poetry and then move into informational books and first hand observation and experience. Literature serves as a springboard for inquiry and discovery about the human experience, the arts and sciences, the world we live in.

The Sea Focus Unit

The study of the sea was introduced to this fourth grade class with the question: "What do you know about the sea?" Readers and listeners make sense of texts and generate meaning by bringing their prior knowledge to the text.[3] The quality of comprehension is determined, in large part, by the nature of this prior knowledge and the reader/listener's ability to utilize it to make predictions and pose questions to generate meaning during interaction with the text. Thus, the teacher introduces a question to facilitate comprehension of fiction and nonfiction about the sea by prompting retrieval of relevant information from the children's memory store. The teacher invites them to bring their prior knowledge to each text they encounter as listeners or readers.

Regular read-aloud sessions are an integral part of the Focus Unit. During these group sessions several key questions are introduced to initiate and sustain an ongoing cumulative dialogue that is the core of the Focus Unit and that provides the social context for collaborative learning. The read-aloud sessions serve as shared experiences in which teacher and students explore, study, and respond to literature and work together to build meaning as partners in the learning process.

Each read-aloud session begins with dialogue initiated by the teacher or students. The dialogue continues at relevant points during the reading of the selection and takes up again after its completion. It eventually extends beyond these group read-aloud sessions and into the life of the classroom in informal conversations, student-teacher conferences, dialogue journals, or small study groups. This cumulative dialogue connects diverse Focus Units introduced throughout the school year. It serves as a model for ways to interact with, think about, and respond to texts as well as a rehearsal for the internal dialogue that solitary readers carry on as they interact with, think about, and respond to texts.

Questions initiated by the teacher or students stimulate and shape the cumulative dialogue. In recent years, investigators have focused on the role of questioning in molding the quality of thinking done by students as they read or listen to written texts.[4] Such studies have offered evidence that the question can be used as a valuable tool to teach reading comprehension strategies and to facilitate critical thinking. The teacher demonstrates questioning strategies for students and invites them to formulate their own questions to guide the reading/thinking process. The art of teaching is, in large part, the art of questioning students so as to stimulate and guide reflection and to form in them the independent habit of inquiry, as John Dewey wrote in 1910.[5] All learning begins with questions. The quality of a reader's interaction with a text depends on the questions he or she initiates to generate meaning.

Teacher-initiated questions introduced during the first few read-aloud sessions are designed to encourage students to draw from and use relevant prior knowledge; to make predictions; to evaluate, confirm, or revise these predictions as the text unfolds. Some questions call attention to story ideas, patterns, themes, and elements; layers of meaning; the language of literature; the author's craft; and diverse literary genres. Some questions invite children to make connections with other stories they've heard or read or to relate the story to their own lives. Some are "hypothesis-demanding questions" that foster a "what if. . ." frame of mind and encourage student-initiated exploratory and hypothetical questions and statements.[6] By the third or fourth session, the students are usually ready to pose their own questions and to assume more responsibility for the content and direction of the dialogue. The ultimate goal is for students to learn the art of questioning and to become independent learners.

Session One

Before reading aloud *A Thousand Pails of Water*,[7] the teacher reviewed with the students their knowledge about tides and whales since this information would be important to bring to this story.

Yukio, the central character, is distressed that his father is a whale hunter. When he finds a whale lodged between some rocks on the beach, Yukio realizes that it has been left behind when the tide went out and will not survive out of the sea. Although Yukio makes a valiant attempt to keep the whale alive by himself, it is his father who helps him save the whale's life.

This moving story elicited thoughtful comments about the conflict between the father and son and the father's decision to help save Yukio's whale. A teacher-initiated question about the possible effect of this episode on the attitudes of and relationship between the father and son stimulated hypothetical statements as the students explored possibilities extending beyond the text. The author had concluded the story at the point when the whale swims out to sea. The children had their own opinions about what would happen next in the lives of the story characters. Several chose to write a sequel.

Another question initiated by the teacher—"What factual information do you think the author used to compose this story?"—prompted the children to draw from their own knowledge about the patterns of tides and the survival needs of whales. They concluded that the author's use of this information helped to make the story realistic. Several children connected the plight of the whale in this story to that of the whales trapped in the ice in Alaska, whose dramatic story had been told and shown by the news media not long before this group session. At this point, the teacher shared with them a brief news item she had clipped out of a newspaper before the publication of *A Thousand Pails of Water*. Under the headline "Bucket Brigade Saves Whale," the writer started this story from Clacton, England, with, "More than 60 children and their parents organized a bucket brigade to save the life of a whale that ran aground at nearby St. Osyth." Since this is exactly what happened in Ronald Roy's story of Yukio, the students concluded that the author had probably based his story on an actual incident. One child said, "We sure have a lot of evidence that this is a realistic story!"

When several children expressed a special interest in tides and whales, the teacher invited them to work together to gather additional information about these topics to share with the class. As a result, two small "research committees" were established. At the close of this session, the teacher called attention to two display tables set up in the classroom: One held a collection of modern and traditional sea stories and poems; the other held a collection of nonfiction about the sea. The children were encouraged to browse and select at least two books from each table for independent reading. The nonfiction table served as a useful resource for the research committees, although they found that the school library contained a more extensive reference collection.

Each child was given a notebook to use as a response journal for personal responses to fiction and nonfiction read aloud or independently in the context of this Sea Focus Unit. The journal took the form of a dialogue journal when the teacher responded to students' comments and questions and initiated ongoing written conversations with individual students.[8] Thus, the dialogue initiated in the group story sessions extended into other oral and written interactions in this "community of readers."[9]

Session Two

Why the Tides Ebb and Flow[10] is a legend about the origin of the tides. Before reading it to the group, the teacher invited the "tides research committee" to share the information they had gathered. After this presentation, the teacher introduced the question "What is a legend?'' to focus attention on the nature of this literary genre and the distinguishing features of the *pourquoi* tales in particular. The resulting discussion reminded the children to view this story as an imaginative and creative explanation of the unknown, the mysteries of nature by the storytellers of old.

After this legend was read aloud, the children speculated about the beliefs held by those who originally told and listened to this old tale and the questions it was intended to answer. When asked to compare *A Thousand Pails of Water* with *Why the Tides Ebb and Flow*, they responded:

> ''The first story was very real. It could be a true story.''

> ''The other one is a legend. You don't expect it to be true. It was made up a long time ago to explain things people saw—like tides coming and going.''

> ''You can tell it's not going to be a true story because of the way it starts out. 'Not in my time, not in your time, but in the old time, when the earth and sea were new. . .' ''

> ''And the old lady talked to a sky spirit! That's another clue—So you know right away you're not supposed to read it like it's true.''

At the end of this second session, a new research committee was established by two students interested in studying sea legends.

Session Three

In William Steig's story of *Amos and Boris*[11] Amos, a mouse, is saved from drowning in the ocean by Boris, a whale. These two mammals become devoted friends. Years later, during a hurricane, Boris is ''flung ashore by a tidal wave and stranded on the very shore where Amos happened to make his home.'' Amos manages to save his friend's life. After listening to this story, the children spontaneously compared the final scenes in the story to *A Thousand Pails of Water*. Several children also recognized the connection between this story and the fable of ''The Lion and the Mouse.''

''I think Mr. Steig got the idea for his story from that fable. Both are about returning a favor. But Amos and Boris is really about friendship.''

One child focused on the literary genres:

> ''We've read three different kinds of stories: a realistic one, a legend, and Amos and Boris is sort of like a fable.''

These children were making literary connections and identifying themes and literary genres without prompts from the teacher. By this third session, they had begun to initiate their own questions and to assume more responsibility for the content and direction of the group dialogue.

At the conclusion of this session, the whale research committee made a progress report and shared some of the information they had gathered. They had decided to create their own book about whales for the nonfiction collection.

Session Four

The Boy Who Held Back the Sea[12] is an unusual retelling of the famous story of the Dutch boy who held his finger in the dike to stop the leak and protect his village from a flood. This new version of an old story is illustrated with striking paintings that reflect the influence of the great Dutch Masters. The teacher brought in a book of Dutch paintings so the children could see the works of Rembrandt and Vermeer, the artists who had apparently inspired Thomas Locker as he created the illustrations for this picture book.

Before reading aloud to the class, the teacher asked if anyone was familiar with the legend of the hole in the dike first told by Mary Mapes Dodge more than 100 years ago. Quite a few had heard this story. One boy volunteered to retell it; another explained the purpose of the dikes in Holland and the threat of floods to those whose land is below sea level. This provided important background information for understanding Hort's retelling.

The children responded to this retelling with interesting observations about the writer's craft. They noted that Hort had created a "story within a story," a literary technique studied in a previous literature unit. They observed that the Dutch boy in this retelling was a more richly developed, dynamic character than the ones in earlier versions:

> "This boy changes. In the end he tried to be a better person."

> "He's sort of like the kid in 'The Boy Who Cried Wolf' because no one believed him about the leak in the dike because he was always telling lies. So he learned a lesson, and he changed."

Several children compared this legend to *A Thousand Pails of Water* in terms of the basic theme. For example, one student commented:

> "Both boys were life-savers. One tried to save a whale, and the other tried to save a village. In both stories the villagers had to cooperate to finish the job but one person got it started!"

Another commented on the role of the sea in these two narratives:

> "In the first story, the sea gives life to the whale. In the second story, the sea can take life—it can destroy everyone if the dikes break."

Another discovery stimulated by this comparative analysis related to the literary craft:

"Both writers used factual information for their stories—about whales, tides, Holland, and whale hunters."

The literary experiences of these students were enriched as they developed the habit of responding to each new text in light of previous texts in their literary histories. Past texts serve as "anticipatory frames" that allow readers to engage in prediction and confirmation. By making connections between diverse texts, the reader can move beyond an immediate literary experience to generate new meanings and build new understandings. As Harste says, "One's history of literacy is an integral part of any literacy event."[13]

The excerpts drawn from the group dialogues reflect and illustrate the cumulative nature of these dialogues and the quality of the children's literary responses as they explored related texts. These children engaged in inquiry and discovery and made use of their growing literary and conceptual background to generate meaning.

Session Five

Hansy's Mermaid[14] is another story of Holland with an element of fantasy woven into it. A mermaid is found stranded on land after a storm and is taken to a farm to be trained as a useful Dutch peasant. Only Hansy is sympathetic and understands that the mermaid longs to return to her home in the sea. Eventually, he finds a way to grant her wish.

After a discussion of the characters in this story, the children initiated a comparative analysis. They noticed, for example, that both the author of this story and the author of the story of the leak in the dike used factual information about Holland to create fiction. They noted that Hansy's mermaid rewarded him for his kindness and compassion, and they recognized this as a recurring theme in folk literature. Several students were particularly interested in the dual nature of the sea captured in these tales:

"The sea is like a villain because it can destroy the villages, and people can drown. But it's also important for life—for fishing and going places—and even having fun!"

"Also in the story of Hansy the sea is like a mysterious fantasy world with merpeople and shell houses."

These comments prompted other students to discuss books they had read independently in terms of this larger theme of the dual nature of the sea. A student who had read *The Wave*[15] commented:

"In this story a tidal wave destroys a village in Japan. So, the sea is the villain. But in Japan, they eat a lot of fish so the sea is also good."

Another student who had read this ancient tale compared it to *The Boy Who Held Back the Sea:*

> "In *The Wave* one old man saved the whole village from drowning, and that's what happened in the Dutch story. The boy saved his village."

At the conclusion of the session, a "mermaid committee" was established by several students, who planned to build a collection of tales about fantasy creatures of the sea.

Session Six

"The Sea of Gold"[16] is a Japanese folktale about Hikoichi, a cook on a fishing boat, who feeds the fish every evening for many long years and is rewarded for his kindness by the King of the Sea. This tale elicited the following comments:

> "This is one of those old stories that's been written down. See, on the front cover it says it was 'adapted.'"

> "And it's like those folktales where someone gets rewarded for kindness."

> "I just read 'Urashima.'[17] It's about this guy who is nice to a tortoise, and the Dragon King of the Sea rewards him. So it has that same pattern about rewarding kindness. Also, those storytellers both believed in a sort of royal kingdom under the sea."

> "It's also like the story I read—*Taro and the Sea Turtles.*[18] This boy saves the sea turtles, and later they save him from pirates!"

Having identified this recurring theme in both traditional and modern stories, the students were curious about the reason for the widespread use of this theme by storytellers and writers across the centuries and miles. After a lively discussion, they concluded that the hidden message or lesson about the value of kindness has continued to be an important one from ancient days to modern times. One student added his own discovery about the nature of story:

> "Stories are supposed to be fun, and also they're supposed to teach you things."

Session Seven

The Jolly Mon written by songwriter and musician, Jimmy Buffett and his daughter, Savannah Jane,[19] was introduced by sharing their dedication as well as the "Storytellers' Note" that precede the story. The authors dedicate their story "To all the people on all the islands in the Caribbean and all the dolphins in the sea below." The first lines of the "Storytellers' Note" provide interesting background for those who read or listen to this tale of a fisherman and his magic guitar:

> It seems that pirates have been throwing musicians into the oceans since the beginning of time, and thankfully dolphins have been around just as long to pluck us out so that we can continue to sing. . . . The poet and musician Arion seems to be the first musician to have gotten the proverbial "hook" as he was traveling and singing his way through Italy around 625 B.C. He was saved by a dolphin who liked music a lot more than the pirates.

The children responded spontaneously with predictions about the story plot as well as with relevant information about pirates, dolphins, Caribbean Islands, and the constellation Orion. As they listened to the story, the children were eager to confirm or revise their initial predictions and to generate new predictions about subsequent events as the story unfolded. At its conclusion, the children focused on the mystery of the magical guitar, the dolphin painted on the back, the words inscribed in gold, and the diamond stars forming the constellation Orion. The discovery that the dolphin on the guitar was the very one that saved the Jolly Mon when the pirates pushed him into the sea reminded many of the children of Japanese folktales read during a previous literature unit. They identified a number of ancient Japanese tales in which an animal had left the surface on which it had been painted and had come to life. Those who had selected *Arion and the Dolphins*[20] for independent reading for the Sea Focus Unit were anxious to share and compare this retelling of an ancient Greek legend:

> "Both stories are about friendship between humans and dolphins."
>
> "And the dolphins save them from evil pirates or sailors."
>
> "And they love music. In one it's the guitar; in the other, it's the lute. I wonder if dolphins really do like music."
>
> "And in both stories the villains get punished by a princess or king."
>
> "You can sort of tell that the writers love the sea. Even the magical guitar comes from the sea."
>
> "Here it is again—that theme about the two sides of the sea. It can be really beautiful and you can swim and sail, but you can also drown."
>
> "And there are friendly animals like the dolphins, but you could also get killed by a shark!"

The seventh session concluded with the establishment of several new research committees: pirates and sunken treasure; dolphins; islands; constellations. Several students recommended titles of books they had discovered in the Focus Unit collections. For example, one suggested *Sunken Treasure,*[21] *Lafitte the Pirate,*[22] and *Pirates.*[23] Another shared these titles with the "island committee": *Bayberry Bluff,*[24] *Island Winter,*[25] *Island Boy,*[26] and *My Island Grandma.*[27]

Session Eight

Jack, the Seal and the Sea[28] is a contemporary story about pollution. Jack, a fisherman, finds in his net a half-dead seal covered with an oily film. He takes care of the seal until its health returns and is rewarded for his kindness. In a dream, Jack hears a voice from the sea pleading for help. This experience changes his life: He decides to devote himself to the fight against pollution and to spread the message he had received from the sea.

The students responded to this story in light of previous encounters with sea tales. They noticed, for example, that the author used traditional folktale patterns to create a story about a current issue.

"This story has that old 'kindness rewarded' theme, and it's also about things in our newspapers and on television!"

"The sea talks—sort of like in those stories where the Sea King rewards someone."

"The story pattern is really familiar so you can pay attention to the important message."

The children also discovered a third perspective for exploring the relationship between man and the sea:

"You can think about the sea as an enemy. Some stories show how the sea can destroy a village or how people can drown in the sea."

"You can also think of it as really great. You can swim in it and get fish to eat or just watch the waves. . ."

"Or you can imagine castles and mermaids in kingdoms under the sea."

"In this story, people are the enemy of the sea because they pollute it and kill the fish and plants! The sea is the victim."

Several children became interested in studying the topic of pollution. They established a "committee" and decided to set up a bulletin board to display newspaper or magazine clippings about this significant problem facing the global community. They invited their classmates to add relevant items to this collection of current events. The "pollution committee" produced posters to call attention to the different kinds of pollution, causes, tragic consequences, and possible ways to prevent further pollution.

The dialogue and activities generated by this brief tale—originally published in German under the title, "Jan und das Meer"—extended out of the classroom and into the rest of the school community. Interest in this important issue spread as the children learned what pollution of our lakes and oceans would mean to them as individuals and to all inhabitants of Earth.

Session Nine

This session was scheduled to allow the members of the mermaid committee to share their collection of stories about fantasy creatures from the sea and to present book talks on such stories as *Greyling*,[29] *The Mermaid's Cape*,[30] *The Kelpie's Pearls*,[31] and *The Black Pearl*.[32] This committee also shared its progress on a book of fantasy sea creatures, which included sketches and descriptions of Kelpies; merfolk; selchies; sea monsters and serpents, including the Kraken and the Midgard serpent of Norse mythology; sea witches; and the monster devilfish in Scott O'Dell's *The Black Pearl*. Their book included original poems and stories inspired by their study of these legendary characters. The enthusiasm of the committee members prompted many of their classmates to select books from their collection for independent reading. Some added their own stories or pictures to the committee's book. In a community of readers, students enjoy sharing what they have read and learning what their peers have enjoyed reading. This interchange of reading experiences provides a dynamic context for literary and literacy learning.

Session Ten

The Wreck of the Zephyr[33] was the last story read aloud to the whole group. The dialogue excerpt that introduced this chapter suggests the nature of the cumulative dialogue toward the end of this series of related literary experiences. By this time most of the students had become active participants in the dialogue and assumed most of the responsibility for its content and direction. They had developed habits and strategies that enabled them to respond critically and creatively to this tale, in particular, and to literature in general. Their contributions demonstrated their ability to utilize relevant prior knowledge to generate meaning as they read and to respond to literary texts as springboards for further inquiry and exploration. *The Wreck of the Zephyr*, like other stories presented in this unit, raised new questions and stimulated new interests. By the end of this group session, three new research committees had been established to explore boats, light houses, and coral reefs.

Synthesis

The final group session of the Sea Focus Unit was designed to help reinforce the concepts developed as it evolved and to invite the students to move from analysis toward synthesis. The students identified threads that seemed to weave through these diverse tales and connected them to each other and to the literature of the world. They noted recurring themes of kindness rewarded and greed and pride punished. They discovered that storytellers around the world interpreted the dual nature of the sea through themes of good and evil; love and hate; life and death. They found that storytellers past and present have been inspired by the beauty and mystery and terror of the sea. They discussed the diverse literary genres represented in the collection and examples of writers' literary techniques and styles. They noticed that contemporary writers used themes and patterns from traditional literature. They explored writers' use of symbolism and allusions to myths, legends, biblical tales, and folktales. They had begun to read like writers and to discover what writers do to create a literary piece.[34]

As these fourth grade students engaged in the process of integrating fact and fiction, they learned to bring relevant conceptual and literary knowledge to each new text to generate meaning. In addition to developing this important reading strategy, the students began to consider each text from the viewpoint of its author: What literary and conceptual knowledge did the author bring to the composition process?

A concrete example of their integration of fact and fiction is the illustrated dictionary produced by the students for a class project: "The Sea Dictionary: Fact and Fantasy." They composed definitions and sketches for each word, beginning with *anemone* and ending with *zephyr.* They included words from legends and folklore about the sea. Members of each research committee contributed key words from their inquiry so that this final product represented a synthesis of their diverse explorations and discoveries about the sea.

Other projects involving synthesis extended the reading/listening experiences into art, writing, and drama. Individuals and small groups drew from their encounters with sea facts and fiction to produce murals, seascapes, and treasure maps; plays about pirates, floods, undersea worlds, and heroic deeds; and stories and poems that reflected their study of the sea and their growing background of literary motifs and themes and techniques.

Literature in the Elementary School Classroom

The literature curriculum described in this chapter is based on literacy research that suggests that the enjoyment and study of literature is a valid and important dimension of the elementary school experience and that literature can be a rich natural resource for literacy learning. Children who learn about literature and ways to generate meaning as they interact with literary texts expand their literacy and thinking skills in the process. As they read and write literature, they learn about language and ways to use language. Literary and literacy skills complement and build on each other.

Cognitive theorists have demonstrated that readers make sense of text by bringing what they know about language, literature, and the world to the text. Researchers in story comprehension developed the concept of "story schema." This story schema is the reader's mental model of the story's internal structure or "grammar" made up of a network of categories and logical relationships.[35] By listening to stories, children develop a story schema that enhances their interaction with narrative texts and their ability to generate meaning.[36]

Studies of "early readers," preschool children who have learned to read without formal school instruction, have highlighted the central role of literature experiences in literacy learning.[37] Gordon Wells suggests that listening to stories "familiarizes [children] with the language of books and with the characteristic narrative structures that they will meet in story books at school."[38] He sees "story" as a genre of written language and argues that ". . . listening to stories read aloud . . . the child is . . . beginning to gain experience of the sustained meaning-building organization of written language."[39] Wayne Sawyer concludes a review of research supporting the significant contribution of literature to reading development with this statement: "Narrative is a fundamental mode of meaning making through language for humans, and probably the main mode for children."[40] He suggests that teaching the strategies necessary to interact with narrative texts is essentially a way of teaching processes of reading comprehension.

The literature curriculum described in this chapter was designed to provide experiences that stretch children's minds and imaginations and touch their hearts. Children are invited to enter into the world of story and to engage in dialogue with authors and artists. They encounter characters who will become their friends; they live through experiences that will remain with them; they discover ideas that will enrich and expand their view of the world.

The literature curriculum provides a context for literacy learning and for developing habits and attitudes associated with lifelong readers. Literature is introduced into the lives of children so they can discover for themselves its power and joy.

End Notes

1. Chris Van Allsburg, *The Wreck of the Zephyr* (Boston: Houghton Mifflin, 1983).

2. Joy F. Moss, *Focus on Literature: A Context for Literacy Learning* (New York: Richard C. Owen Publishers, Inc., 1990). Joy F. Moss, *Focus Units in Literature: A Handbook for Elementary School Teachers.* (Urbana: NCTE, 1984).

3. See David E. Rumelhart, *Toward An Interactive Model of Reading* Technical Report No. 56 (San Diego, California: Center for Human Information Processing, University of California, 1976); Marilyn Adams, and Allen Collins. *A Schema-Theoretic View of Reading* (Boston: Bolt, Beranek, and Newman, 1977); Frank Smith, "Reading Like a Writer," *Composing and Comprehending,* ed. Julie Jensen (Urbana, Illinois: ERIC, NCRE, 1984): 47–56; Frank Smith, *Understanding Reading. A Psycholinguistic Analysis of Reading and Learning to Read,* 2nd ed. (New York: Holt, Rinehart & Winston, 1978); and Kenneth Goodman, "Unity in Reading," *Theoretical Models and Processes of Reading,* 3rd ed., ed. Harry Singer and Robert Ruddell (Newark: IRA, 1985).

4. David Ausubel, "The Use of Advance Organizers in the Learning and Retention of Meaningful Verbal Material." *Journal of Educational Psychology* 51 (1960): 267–72; Lawrence Frase, "Learning from Prose Material: Length of Phrase, Knowledge of Results and Position of Questions." *Journal of Educational Psychology* 58 (1967): 266–72; J. Carroll, and R. Freedle, *Language Comprehension and the Acquisition of Knowledge.* (Washington, D.C.: V.H. Winston & Son, 1972); and E.Z. Rothkopf, "The Concept of Mathemagenic Activities." *Review of Educational Research* 40 (1970): 371–93.

5. John Dewey, *How We Think* (Boston: Heath, 1910).

6. Douglas Barnes, *From Communication to Curriculum* (Hammondsworth: Penguin Books, 1975).

7. Ronald Roy, *A Thousand Pails of Water* (New York: Alfred Knopf, 1978).

8. Jana Staton, "Writing and Counseling: Using a Dialogue Journal." *Language Arts* 57, no. 5 (May 1980): 514–518; Nancie Atwell, "Writing and Reading from the Inside Out." *Language Arts* 61, no. 3 (March 1984): 240–252.

9. See Susan Hepler and Janet Hickman, "The Book Was Okay. I Love You—Social Aspects of Response to Literature." *Theory Into Practice* 21.4 (Autumn 1982): 278–83 for a discussion of "community of readers".

10. Joan Chase Bowden, *Why the Tides Ebb and Flow* (Boston: Houghton Mifflin, 1979).

11. William Steig, *Amos and Boris* (New York: Farrar, Straus and Giroux, 1971).

12. Lenny Hort, reteller, *The Boy Who Held Back the Sea* (New York: Dial, 1987).

13. Jerome Harste, "Cognitive Universals in Literacy and Literacy Learning: Toward Practical Theory," Paper presented at Spring Conference on Teaching English and the Language Arts, Columbus, Ohio, April 14, 1984.

14. Trinka Hakes Noble, *Hansy's Mermaid* (New York: Dial, 1983).

15. Margaret Hodges, adaptor. *The Wave* (Boston: Houghton Mifflin Co., 1964).

16. Yoshiko Uchida, "The Sea of Gold." *The Sea of Gold and Other Tales from Japan* (Boston: Gregg, 1980).

17. Lafcadio Hearn, "Urashima" *The Boy Who Drew Cats* (New York: Macmillan, 1963).

18. Arnold Dobrin, *Taro and the Sea Turtles: A Tale of Japan* (New York: Coward-McCann, 1966).

19. Jimmy Buffett, and Savannah Jane Buffett. *The Jolly Mon* (New York: Harcourt Brace Jovanovich, 1988).

20. Lonzo Anderson, *Arion and the Dolphins* (New York: Charles Scribner's Sons, 1978).

21. Gail Gibbons, *Sunken Treasure* (New York: Thomas Crowell, 1988).

22. Ariane Dewey, *Lafitte the Pirate* (New York: Greenwillow, 1985).

23. Karen McWilliams, *Pirates* (New York: Franklin Watts, 1989).

24. Blair Lent, *Bayberry Bluff* (Boston: Houghton Mifflin, 1987).

25. Charles E. Martin, *Island Winter* (New York: Greenwillow Books, 1984).

26. Barbara Cooney, *Island Boy* (New York: Viking Kestrel, 1988).

27. Kathryn Lasky, *My Island Grandma* (New York: Frederick Warne, 1979).

28. Joanne Fink, adaptor, *Jack, the Seal and the Sea* by Gerald Aschenbrenner, (Englewood Cliffs, New Jersey: Silver Burdett Press, 1988).

29. Jane Yolen, *Greyling: A Picture Story from the Island of Shetland* (Cleveland: World, 1968).

30. Margaret Wetterer, *The Mermaid's Cape* (New York: Atheneum, 1982).

31. Mollie Hunter, *The Kelpie's Pearls* (New York: Funk and Wagnalls, 1966).

32. Scott O'Dell, *The Black Pearl* (Boston: Houghton Mifflin, 1967).

33. Van Allsburg, 1983.

34. Smith, 1984.

35. Nancy Stein, and C.G. Glenn, "An Analysis of Story Comprehension in Elementary School Children," *New Directions in Discourse Processing*, 2, ed. R. O. Freedle (Norwood, New Jersey: Ablex, 1979) 58.

36. John Guthrie, "Research Views: Story Comprehension." *The Reading Teacher* (February 1977): 574–77.

37. Dolores Durkin, *Children Who Read Early* (New York: Teachers College Press, 1966); see also Margaret Clark, *Young Fluent Readers* (London: Heinemann, 1976); Gordon Wells, *The Meaning Makers: Children Learning Language and Using Language to Learn.* (Portsmouth, New Hampshire: Heinemann, 1986); Gordon Wells, "Story Reading and the Development of Symbolic Skills." Paper presented at the Reading '82 Conference, York University, Toronto, February 18, 1982. (Cited in Wayne Sawyer, "Literature and Literacy: A Review of Research," *Language Arts* 64.1 (January 1987): 33–39).

38. Wells, 1982, 11.

39. Wells, 1982, 5.

40. Wayne Sawyer, "Literature and Literacy: A Review of Research." *Language Arts* 64.1 (January 1987): 37.

9

Children's Literature and Popular Culture, or, Potatoes, Potatoes Meets Tyrannosaurus Rex

Frances Nolting Temple

Frances Temple teaches a combination of first and second grades at the Children's Hours School in Geneva, New York. She has coauthored several books on using literature to teach children to write and writes novels, stories, and poetry for children. In this chapter she addresses a troublesome topic: the competition between the violent characters and images from the mass media and the more subtle voices from children's books.

Scenario

For five mornings running, Roger has ambushed his first grade teacher. Leaping out of the closet as Mrs. T. makes her way to hang up her coat, he screeches and snarls, claws outstretched and saber-teeth bared.

"Freddy Kruger? Dinosaur?" asks a co-worker, greeting Mrs. T. with a sympathetic pat on the back.

I AM A SABR TUTH TGR. I FIT. I KL.

"That's the blood," explains Roger, showing off his illustrated story with satisfaction.

And on the playground, a shrill complaint from Amy: "Teacher! Roger ripped my leg!"

Mrs. T., who normally loves teaching, reveling in the bounce of energy and the flashes of realization among her students, today feels resentful. Before the bell rings, she collects treasures the children have brought from home to show their friends: laser-guns, tanks, intricately armed Ninjas. The well-meaning and indulgent gifts of parents who both work. Tokens of affection but somehow not healthy.

Worried, Mrs. T. flips through Roger's writing folder, September through December, first grade.

> ROGER IS TREX. ROGER FITS. TREX KILS. ROGER WINS.
> GODZILLA CAM TO THE CITE. GODZILLA DSTROED THE CITE.
> KING KONG KILD GODZILLA.
> BATMAN COME KWIK! THE BAD GYS FIT. THE BAD GYS WIN.
> GEEDRA IS RAMPAG. THE CTE IS DSTROED. THE BAD GIS DED.

Reading this kind of work day after day, Mrs. T. has watched the handwriting and spelling gradually improve. Skills have improved, but the thoughts remaining depressingly the same. She thinks of the discouraging conclusions Sylvia Ashton-Warner reached about America during the year she left her native New Zealand and taught first grade in Colorado. The imaginative force, said Ashton-Warner in *Spearpoint*,[1] the power of curiosity and initiative that drove children's reading and writing, the vivid native imagery that she counted on finding, had been replaced in American children by something sinister, something that was like native imagery but profoundly different. The deeply harbored images and symbols of children's imaginations had somehow been rooted out and replaced by the carefully contrived and mass-manufactured creations of popular culture. Unable to work creatively with what she concluded were synthetic imaginations, Ashton-Warner went home.

Mrs. T. can't afford to reach the same conclusion as Ashton-Warner. She is home. She forces herself to watch Saturday morning TV, to get a closer look at this "synthetic imagination."

Undeniably, the imagination being promoted there is geared toward empowerment through ownership, or through identification with monsters or powerful machines (often combinations of monsters and weapons). These programs are geared to sell. Because an inventive, caring, connected human doesn't need to buy much, there is little in the cultural smorgasbord offered children, little in all the toys, the video games, the movies, the TV shows and ads, that encourages invention and compassion.

Dialogue between Mrs. T. and Roger, December 4th:

> *Roger:* Teacher, can I share today? I didn't share yesterday, really I didn't.
> *Teacher:* I thought you shared a story about Guidra yesterday.
> *Roger:* NO! No, today my story is about Guidra.
> *Teacher* (losing her composure): Roger, every single day your story is about somebody fighting and somebody killing somebody, and I can't keep them

straight anymore. Could you please just try to write a different story? A story where there is no fighting?

    Roger (looking pale): But I've always written about fighting!

    Teacher: So many other interesting things happen in the world!

    Roger: Not interesting to me.

    Teacher: People dive down deep under the sea, to look for fish no one has ever seen. People climb tall rocky mountains and risk their lives to rescue someone who has fallen in a crack in the ice, a crevasse might close up at any minute...

Mrs. T. mutters these things as she bumbles around the room cleaning up, resentfully ransacking the storehouse of her memory for the situations she liked best to pretend when she was six, for the sake of a six-year-old who simply isn't interested, a child who finally says wearily, "Oh, OK then," and comes up with the following story.

A TRESR SHIP SENK IN THE OSHUN 300000000 YERS AGO. THERE WAS GOLD ON IT. LOTS UV GOLD. ENUF TO BY THE HOLE WORLD.

"What do I do now," the teacher asks herself. "Ban money?"

Again, she feels Ashton-Warner's frustration, her fear. Suppose all of the achievements of human character and culture, of selflessness and bravery, of the struggles against great odds seem downright uninteresting compared to the thrill of seeing Godzilla smash apart a whole city with one sweep of his tail? Or the strange hope of being rich beyond your wildest need.

The Primary School's Dilemma

Mrs. T.'s students are in school six hours a day. Even assuming that they are exposed to lots of mass culture in their off hours, school is still the core of their day. Time, perhaps, to recreate a culture. The dilemma for the primary school teacher, the dilemma Ashton-Warner found so daunting, is that the best of primary teaching is based not so much on pouring in as on drawing out—helping children discover new channels for their growing energies: the power of art, of dance, of numbers, and most of all, the power of words. Ashton-Warner's approach was simply to use what was already there, deep in her students' imaginations. Probing, she found the word most often likely to strike a chord deep enough to be a key word, one that written down would begin to unlock the whole system of writing for a child in New Zealand—KISS. Here in the U.S.A., for too many children that key word would be: KILL.

The challenge, then, is to present during school hours a cultural complement to mass culture, rich in areas where the mass culture is poor (for instance in subtlety, in human dilemmas and feelings).

Primary school teachers are further challenged to present what amounts to a counterculture in response-provoking ways, adding to the children's storehouse of energy and imagination, helping them integrate their various sources of knowing, and helping them, as well, to express the various syntheses. A steep order.

Action

Recreating our culture in the classroom means, in part, calling upon literature and delivering it to the children. Thoughtful teachers, child advocates, and seekers in general have put their thoughts in books and stories, but often it is up to classroom teachers to introduce them to children.

Teachers and children alike need hero-images of themselves. Children need stories that help them empathize with explorers, hobos, artists, planters of seeds. They need time and guidance in thinking their way into the characters and conflicts and causes that are all around them, the stuff of good stories, and the essence of independent culture. To recreate themselves, children need not just to read but a chance to grapple with ideas and make the stories and heroes their own, through responding, writing, dreaming, and play-acting.

On a day-to-day level, there are two things a teacher needs to do to use literature well in her classroom. He or she needs to:

- Make available, accessible, and, to some degree, unavoidable literature that will nurture children, including books, poetry, songs, and the oral tradition.
- Give children every opportunity to make the stories, ideas, heros, situations, thought processes and language theirs, through guided discussion, response journals, acting out stories, writing their own, acting out their own, creative play, and references to experiences and characters from literature in everyday conversation.

Some of these things occur spontaneously, while others require intense planning on the part of the teacher.

Available, Accessible, Unavoidable

Making good literature available means finding it, choosing it, and bringing it in—poems read and recited, taped on the walls for future reference; resource books and magazine articles for science or social studies ready at hand; songs learned and typed and sung again throughout the year.

Having literature accessible also sometimes means taking things away, so that all is not lost in clutter, and reintroducing a book judiciously. It means trips to the library, an awareness of authors' names and card catalogues, an awareness of the shelving system of libraries so that a child can know where to look for a book on ants or a "princess story." It means that there is some time in the day set aside for reading and that some books may be taken home.

In another sense making literature accessible can be a question of getting a child who has been conditioned to "consume" or just receive stories to participate more in their unfolding, to question, and to anticipate. There are, of course, entertaining stories on TV. In children's movies important themes are stacked as thickly as the layers in a Dagwood sandwich, so thick nobody can get their jaws around them all. The children peering over their parents' shoulders at the videos they bring home would have their emotions and their powers of reasoning exhausted if they did not soon learn to be passive and just wait and see what happens next. Slowly, however, this conditioning towards passivity needs to be turned around, and some books are especially good for the purpose; for instance Meinhart Dejong's *The Wheel on the School*,[2] in which each development is carefully weighed for its importance by all the children in the story, inviting the reader to join in.

In almost every group of children there will be one or two who will avoid reading at first if they can. Making literature unavoidable means using teacher-leverage to open some new doors. It means supplementing the fifteen minute free reading time with reading assignments: children might take home books they are working on and their response journals. Both teacher and students write questions and comments in the journal about the stories.

It might mean sending children out in the hall in pairs to read over their poems or assigning groups of two or three to develop choral readings to present to the class, using the enthusiasm of strong readers to rope in the reluctant. It means, in Mrs. T.'s class, that the teacher reads aloud from a chapter book during part of the children's lunchtime.

Helping Children Make the Literature Theirs

Guided Discussion

The habit of thinking and talking about what we read needs to be developed casually in the early grades, speculatively, over lunch or on the playground or more formally in groups during class time. (There is much good material in this book, and particularly in this section, about discussing texts with children.) Among the recordings of class discussions from Mrs. T.'s class, many shed interesting light on the worries Mrs. T. had over Roger's obsessions.

For instance: Some psychologists maintain that jewels and gold are understood by the readers of fairy tales to represent treasures of the spirit, such as wisdom and grace. Mrs. T.'s first and second graders do not back this up. They tend to think of things concretely: gold is gold. The following discussion took place after Mrs. T. had read aloud *Everyone Knows What a Dragon Looks Like* by Jay Williams.[3] In this story a young street sweeper shares his meager livelihood with an old man and in the end is rewarded with jewels.

> *Teacher:* That was quite a story. Something puzzles me about it.
> *Ann:* I didn't like the end.
> *Teacher:* Can you think why?
> *Ann:* Because they rewarded him with gold and jewels, but he didn't care about gold and jewels before, he just cared about other people. So he was nice before. Now, he might get spoiled and then he won't even be nice any more.

The second discussion came in response to a question Mrs. T. uses often: What does____want most in this part of the story?

> *Teacher:* So, in ''Jack and the Beanstalk,'' what do you think Jack wants most?
> *Roger:* Gold.
> *Teacher:* What for? (She catches a withering look from Roger, but. . .)
> *Amy:* To get a good house for his mother to live in.
> *Nora:* Well. In the beginning, the giant had stolen the gold from Jack's father, so he just wanted to get it back. . .
> *Teacher:* So he wanted . . .
> *Nora:* For it to be fair.
> *Teacher:* What some people call . . .
> *Nora:* Justice. He wanted justice.

It's not a question of leading the students toward the light in these discussions. Mrs. T. has her own interpretation of Jack's character: an adventurer with a strong dash of greed. What children are being led toward is thoroughness of thought and of expression. Children who don't accept the easy answer ''gold'' as a complete motive are not likely to be susceptible to shallow stereotypes. Nor are they likely to take Uncle Scrooge as hero.

There is a pleased and bemused expression that appears from time to time on the faces of the children in Mrs. T.'s room. It happens when a child suddenly realizes that a story can be not only a vicarious experience but also a play-toy of the mind, as fun to explore as a new transformer. When that moment strikes, the child has taken a giant step away from dependence on material things.

Response Journals

Referred to above as one way to make literature unavoidable, response journals have other even greater usefulness (see also Diane Barone's chapter). They allow the teacher to correspond individually with children whose ideas might not get expressed in a discussion group. When they're used for homework, as in Mrs. T.'s class, they establish a link through books with the child's family and/or after school caregiver. They generate not only more reading but more thinking and writing as well. Here is a typical first grade entry (at this level, the teacher frequently does more writing than the child):

> *Teacher's entry:* 1/20 Nora, I loved your comment about *Nicky's Noisy Night.* Those sounds were really spooky to Nicky! Tonight, read *Lollipop,* by Wendy Watson.[4] When you get through, turn back to page 14. Why do you think Bunny's mother "hugged him and spanked him" at the same time?

> *Nora's entry:* SHE WAS WORRIEED IS WHY.

Roger, having been assigned Anita Lobel's Potatoes, Potatoes, writes: "I WOD NOT GO TO WAR. IT IS TOO DANGRIS," which sheds a new light on his classroom ferocity.

Acting Out Stories

The halls and broom-closets of school are often occupied by groups of three or four who are "working out a story." Mrs. T. hands them a book one of them has liked, asking them to "see if this will work up into a good play." She floats from group to group giving minimal suggestions, helping read hard words, and then calls all the children together.

As the "actor children" put on their plays, the "audience children" are asked to comment on the plays specifically and positively: They say what parts they liked and why. Best of all, they respond directly by laughing, clapping, or just listening.

The exercise serves equally well whether or not the actors stay close to the text. The fact that they've been asked to follow a text makes the audience children more attentive both to the play and to the text, which the teacher sometimes shares aloud after the performance. (See Patrick Collins' chapter in this book; also, a detailed guide for kindergarten and primary teachers on this approach to language and learning can be found in Vivian Gussin Paley's excellent book, *Wally's Stories.*[5])

Writing Their Own

There is probably nothing that makes children appreciate good literature more than writing their own. Writing puts them squarely and sympathetically in the company of authors. The children in Mrs. T.'s class borrow shamelessly, both from each other's work and from the stories they read. (It is as inappropriate to accuse a six-year old of plagiarism as it is to accuse a two-year old of stealing.) Because there is no sense of shame attached, most children readily share their sources:

I GOT THIS IDEA FROM JULIAN, IT'S ABOUT. . .

When one child shares a story with a beginning so striking that several children comment on it, she calmly says:

I REMEMBERED THIS STORY FROM A CRICKET MAGAZINE I READ LAST YEAR.

Children who love certain stories immerse themselves in them so fully that they are not aware of boundaries between their own ideas and those written by another person.

Some of the questions asked at writers' sharing time in Mrs. T.'s class sound very much like the ones asked in guided discussions of literature:

WHAT MAKES THE BAD GUYS BAD?

WHAT DOES THE UNICORN REALLY WANT?

But because the author is right there, the teacher also models gentler and less judgmental approaches:

"Let's try closing our eyes while Amy reads this passage, and then we'll tell her what her words made us see in our mind's eye."

I SAW LOTS OF COLORED LIGHT, WHEN SHE SINKS DOWN UNDER THE OCEAN YEAH, IT WAS VERY SOFT, FLOATY, AND THERE WERE SOME BIG SHELLS

Amy (who had not mentioned the shells in her story) nods authoritatively:

"Yep, those were the uncle's palace."

Creative Play

Last month, Mrs. T. read Lynn Reid Banks' *The Indian in the Cupboard* to her class during lunch.[6] At the same time, the situation in the woods, where the children go by choice for their free play, was getting out of hand (quarrels over forts; sticks carried as weapons; heartfelt anger; aggression; anguish released or generated, who knows, but dangerous). Mrs. T. called the children together and unilaterally banned war-games.

> *Roger:* But it's exciting! And I want to be in a war!

It was Tommy, a British World War II medic, hauled straight out of the trenches by magic in Ms. Banks' book, who saved the day.

Teacher: There are lots of things that need doing in a war besides fighting. Remember Tommy?

That was enough. For days after the woods echoed with the sounds of exploding shells, desperate orders to orderlies and doctors, the whine of ambulance sirens.

And Roger wrote this story:

BOOM! PIIIIRRRNN...BANG! QUICK YOU IDIITS BRING A STRECHER OVR HIR! THIS MAN NEEDS HELP AND HE NEEDS IT FAST YOU NUTHEDS. SMOKE IS GETIN IN AR WAY SO WE CAINT SEE. HERE! OH BE CAREFULL HE IS HURT BAD.

There've been plenty of rough days since, but that was a moment of glory for Roger and Mrs. T.

End Notes

1. Sylvia Ashton-Warner, *Spearpoint* (New York, Knopf, 1972).
2. Meinhart Dejong, *The Wheel on the School* (New York: Harcourt Brace Jovanovitch, 1954).
3. Jay Williams, *Everyone Knows What a Dragon Looks Like* (New York: MacMillan, 1976).
4. Wendy Watson, *Lollipop* (New York, Scholastic, 1976).
5. Vivian Paley, *Wally's Stories* (Cambridge, Harvard University Press, 1981).
6. Lynn Reid Banks, *The Indian in the Cupboard* (New York, Doubleday, 1985).

10

Before, During and After: Using Drama to Read Deeply

Patrick M. Collins

Pat Collins is a former primary teacher who is an Assistant Professor of Education at Hobart and William Smith Colleges. In addition, Collins has almost twenty years of experience teaching and directing theatre and drama with children. In this chapter Collins explores ways in which a teacher can use drama to help children gain a deeper understanding of the stories they read.

Teachers have long recognized classroom drama as a potentially effective means of helping children explore literature. Some, such as Winfred Ward,[1] have pointed to the ability of drama to help children develop empathy with the characters and contexts in the stories they read. Others, such as Dorothy Heathcote, have viewed dramatic activity as a means of helping children discover the "universal" themes, problems, and motifs developed in literature,[2] while still others, the more pragmatic, have argued that dramatizing stories may not only foster reading comprehension but also be used as a means of assessing comprehension.[3] Despite widespread recognition of the potential of classroom drama, extended dramatization of literature is still a relatively rare event in most classrooms. In this chapter I hope to broach this disparity between intention and practice by describing some basic ways in which teachers can use drama to help children read more deeply.

The act of reading a story and the act of dramatizing a story are similar in a variety of ways.[4] Both are constructive acts: Just as the actor (or child) reconstructs a story on the stage (or in the classroom), the reader uses a text to reconstruct a story on the stage of the mind. Both acts require imagination as well as the ability to reflect upon appropriate personal experience. Both depend upon powers of projection and identification: The reader must be able to find connections between his or her own experiences and the experiences of Cinderella, Jack, or Charlotte; it is through making similar connections that the actor brings those characters to life. Reading stories and dramatizing stories are both ways of knowing; both are ways of making and remaking the world.

The educational potential of combining story reading with story dramatization, however, is not so much a function of the similarities between these two ways of worldmaking as it is a result of recognizing that reading and acting are two different ways of worldmaking. The primary difference between the two has been succintly articulated by James Moffett.[5] Moffett describes the difference between drama and narrative as the difference between what is happening and what has happened. Stories are generally narratives in nature: They are told (or written) as accounts of events that have already happened and are told in the past tense. Drama, on the other hand, "is any raw phenomena as they are first being converted to information by some observer" (Moffett, 61). Drama is action in the present tense. This suggests that dramatizing a story is a more concrete (or at least less abstract) experience than reading a story.

It is because drama works on a different (more concrete) level of abstraction that it can be a powerful means of helping children approach literature. Drama provides the teacher with a means of taking "the long ago and far way" and bringing it into the present, into the here and now, into the classroom. Dramatic activity provides children with a means of living through stories in a way that, if properly nourished, can only deepen their understanding and appreciation of the stories in question as well as the process of storymaking at large.

But how, specifically, can teachers use classroom drama to deepen children's responses to literature? There are three basic ways to structure the dramatic exploration of literature with children: *reenactive dramatization, exploratory dramatization,* and *preparatory dramatization.* Generally speaking these three approaches may be thought of as occurring at three different times during the process of reading: Reenactive dramatization occurs *after* a story has been read, exploratory dramatization may take place at any time *during* the reading of a story, and preparatory dramatization is undertaken *before* reading a piece.

While each of these approaches enhances reading in different ways and makes different pedagogical demands on the teacher, there are some techniques and issues that teachers should consider in planning almost any classroom drama. Before describing the reenactive, exploratory, and preparatory approaches we need to consider some more generic aspects of using drama in the classroom.

Warm-ups

There are a few gifted teachers (such as Dorothy Heathcote) who are able to walk into a classroom full of students and say, "So you would like to do a drama about *Charlotte's Web* today—where shall we begin?" and start the dramatic work without the use of any conventional warm-up activities. In most cases, however, teachers and students are not comfortable simply jumping into a drama. Just as the athlete warms up before a practice or a game, the singer warms up his or her voice before a concert, and the actor limbers up before a performance, a classroom full of children needs to loosen up at the beginning of any dramatization.

In selecting warm-up activities the teacher needs to be concerned with helping children loosen up physically, vocally, and emotionally (or psychologically). Classroom drama demands that children use both voice and body in a relatively self-conscious fashion—in a fashion that many (especially older) children may initially find a bit awkward. It is through the use of nonthreatening physical and vocal warm-ups that teachers can help children become more comfortable with the emotional and psychological demands of make-believe. The best warm-up activities are those that warm-up body, voice, and psyche all at the same time.

The warm-up period should be short and sweet. It should probably last not much more than five minutes and should utilize activities that children can master quickly. Almost any text on acting will provide a variety of ideas for warm-up activities, but one of the most useful books for teachers is *Theatre Games for the Classroom* by Viola Spolin.[6] Spolin has developed what has been called the "theatre games approach" to teaching acting, and in her books she has adapted many of her theatre games for use by classroom teachers. Most teachers, however, already possess an entire arsenal of warm-up activities. Many children's games and songs such as "The Hokey Pokey," "Duck, Duck, Goose," "Simon Says," "Row, Row, Row Your Boat," "Freeze Tag," and variations on "Follow the Leader" all provide ample opportunity for physical, vocal, and emotional warm-up. Many of these activities may seem a bit juvenile or silly to the older child (eleven or twelve-year-olds) but often the sillier the better. Remember the goal of the teacher at this point is simply to loosen up body, voice, and mind while also helping children overcome any inhibitions they may have about using body, voice, and mind to tell stories. In this case the silly can often serve a serious purpose.

Classroom Planning

In addition to helping students loosen up, teachers also need to help students plan and organize their dramatic experience: They need to help the class set the scene. Just how a teacher goes about setting the scene depends on the goals in using drama. Generally speaking, it is wise to use a combination of large and small group discussions to help students plan the shape of their drama. There are at least three basic questions that need to be considered at this point: What is the story? Where does it take place? Who are the principle characters in the story?

At the very least, teachers need to be sure that students agree on how they are going to begin their drama. If, for example, a class is working with *The Lion, the Witch and the Wardrobe*, the students need to agree on whether they are going to begin their dramatization with the arrival of Peter, Susan, Edmund, and Lucy at the professor's house, with Lucy's first meeting with Mr. Tumnus, or with the first visit of all of the children to Narnia. While it may be sufficient merely to determine the starting point of the drama, at other times the teacher may need to help students generate an entire scenario (or outline) of the action before even beginning the drama. This is especially the case when the primary goal of the teacher is to strengthen basic comprehension through reenactment. Even if faithfulness to the text is not a priority, children need to talk about the general contours of the storyline they hope to dramatize. In addition to agreeing on a basic plot, students need help fleshing out the setting and characters. The teacher needs to lead the class in a discussion of where the story takes place, the historical period of the story, the time of year, the weather, and the kind of atmosphere or mood they wish to create. At times setting the scene requires more than mere discussion. Children often find it helpful to draw pictures, floor plans, or maps of their setting. At times it is also helpful to have children actually get up and physically create their space by using pantomime to render the setting physically. The goal at this point is to help students visualize as much detail as possible about where their drama will take place while minimizing the use of actual scenery and properties.

Finally, the teacher must help students explore the characters they will need to develop in the course of creating their drama. This entails more than simply agreeing on what characters will be needed in the drama and deciding who will play each character. It also means that the teacher must help the class determine the basic personality, motivations, and personal and historical background of each character. Once again this may be done by discussing a number of basic questions about each character. In working with the character of Edmund in *The Lion, the Witch and the Wardrobe* the teacher may ask questions such as: How old is Edmund? Where were he and his brothers and sisters born? What kinds of hobbies do you think Edmund would have? Who are his friends? Is Edmund as self-centered as he appears or is he simply insecure? What in his past has made him either insecure or self-centered? Why is he such a skeptic? Some of these questions will require a close examination of the text while others will call for children to create their own details of a character. Once again the goal is to help children generate as many details about their drama as possible before they jump into it. Teachers often think of classroom drama as essentially improvisational and off the cuff, but the fact of the matter is that good improvisation requires preparation; in the classroom that means careful planning by the teacher and students.

Control: Teacher as Actor, Coach, or Director

Classroom drama also requires leadership. One of the ways in which classroom drama is distinguished from the natural dramatic play of children is that classroom drama is controlled by a leader—by a teacher. Many teachers, however, have difficulty deciding how to control dramatic activity without stifling the inventiveness and enthusiasm of their young charges. It is true that teachers need to think carefully about how best to strike a delicate balance between ''creativity'' and control, but the teacher should never totally abdicate authority in the name of creativity.

Every teacher must grapple with the problem of control in his or her own way. As Dorothy Heathcote[7] suggests, each teacher must decide what his or her ''teaching thresholds'' are. Teachers must decide for themselves how much noise, how many students, how much activity, and how much student freedom they can tolerate, and they must find ways to work within these thresholds. For some teachers this may mean that they need, at least initially, to function as directors, closely guiding almost every move made by their students. It is probably more common, however, for teachers think of themselves as guides, coaches, or tipsters who carefully lead children through a dramatic activity. Even here teachers have a choice to make: Do they want to guide the drama from the inside, as an actor, or from the outside, as a coach?

Both approaches (teacher as actor and teacher as coach) have their advantages. Playing in a role provides teachers with a means of controlling both the drama and the children in a subtle but effective way. For example, the teacher who casts herself or himself as one of the older children (Peter or Susan) in *The Lion, the Witch and the Wardrobe* is not only able to control the direction of the story by virtue of being the teacher but also gains the natural authority of being one of the older siblings in the drama. Playing a role permits the teacher to control the drama without interrupting it: The teacher in a role often gains authority without being authoritative.

Many teachers, however, are not comfortable playing a role and should not feel compelled to do so. Most teachers probably feel more comfortable (at least at first) standing on the side and functioning as what Spolin calls a side-coach. As side-coach the teacher observes the drama from the outside (as teacher) and occasionally asks questions and provides suggestions that help move the drama forward. The advantage here is that this approach may provide the teacher with a more objective view of the activity and it may provide children with the security of knowing that the teacher is still in charge (as teacher). Both approaches (acting and coaching) can be effective, and both may be used by the same teacher at different times. Once again, the key to determining which approach is best for you is recognizing your limits as a teacher, recognizing what we might call in this case your acting threshold.

A final note needs to be made about control. It is perfectly permissible, indeed often necessary, to stop a drama at any point. In addition to stopping a drama anytime it reaches a teaching threshold, there are at least two other critical reasons for stopping a drama. Anytime you sense that children are losing their concentration, that they are no longer believing in what they are doing, or that they are not taking the activity seriously, you need to stop the action and find a way to help the class get back on track. Also, there are often moments in a drama, often highly emotional moments, that you want students to stop and dwell on. While you should be careful not to stop too often for these moments, you sometimes do want to slow a drama down (via discussion) so that children have more time to think about the event they have just experienced.

The Reenactive Dramatization of Stories

Reenactive dramatization is probably the most commonly used approach to story dramatization in the elementary classroom. The primary aim of reenactment is to retell, re-create, or re-present a piece of literature in dramatic form. As such reenactive dramatization almost always occurs after reading a book or story. However, while this approach to dramatization places a premium on being true to the text in question, reenacting a story does not require absolute fidelity between drama and text. As Nancy King[8] points out, one of the dangers of this approach to dramatic work is that personal and emotional response may be sacrificed for the sake of accuracy and authenticity, which in turn may place undue pressure upon children to recall and re-create all the details of what they have read. Teachers need to realize that reenactment is not simply retelling a story; it also involves interpretation.[9] No two groups of children will reenact *The Lion, the Witch and the Wardrobe* in the same way. Each group will interpret the story a bit differently. What sets off reenactment from other approaches to drama (exploratory and preparatory) is that it aims at an honest retelling of the story in question.

Reenacting a story may be appropriate under any number of circumstances, but there are two needs that are most clearly met by acting out a story after it has been read: Reenactment helps children consolidate their basic comprehension of a story, and it may help them identify with the characters and circumstances of a story. As we have already seen, dramatization always requires planning on the part of teachers and students; in the case of reenactment this planning generally requires students to generate an outline of the story they are to dramatize. At the very least, such an exercise forces children to read carefully in order to be able to sequence the events of the story for the dramatization adequately. More important, planning a reenactment often forces students to read more deeply in order to be able to make judgments about which events should (and should not) be included in a drama; it also forces them to make connections between the key events in a story. Reenactment can help children consolidate and operationalize their understanding of a story and, at the same time, provides the teacher with a means of evaluating that understanding.

Reenactment also helps children identify with the characters they read about by providing them with an opportunity to walk vicariously in someone else's shoes. Upon first reading about Edmund's misadventures in Narnia children may have little sympathy for him, but they may develop a much fuller understanding of what drives Edmund if they have an opportunity to reenact the character of Edmund themselves. Reenactment may not only consolidate but also deepen a child's basic understanding of a story.

Classroom reenactment is a relatively straightforward process with which most teachers have at least experimented. A few pedagogical comments, however, may be helpful here. First, while we often talk about reenacting a story, reenactment does not necessarily imply dramatizing a whole story. Though it may be appropriate for a group of first graders to reenact all of *Where the Wild Things Are*,[10] it is rather unlikely that a group of fifth graders will be able to reenact all of *The Lion, the Witch and the Wardrobe*. Indeed, it is often more productive to dramatize a selected part of a story rather than an entire story. Even when trying to dramatize an entire story it is seldom possible (or appropriate) to re-create every event described in the text. Drama tends to be more selective than narrative in the events it portrays. This should be some relief for the teacher who would like to use drama to extend reading but can't find the time. You can't do it all—you need to be selective in what you decide to reenact.

Second, whether you dramatize a story in a large group or a small group will depend in large part on the nature of the story in question (e.g., Does the story require four characters or twenty-four?). While it may be easier for the teacher to control and influence the work of a large group, there are some advantages to doing multiple, small group reenactments of a story. If four or five small groups work on reenacting Edmund's first encounter with the White Witch you are likely to wind up with four or five different renditions of that scene. This provides a wonderful opportunity for students to justify various interpretations of the text. Interpretation becomes a topic of discussion—it becomes an intentional activity.

Finally, in addition to doing multiple, small group reenactments, it is often beneficial to have the same group replay the same scene a number of times while rotating roles each time. For example, the child who played the White Witch in the scene noted above might play Edmund the second time around while the student who initially played Edmund may take on the role of the White Witch. This rotation of roles helps children realize that any story, any piece of reading, may be approached from a variety of perspectives. Drama helps children experiment with multiple points of view.

The Exploratory Dramatization of Stories

While we may generally think of reenactment as a dramatic activity that occurs after reading a story, exploratory dramatization may occur at any time during the process of reading. Exploratory dramatization is what John Stewig calls "improvisation."[11] While reenactment is primarily concerned with retelling a story in a relatively accurate manner, exploratory drama aims at deepening one's understanding by improvising on the text in question—by using the text as a point of departure rather than as an outline (Stewig 88-9). Stewig suggests two ways in which this approach may be used to explore a story.

First, drama may be used to extend a story either forward or backward in time. As Figure 10-1 illustrates, this allows the teacher to use drama to help children hypothesize about what happened before the story begins as well as about what may happen after the story has ended.

Figure 10-1. **Plot Extension of *The Lion, the Witch and the Wardrobe***

Extend story backward in time.		Extend story forward in time.
	Actual Time Described in Story	
Where in London did the children live?		Will the children be able to return to Narnia?
Were they victimized by many bombings?		How might they return?
What was life like before the war?		What will they find if they return?
What kind of school did the children attend?		What will the children do when they return to London?
What kind of relationship did the children have with their parents?		How will other people react to their story about Narnia?
The story begins when the children arrive at the professor's house.		The story ends when the children return from Narnia.

Adapted from: John Stewig. *Informal Drama in the Elementary Language Arts Program.* New York: Teachers College Press, 1983, p. 89.

Extending a story backwards, into the past, can be an effective way of helping children envision the circumstances that may have led to (or caused) the events narrated in the story itself. In the opening paragraph of *The Lion, the Witch and the Wardrobe* we are told, in just one sentence, that Peter, Susan, Lucy, and Edmund were sent to the professor's house to escape the air raids in London during the war. But what are the implications of this for what follows? The teacher who wants her or his students to consider the possibility that the children's war experience affected the nature of their fantasy may begin by having the class improvise the children's wartime experience in London by having them act out those air raids, and by having them live through what it must have felt like to say goodbye to their parents and get on a train to an unknown destination. In this case the use of exploratory drama may provide children with a backdrop for what they are reading.

Using drama to extend a story forward in time does not provide a backdrop as much as it encourages students to think hypothetically and predictively about what they read. Whether or not the children will be able to return to Narnia and what they might find upon their return are especially pertinent questions for exploration given the fact that *The Lion, the Witch and the Wardrobe*[12] is only the first of several stories about Narnia. But a sequel is hardly necessary to justify this kind of hypothetical exploration. It is now common practice to help children think hypothetically about what they are reading. What we take from a text depends, in part, on what we expect to find, and drama provides children with an active means of discovering their own expectations, of predicting what will happen next.

With this in mind it is important to underscore the point that this kind of dramatic exploration may take place at any point in the reading of a story. Indeed, it is probably more useful to stop at key points in a story and act out what the class thinks will happen next than it is to wait until the end of the story and then extend the entire story into the future. Extending a story before students have completed it allows students to compare their hypothetical outcomes with those eventually unveiled by the author.

Stewig also suggests that exploratory drama (improvisation) may be used to extend a story by adding, deleting, or altering characters. Exploring the relationship between characters in a story with those not included in the story may prove to be a valuable means of helping children gain a better understanding of why the people in the story behave the way they do. For example, in exploring the background of the four children who go through the wardrobe a teacher may have children create a whole range of characters not mentioned in the book (see Figure 10-2). While at times it may be interesting to introduce new characters into the story itself (e.g., What if the children ran into their older brother in Narnia?), it is generally more useful to explore the relationship between actual and invented characters outside of the story as a way of developing background information about the characters in the story. Adding, deleting, or altering characters in the story, however, might also prove to be enlightening. What would happen, for example, if Lucy met her cat rather than Mr. Tumnus? Or what would happen if there were only three children: Peter, Susan, and Lucy? Or what would happen if Lucy was the self-centered skeptic rather than Edmund? Using drama to explore these kinds of questions can help children develop a better understanding of why stories are structured the way they were.

Figure 10-2. **Character Addition Based on** *The Lion, the Witch and the Wardrobe*

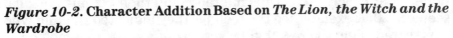

```
                              ┌ ─ ─ ─ ─ ─ ─ ─
                              │  The children's mother
         ┌ ─ ─ ─ ─ ─ ─ ─ ─ ─ ┤  The children's father
         │                       The children's grandparents
         │                    │  Max—The children's older brother
         │                    └ ─ ─ ─ ─ ─ ─ ─ ─

                                ┌─────────────────────────┐
 Possible                       │  Peter                  │
 Additional                     │  Susan       Actual characters
 Characters                     │  Edmund      in the story
                                │  Lucy                   │
         │                      └─────────────────────────┘
         │
         │                    ┌ ─ ─ ─ ─ ─ ─ ─
         │                    │  Mariet—Peter's fiancée
         └ ─ ─ ─ ─ ─ ─ ─ ─ ─ ┤  Doreen—Susan's best girlfriend
                                 Dick—Edmund's buddy from school
                              │  Mittens—Lucy's pet cat
                              └ ─ ─ ─ ─ ─ ─ ─ ─
```

Adapted from: John Stewig. *Informal Drama in the Elementary Language Arts Program.* New York: Teacher's Colleges Press, 1983, p. 90.

Nancy King[13] suggests two other ways in which drama may be used in an exploratory fashion: to explore point of view and to explore emotional response. Children may explore point of view by reenacting a story a number of times as they rotate roles, as noted above, although King suggests a slightly different approach. She suggests that children do multiple improvisations of a story or scene in which they consciously change the point of view from which the story is told. Rather than retelling the adventures of Narnia as they are narrated by an anonymous third person, children may improvise the story as it might be retold by Edmund, or Aslan, or even the White Witch. In this case students are not so concerned with being faithful to the text as they are with being faithful to the point of view from which they are trying to work. The emphasis is on exploration of character and point of view.

King maintains that drama can also be used to help children discover, understand, and articulate their own feelings about what they have read. In this case exploratory drama is used not to improvise upon the story itself but to act out the emotions children experience when reading a story or passage. After reading of Lucy's first excursion into Narnia a teacher may ask the class how such an experience would make them feel (scared, curious, lightheaded, intrigued, hopeful, at peace, etc.). The children could then act out personal scenarios that exemplified the feelings they indicated. A child who was scared might express that by acting out a scene in which he or she was lost in a department store, while the child who was curious might improvise a scene about exploring the toy section in that same store. Drama does not only provide children with a means of exploring stories but also provides them with a means of exploring their own feelings about those stories.

These are only a few examples of how drama may be used to explore literature. The important point to remember is that the dramatic exploration of stories is not limited merely to reenacting stories. Exploratory dramatization suggests that teachers may use drama to improvise, extend, alter, and otherwise play around with what children have read. This is not to suggest that anything goes. The primary goal of the teacher must always be to help students develop a better understanding of the text they are reading. But as long as this goal remains a guiding force teachers should feel free to use exploratory drama in any way that will help children read more deeply.

Preparatory Dramatization and Stories

Thus far we have looked at ways in which drama can be used during and after reading a story. Drama, however, may also be used before children read a story. If it is true that children's personal experiences affect what they read (or see) in a story, then, in so far as drama provides teachers with a means of creating vicarious experiences for children, it becomes, if carefully structured, a viable means of providing children with experiential structures (schemata, mindsets, scaffoldings, backdrops) that may inform their reading. I would like to end by exploring drama as a prereading activity, as a means of helping children prepare for reading.

How can children dramatize a story before they have even started to read it? They can't (at least not consciously), but teachers can structure dramatic experiences that parallel (in various key ways) stories that children are about to read. In order to do so a teacher must:

1. Determine how he or she wants the drama to prepare the children for the reading they will do—determine the objective of the dramatic activity;
2. Determine the key elements of the story (or scene) in question;
3. Determine how these key elements are particularized in the story;
4. Develop a parallel situation (drama) and dramatize it with the class;
5. Ask key follow-up questions about the drama;
6. Read the story;
7. Ask questions that relate the story back to the drama.

This method can once again be illustrated by way of an example from *The Lion, the Witch and the Wardrobe* (see Figure 10-3). Let us say that a teacher is reading this book to a group of second graders. As the class approaches the chapter in which the four children first meet Aslan, the teacher becomes concerned that the students may not feel the full impact of this first meeting. The teacher may therefore decide to create a drama that will help sensitize the class to the feelings Peter, Susan, Edmund, and Lucy may have upon first meeting Aslan. Having determined the objective of the drama the teacher then lists the key elements of the scene in question (hope, fear, uncertainty, excitement, nervousness, anxiety). The teacher then lists ways in which these key elements are particularized in the children's first meeting with Aslan (Aslan can defeat the White Witch; Aslan may reprimand the children; Aslan is a king, but what kind of king is he?).

The teacher then creates a similar situation and develops details that will parallel the details in the original story. In this case the teacher may ask the students to act out a group of younger children meeting Santa Claus for the first time. It is important that the teacher be aware of how the meeting with Santa parallels the meeting with Aslan so that he or she (the teacher) will be sure to develop these points fully when working with the class. The emphasis in this case would not be so much on actually meeting Santa as it would be on living through the days, hours, and minutes leading up to that first meeting.

Immediately following the drama the teacher asks questions that help the children become conscious of the key elements of the drama: How did you feel before you met Santa? Why were you afraid of Santa? Why were you excited about meeting Santa? How did you feel when you actually met Santa?

Figure 10-3. **Plan for Preparatory Drama based on *The Lion, the Witch and the Wardrobe***

Meeting Aslan	Key Elements	Meeting Santa
Aslan can defeat the White Witch.	Hope	Santa can bring children presents.
Aslan may reprimand the children.	Fear	Santa may scold children and not bring them anything.
Aslan is a king, but what kind of king is he?	Uncertainty	Santa is a jolly fellow, but does he ever get upset with children?
The children are going to meet a king.	Excitement	Santa is one of the most famous people in the world.
The children don't know how to greet this king.	Nervousness	What does a young child say to Santa when meeting him for the first time?
The children have walked a long way to meet Aslan.	Anxiety	The children have been waiting all year to visit with Santa.

Finally, the class is ready to read (or, in this case, listen to) the scene in which the children meet Aslan. (This is likely to be done the next day, or even a few days later.) Before reading the text the teacher may tell the students to keep their Santa Claus drama in mind as they listen to the story. After reading the text the teacher then asks questions that help the children relate the story back to the Santa Claus drama: Have you ever been in a situation like Peter, Susan, Edmund, and Lucy? How do you think you would feel just before meeting someone like Aslan? Can you think of times when you have felt this way?

While this example focuses on developing an entire drama that is similar to a story the children are yet to read, the same approach may be used in using preparatory drama to provide children with the vicarious experience they need to understand a specific character or a specific setting: Drama can be used to develop parallel people and places as well as parallel stories. Once again, what is important is that teachers realize that drama provides them with a tool for helping structure the kinds of experiences children bring to their reading: That dramatic activity may be as useful before reading as it is after reading.

Curtain Call

It is only in using drama before, during, and after reading that classroom drama can have its most profound effect upon how children make and take stories. It is only in utilizing the full range of dramatic activity that teachers will come to realize that drama is not just a frill to be relegated to 2:30 p.m. on Friday afternoon but that it can play an integral role in helping children understand the tales they are told, the stories they read, and the worlds in which they live.

End Notes

1. Winifred Ward, *Stories to Dramatize* (New Orleans: Anchorage Press, 1952).
2. Betty Jane Wagner, *Dorothy Heathcote: Drama as a Learning Medium* (Washington D.C.: National Education Association, 1976).
3. Mary Jett-Simpson, "Reading Comprehension Through Creative Dramatics," *Using Literature in the Elementary School*, eds. J. Stewig and S. Sebesta (Urbana: NCTE, 1978).
4. John McInnes, "The Drama of Reading." *Creative Drama in a Developmental Context* ed. Judith Kase-Polisini (Lanham, MD: University Press of America, 1985).
5. James Moffett, *Teaching the Universe of Discourse* (Boston: Houghton Mifflin, 1983).
6. Viola Spolin, *Theater Games For The Classroom* (Evanston: Northwestern University Press, 1986).
7. Liz Johnson and Cecily O'Neill, eds. *Dorothy Heathcote, Collected Writings on Education and Drama* (London: Hutchinson Publishing, 1984).
8. Nancy King, "From Literature to Drama to Life," *Children and Drama.* ed. Nellie McCaslin (Lanham, MD: University Press of America, 1985).
9. What I am calling reenactive drama here is called "Interpretation" by John Stewig in *Information Drama in the Elementary Language Arts Program* (New York: Teachers College Press, 1983).
10. Maurice Sendak, *Where The Wild Things Are* (Harper & Row: 1963).
11. Where I use the term "exploratory" Stewig (1983) would use the term "improvisation." Much of the following discussion of exploratory drama is adapted from Stewig.
12. C.S. Lewis, *The Lion, the Witch and the Wardrobe* (New York: Macmillan, 1950).
13. King, 1985.

11

Among Nonreaders: Voluntary Reading, Reading Achievement, and the Development of Reading Habits

Paul Wilson

Paul Wilson teaches courses on reading and literacy at Western Michigan University. While at the Center for the Study of Reading, he co-authored, with Richard Anderson and Linda Fielding, an influential series of studies on children's bookreading habits. The findings, in short, were alarming: Most children don't read. Our methods and programs have provided children the skills of reading but have not made them readers. Making children readers should be the goal of reading instruction, Wilson argues. But what kind of readers: readers for pleasure or critical readers? Wilson offers his own surprising answer to this question, based on a new view of how reading abilities develop, and then sets out several proposals for making all children readers.

Introduction

As more schools move towards integrating literature into their reading curricula, two issues must be addressed. In the short term, the American public, school administrators, and responsible educators must have assurances that the reading achievement of America's children will not be jeopardized; this is an important but limited perspective when we consider how achievement is currently standardized and measured. A broader issue also arises about the most desirable long-term outcomes of American reading instruction: What kinds of readers should the schools be producing, and how can the use of literature contribute?

This chapter addresses both issues. First comes an encouraging review of the best evidence about the beneficial effects of reading trade books on various measures of reading achievement. This is followed by a discouraging account of how little voluntary reading children actually do. Based on this evidence, the argument is made that the most important goal of American reading instruction should be to produce more avid readers. The chapter goes on to a discussion of factors that might be useful in stimulating avid reading: required reading, Sustained Silent Reading, extrinsic incentives, peer interaction, and the presence of books in the classrooms. The chapter concludes with speculations about the role of literature in the development of avid reading and the consequences of avid reading for reading fluency.

Voluntary Reading and Reading Achievement

Voluntary reading, the amount of time children spend each day reading books of their own choice on their own time, has significant positive effects on growth in comprehension, vocabulary, and reading fluency. That is the incontrovertible finding reported by Anderson, Wilson, and Fielding[1] after an extensive investigation of fifth graders' out of school habits.

For periods ranging from eight to twenty-six weeks, 155 fifth grade children filled out daily log forms on which they reported the numbers of minutes they spent on their various out of school activities. The activities included (among others) doing homework, watching television, going out, playing with their friends, eating dinner, listening to music, reading newspapers and magazines, and reading books. Book reading time was verified by having the children report the title and author of the book they had been reading on the previous day.

The children's fifth grade reading achievement was measured with tests of comprehension, vocabulary, and reading rate. In addition, school files were used to obtain an overall measure of their reading achievement in second grade. Two different kinds of analyses were undertaken to interpret the relationships between habits and reading achievement. First, fifth grade habits were related to fifth grade reading achievement. Second (assuming that fifth grade habits represented enduring student traits), fifth grade habits were related to gains in reading achievement between second and fifth grade.

Of all the out of school activities engaged in by these children, book reading had by far the most positive influence on fifth grade reading achievement. Book reading also had the most positive influence on gains in reading achievement from second to fifth grade. In both analyses, average daily book reading time contributed significantly to comprehension, vocabulary, and reading rate.

In sum, voluntary out of school reading of trade books has beneficial effects on school measures of reading achievement. Those children who spend more time reading books do better on reading tests. If more children can be motivated to do more voluntary reading, they too will do better on school reading tests. Results from this study suggest that an average of ten to fifteen minutes per day spent on reading books could produce achievement gains for many children. A worthwhile, indeed vital, outcome of school reading programs would be for American children to do more voluntary reading: Reading achievement is not jeopardized by more book reading; it is enhanced by it.

How Much Voluntary Reading Do Children Do?

Although the influence of voluntary book reading on reading achievement is salutary, the amount of voluntary book reading that children actually do is distressingly low. The children in the Anderson, Wilson, and Fielding investigation were a reasonably representative sample, yet most of them did very little voluntary reading.

If avid reading were defined as spending thirty minutes or more each day with a book, fewer than 10 percent of these children were avid readers. Across the whole period during which their habits were tracked, fully 50 percent of them averaged less than five minutes of voluntary book reading per day; 70 percent averaged less than eleven minutes per day; 90 percent averaged less than twenty minutes. If you were going to predict how much reading any child, picked at random, might do on any particular day, the best guess would be none; 50 percent of these children read from a book only one day out of every five. If you predicted no book reading for any child on any particular day, then you would be right as often as four days out of five.

The Anderson, Wilson, and Fielding data fit very well with the other recent large scale assessment of American children's engagement in reading. Walberg and Tsai,[2] using data from the *National Assessment of Educational Progress*, found that on the day preceding the administration of the NAEP inventory, 44 percent of the children responding had done no book reading at all.

The data from these studies make two points very clear: first, there is much to be gained in terms of all measurable aspects of reading achievement—comprehension, vocabulary, and reading rate—by increasing the amount of book reading that American children do; second, there are many children who gain no benefit from book reading because they are doing none. When you visit the typical classroom, you find yourself truly among nonreaders.

Required Reading Does Not Become Avid Reading

The development of avid reading habits is everybody's responsibility. Fielding, Wilson, and Anderson[3] interviewed avid readers about how they became interested in reading. Most avid readers reported a significant home influence; in particular, there was at least one other person at home whom they could talk with about their reading and from whom they received ideas about what they could read next. Anderson, Wilson, and Fielding found that there could also be a significant teacher influence on avid reading. Among the seven classes in their study, the most avid class read three and a half times longer each day than the least avid.

Both the home and the school can influence the growth of avid reading habits, so both have a role to play in fostering reading achievement. Describing their coordination is desirable, though beyond the scope of this chapter. However, efforts in schools must proceed apace because the school effect on increasing voluntary reading may be independently beneficial.

The first lesson for school programs comes from considering the dismal results of current school practices. School programs have relied primarily on mandated, regimented reading, even when implementing Sustained Silent Reading. The result, regardless of any judgment about final responsibility, has clearly been that American children are doing very little reading. Required reading, by itself, does not work.

Children do not become avid readers through reading only assigned texts. This is particularly true for the lower ability children who almost never get the chance to read anything other than assigned school textbooks. The common practice of rewarding those who finish their work by letting them read ensures that only the more able students get to do any book reading. The rich continue to get richer, and the poor stay poor.

School reading programs must influence student choices about how to spend discretionary time. More students must come to see reading as something that they want to do, rather than as something they have to do. The crux of the matter is how to get students to engage in reading without requiring it.

Extrinsic Incentives and Sustained Silent Reading

Children, of course, should be informed about the beneficial influence of reading on test scores. Let us not discount the pragmatism of our children. Some children want to do better but don't know how to; some children want to do better but don't want to spend any more time on school work—they don't want to do any more required work. Reminders that reading books they enjoy is a good way to do better on tests may influence some children to read more.

Sustained Silent Reading continues to be a way to provide children with an opportunity to read and thus to develop a reading habit. Much of the research on Sustained Silent Reading, however, has yielded equivocal or even disappointing results.[4] Sustained Silent Reading is surely better than nothing, at least in the sense that it often produces positive attitudes toward reading among both students and teachers. However, clear cut academic benefits have seldom been documented. Collins[5] and Manning and Manning[6] report two of the few exceptions. None of the work on Sustained Silent Reading has directly addressed the issue of whether there has been any long-term influence on children's voluntary reading habits.

I believe that the same could be said for most of the extrinsic motivation plans intended to influence children's reading. Pizza Hut's Book It! program, for example, has achieved two worthwhile goals: It has drawn attention to the value of reading, and it has provided short term extrinsic rewards for those children who participate. Laudable as such efforts are they fall short of influencing the long term growth of children's reading habits. Becoming an avid reader involves more than a few months of reinforcement that recurs only once a year.

Children need support year round to become avid readers. If socially and educationally conscious corporations were to cooperate in providing year round incentives, with each perhaps sponsoring one month of activities, then extrinsic incentives might have more efficacy. School programs, on their own, can and should include extrinsic motivation components—like popcorn parties, challenges from the principal, or competitions between classrooms or schools. The criterion, of course, must be the amount of time spent on reading so that children of all ability levels can participate. For these extrinsic incentives to have an effect on reading habits, schools should be prepared to provide them both throughout the school year and for the summer months.

As a logistical factor, providing time for reading in school is crucial. If most children are choosing not to read outside of school, we cannot expect that simple admonitions or extrinsic rewards will turn them around. Children choose their preferred activities because they are comfortable, familiar, and thus less effortful than something different. Habituation is a powerful force in governing how any of us spend our time. We are most likely to choose what we are habituated to. In order to overcome the inertia of our children's present habituations, schools must provide children ample opportunities for book reading. Time set aside for daily reading, as in Sustained Silent Reading, is a necessary, but not sufficient, condition for changing children's reading habits.

The traditional approach to fostering children's reading habits through school reading programs has involved a combination of Sustained Silent Reading and external incentives. The remainder of this chapter will pursue a discussion of other factors that are also necessary if school programs are to succeed.

The Culture of Reading

Manning and Manning[6] have reported an unusually comprehensive, year long comparison of the effectiveness of approaches to implementing Sustained Silent Reading. They studied fourth grade classes in twenty-four schools of differing socioeconomic levels. There were six classrooms in each of four conditions: a control group, which did no reading; a traditional Sustained Silent Reading group, in which everyone (including the teachers) read silently every day; a teacher conference group, in which (like the traditional Individualized Reading approach) the students had weekly, individual conferences with the teacher about their reading; and a peer conference group, in which the students talked regularly with each other about their reading.

Manning and Manning measured attitudes toward reading and reading achievement using a pretest post-test design. They found that both the teacher conference group and the peer conference group developed more positive attitudes about reading than the control and traditional Sustained Silent Reading groups. Just in terms of developing positive attitudes toward reading, then, it is necessary to go beyond the traditional approach to Sustained Silent Reading.

Much more important than the attitude results, however, were the effects on reading achievement. Only the peer conference group had superior reading achievement gains. Only when the students were talking regularly with each other about their reading did their reading achievement scores go up.

In the best of all possible worlds, Manning and Manning would also have measured increases in amount of out of school reading. Since they did not, we must make inferences about why the peer conference group had significantly greater gains in reading achievement. Consider, first, that the Sustained Silent Reading, teacher conference, and peer conference groups had equal amounts of time allocated to reading in class; thus, in-class reading could not have accounted for the gain in achievement. Recall also the Anderson, Wilson, and Fielding finding about how the amount of voluntary reading influences reading achievement gains. It would seem, then, that the peer conference approach caused more out of school voluntary reading, which, in turn, caused the superior gains in achievement.

This makes sense when we think about Fielding, Wilson, and Anderson's interviews with avid readers: They became avid readers—that is, their amount of reading increased—because they had somebody else to talk with about their reading. They were able to share their reactions to books.

One necessary addition to school reading programs, then, is peer interaction—time and encouragement for students to talk with each other about what they are reading, to read together, to work together on projects of their choosing related to their favorite books. Morrow[7] describes a number of such worthwhile activities. The satisfaction and enthusiasm that are expressed through these activities are reinforced through the expression. When students also express dissatisfactions (as we must expect they will), they can get new ideas from their friends about other books to read. Reading becomes something that students do because of friendship, because their friends read. More important, sharing their thoughts and feelings about books becomes part of the intellectual currency of their social relations within the classroom. Reading becomes part of the culture of the classroom.

The Role of Books in the Culture of the Classroom

If a school reading program is to be effective at increasing voluntary reading, the other essential addition besides time to read and peer interaction is books—real books. In order to have reading become part of the culture of the classroom, students must have ready access to books, and plenty of them. Studies by Elley and Manghubai[8] and Ingham[9] have shown positive effects on reading achievement associated with flooding classrooms with books. Being around books, handling books, and learning to browse through them in order to make decisions about what to read are necessary facets of becoming an avid reader. Without a sufficient number of books in every American classroom, it will be very difficult to motivate children to read more.

In preparing this chapter, I conducted some informal research on the development of reading habits by questioning more than two hundred graduate and undergraduate students in reading education courses. The two issues I addressed were class visits to the school library and browsing habits.

The graduate students already involved in teaching have observed that during library visits, many of their students appear listless and unmotivated when it comes time to choose a book for themselves; they talk with each other instead of choosing. The lower level readers, especially, need to be urged to get a book. They don't seem to know how to choose meaningfully, with the consequence that once they get a book back to the classroom, they may not be very interested in it; yet they are often stuck with that book for a week or two (or longer) without an easy opportunity to make a change.

Virtually all of the students I questioned, both graduate and undergraduate, indicated that they were browsers. They browse both in book stores and in libraries. More than 95 percent of them indicated that they buy less than one book for every five books that they browse. Among the library users, the figures were very similar: They browse many more books than they actually check out. Interestingly, there were more book buyers than library users. This finding in itself may represent an indictment of how both parents and schools fail to build an appreciation in most children of the value of libraries.

I also asked how many books these students actually finished reading. More than half of them said that they did not finish every book, either from the book store or from the library. Several people made informal comments about how sometimes they finished reading a book out of guilt, even though they really didn't want to, because they had bought it.

My point in pursuing these questions was to verify the fact that most avid readers are extremely selective in their reading. They do not read everything that is put into their hands. They do not read everything that they stumble across by chance. Instead, they make very meaningful personal choices about what to read, and many of them are not afraid to admit that they have chosen incorrectly: Avid readers don't finish everything that they start reading. They feel good about reading, and they continue to choose reading as a way to spend their time, in part because of the degree of choice that they are able to exercise as they read.

There must be enough books—enough different books—in every classroom for our children to be able to learn to make meaningful choices about what they are going to read and change their minds at a moment's notice, without penalty and without duress. If books are not available, students cannot learn to make the meaningful, personal choices that all avid readers make daily. There must be enough books for students to have the luxury of being selective. Teachers must single out those students who read the least and give them significant involvement in arranging, displaying, advertising, and managing the classroom collection of books. These are the students who most need to learn how to handle books, how to browse with books. These are the students who most need to learn to indulge in the luxury of being selective, in the luxury of a large collection of books.

All Books Are Not Literature

Part of the motivation for almost everyone involved in the movement toward literature-based reading programs comes from a painfully obvious realization: Because text books are not literature—i.e., because they are often poorly written and uninteresting—children are not very motivated to read and write when using them. Many children work with textbooks out of a sense of duty rather than with a sense of joy about learning.

The conclusion then follows that children's sense of joy about learning can be better stimulated and engaged through literature. While I believe that this conclusion is warranted in part, I also believe that it represents an incomplete vision of what should be happening in our classrooms. The point of departure for a workable new initiative must be the children's sense of joy, not the materials.

Victor Nell's recent work, *Lost in a Book: The Psychology of Reading for Pleasure*,[10] proves revealing on this point. Nell makes an important distinction between two different types of avid readers: the Type A reader and the Type B reader.

Type A readers are primarily escapist in their orientation. They read to dull their consciousness, to hold at bay their awareness of everyday life. They bolt their reading, like speed eaters, and remember relatively little detail from what they read. Of particular importance, they frequently read formulaic texts that fall safely and predictably within the confines of defined genres. Charles Temple (personal communication) has referred to such texts as soap operas in print.

Type B readers are primarily involved savorers. They read to heighten their consciousness, to explore and resolve problems they are pondering, rather than to block them out. As in Bacon's metaphor, they chew slowly and digest more completely what they read. They maintain a high level of involvement with what they have been reading, even when they do not have a book in their hands. As a consequence, they remember plenty of detail from what they read. The bulk of their reading is not confined to particular genres but ranges widely in relation to both their interests and their needs.

Both Type A and Type B readers read a great deal, and they are very fast, fluent readers. Given appropriate circumstances, Nell discovered, they are perfectly capable of shifting from their preferred mode of reading to the other mode; they are flexible and able to meet the demands of any reading task. Nonetheless, they tend to return regularly to their preferred mode of reading.

Because Nell did not delve into the developmental histories of the Type A and Type B readers, I did some introspection about it, interviewed two of my colleagues, and discussed the two types of readers with a graduate class. One of my colleagues and I were both Type A readers throughout elementary school. Later, we shifted to Type B reading, my colleague after tenth grade and I during the transition from high school to college; both of us were influenced by the example of one or more teachers. Once or twice a year, I will shift into Type A mode and read a thriller, but virtually all my reading, like that of my first colleague, is now done in Type B mode. My other colleague has remained exclusively a Type A reader at home and never has been successful at doing Type B professionally related reading in the home setting. This colleague finds that it is quite possible, however, to move into the Type B mode in the office. No one in my graduate class could remember being a Type B reader in their early years of schooling.

My hypothesis is that developmentally, for many students, the Type B mode of reading is something that evolves over time after the Type A mode has been established. If it is true that most students naturally engage first in the Type A mode, doesn't it seem paradoxical that the academic demands of school render the highest rewards to students who display the Type B mode of reading? Schools tend to demand and reward Type B reading, while, developmentally, many students may have the natural inclination to be Type A readers.

Unequivocally, we must have worthwhile literature in every American classroom. Otherwise it will be impossible to move children toward developing a taste for it. The overriding priority for classroom library collections, however, must be the inclusion of many books that children really want to read. Children's choices for what to read are frequently different from teachers' choices, from parents' choices, and from the canons of cultural literacy. When our "literature" differs from what the children value as literature, their preferences must be honored.

Nilsen, Searfoss, and Peterson (1980) explain this point nicely. They argue that classroom libraries should contain three levels of books—verbal, behavioral, and transcendent. Verbal level books like Dr. Seuss are "page turners." Children want to keep on reading, and the reading is not very effortful. Adults often are less impressed with verbal level books than children. Behavioral level books, like those by Beverly Cleary or Judy Blume, emphasize characters that children can readily identify with. Children are eager to read such books because of the character identification and life issues that correspond to their own experience. Both adults and children may be impressed with such books. Transcendent level books are children's books that adults value highly because of their literary qualities. The aesthetic experiences that adults have with these books may be beyond the reach of children; thus, adults need not only to read such books aloud to children but also to discuss why the books are so good.

If we want children to develop into purposeful, choice making, avid readers, we must allow them the freedom to choose what they really want to read. The easiest way to do this is to involve children regularly in choosing new acquisitions for the classroom library. As their Type A reading needs for genre books (Hardy Boys, Sweet Valley High), comedy, and page turners are satisfied and they develop the habits of avid readers, we can then begin to interest them in more Type B reading of the literature that we ourselves have come to value more highly.

Conclusion: Avid Reading and the Headlong Rush Toward Meaning

As one who did considerable advanced graduate work in English, I value and savor literature as one of life's true pleasures. Yet I have arrived at a strange new position regarding the reading children do in their early years. If we have to choose between quantity and quality, we must choose quantity. If we have to choose between the reading we want to require and the reading that the children prefer, we must honor the children's choices. To do otherwise would be to seriously impede the development of avid reading, and avid reading is important, primarily because of its effect on fluency.

Anderson, Wilson, and Fielding[11] found a positive relationship between the amount of voluntary reading and reading rate: Children who read more read faster and thus could be considered more fluent readers. I want, however, to think about fluency in a broader sense as the ability to be completely absorbed in the process of creating meaning with a text, with no conscious thought given to amy of the mechanics of reading.

Think about how you yourself got hooked on reading. Didn't it have its roots in those times when you were so interested in some favorite book that the headlong rush to find out what was going to happen blotted out every other aspect of your conscious experience? As children begin to sense the possibility of that headlong rush, and then as they come to crave it, they see for themselves the value of fluency, the desirability of being able to do it—to read—on their own. We will turn children into avid, fluent readers in direct proportion to the frequency with which we can give them that experience of the headlong rush toward meaning.

To make the demand on children too early to be Type B readers can induce laborious strategies that forever impede the development of fluency. The reason that the genre reading typical of Type A readers is so helpful is that, within the genre, text structure and often significant elements of the content are predictable to children. Thus it is easier for them to slip into the headlong rush toward meaning. For those who are slower to develop, repeated readings of favorite books, both silent and oral, may substitute, early one, for genre reading; repeated reading, like genre reading, can provide that same sense of security, that same sense of growing fluency and competence so necessary for the reading habit to thrive.

In conclusion, then, we must face the fact that when we visit the typical elementary classroom, we find ourselves, at present, among nonreaders. Knowing this, our first goal for school reading programs must be to cultivate literacy, to cultivate that headlong rush toward meaning that leads to large volumes of motivated voluntary reading. It is large volumes of reading that lead directly to improved reading achievement. It is large volumes of reading that provide the base of fluency for all subsequent reading that students will need or want to do. It is large volumes of reading that support the culture of literacy.

End Notes

1. Richard C. Anderson, Paul T. Wilson, and Linda G. Fielding, "Growth in Reading and How Children Spend Their Time Outside of School," *Reading Research Quarterly* 23.3 (1988): 285–303.
2. Herbert J. Walberg, and S. Tsai, "Reading Achievement and Diminishing Returns to Time," *Journal of Educational Psychology* 76 (1984):442–451.
3. Linda G. Fielding, Paul T. Wilson, and Richard C. Anderson, "A New Focus on Free Reading: The Role of Tradebooks in Reading Instruction," *The Contexts of School-Based Literacy,* ed. T. Raphael (New York: Random House, 1986).
4. For a review of this research, see Anderson, Wilson, and Fielding (1988), and J.C. Moore, C. J. Jones, and D. C. Miller, "What We Know After a Decade of Sustained Silent Reading," *The Reading Teacher* 33 (1980):445–450.
5. C. Collins, "Sustained Silent Reading Periods: Effect on Teachers' Behaviors and Students' Achievement," *Elementary School Journal* 81 (1980): 108–114.

6. G.L. Manning, and M. Manning, "What Models of Recreational Reading Make a Difference?" *Reading World* 23 (1984): 375–380.
7. Lesley M. Morrow, *Literacy Development in the Early Years: Helping Children Reading and Write* (Englewood Cliffs: Prentice Hall, 1989).
8. Elley and Manghubai.
9. Ingham.
10. Victor Nell, *Lost in a Book: The Psychology of Reading for Pleasure* (New Haven: Yale University Press, 1988).
11. Nell, Victor, *Lost in a Book: The Psychology of Reading for Pleasure* (New Haven: Yale University Press, 1988).

12

Teaching as Story Telling
Kieran Egan

Kieran Egan is Professor of Education at Simon
Frasier University in Burnaby, British Columbia.
A longer treatment of the fascinating thesis put
forward in this chapter is available in his
Teaching as Storytelling, published by the
University of Chicago Press.[1]

Introduction

This chapter is not, as the title may lead you to believe, about using
fictional stories in teaching, nor about how to tell stories more effectively. Rather, it is about how to use the power of the story form in
order to teach anything more engagingly and meaningfully. What I
want to try to do is take some of the features of stories and see whether
it is possible to abstract them from their roles in fiction and apply them
to regular curriculum content in language arts, social studies, science,
and mathematics. My aim is to build a planning framework that
teachers might use in order better to engage students' imaginations
and emotions in learning.

We might note that the story form is not just something of casually
entertaining value. Stories are one of the few cultural universals—
they are found performing various roles in all cultures we know about.
Why are they so pervasive, and what implication might the reasons
have for education?

In all oral cultures we find stories performing literally vital roles.
Oral societies encode their most important lore into myth stories that
are then passed on, often in sacred rituals, generation by generation.
Why not simply pass the lore on in more straightforward and explicit
ways? In oral cultures one knows only what one can remember, and
so the techniques that can aid memory and preserve meaning, and

171

preserve a sense of the importance of that meaning, are highly prized. It is these techniques that carry the lore that contains the identity of the social group and the rules that sustain its coherence, and the customs that determine for each member his or her own sense of identity. It was discovered early that patterning sound—rhyme, rhythm, meter—made the messages it contained more easily memorable. Such techniques then become of considerable social importance. Vivid images, too, were found to be great aids to memory, and so began that close association between memory and imagination that has been disturbed only in this century with the hostility to "rote-learning." That the human mind is not well used if treated like a computer or other factual storage device seems to have blinded many to the absolutely vital role of memorization for the stimulation of the imagination.[2]

Perhaps the most important technical discovery of oral societies throughout the world—made so long ago that we cannot guess its origin—was that if the lore could be encoded into a story form its memorability was enhanced enormously. Recent research is confirming in a trivial way what has been known for millenia: that the story is the greatest tool we have for ensuring meaningful memorization of its contents. The story does something even more wonderful for oral cultures. Not only can it aid secure memorization, but it can also orient the emotions of those who hear it toward its contents. That is, not only can it convey the lore of the tribe to young and new members, but it also can ensure their emotional commitment to it.

My aim in drawing on the story form to aid planning teaching, then, is to see whether or not we cannot draw particularly on those techniques that encourage meaningful memorization, imaginative stimulation, and affective engagement. If we can begin to see teaching a little more as telling the great and wonderful (true) stories of our culture to the young (and a little less as attaining sets of objectives), we might also encourage teachers to see themselves as a part of the long and enchanting tradition of storytellers, rather than technicians on an assembly-line turning out schooled "products."

I will begin by sketching a framework that embodies some features derived from stories. Obviously, this is just one attempt, and many different frameworks might be constructed with a bit of ingenuity. Rather than try to describe it in the abstract, I will work through how it might be used in planning a teaching unit. This will be a social studies unit on North American Indians, chosen only because the subject matter will be familiar and accessible to everyone.

The Story-form Framework

A set of questions that can guide our preparation of a unit or lesson follows:

1. Identifying importance:
   What is important about this topic? Why should it matter to children? What is affectively engaging about it?
2. Finding binary opposites:
   What powerful binary opposites best catch the importance of the topic?
3. Organizing content in story form:
   3.1 What content most dramatically embodies the binary opposites, in order to provide access to the topic?
   3.2 What content best articulates the topic into a developing story form?
4. Conclusion:
   What is the best way of resolving the dramatic conflict inherent in the binary opposites? What degree of mediation of those opposites is it appropriate to seek?
5. Evaluation:
   How can one know whether the topic has been understood, its importance grasped, and the content learned?

Two of the elements of this framework might benefit from separate discussion before we consider the examples. Explaining the modern uses of the story form might be helpful, and the reason for so prominently including "binary opposites" should be justified.

Story Form and Binary Opposites

The story is one of the basic forms in which we organize events and facts to make them meaningful. The story form is something we impose on events to assert a beginning, from which the meaning starts; through a middle, which complicates it; and to an end, which satisfies us by establishing clearly the meaning of all the events that make up the story. Stories have this crucial feature, which life and history lack, that they have beginnings and ends and so can fix the meaning of events. The difficulties of our lives, or one set of difficulties, is that not knowing the end we cannot be sure of the meaning of the events that make up our lives. "Call no man happy until he is dead," the Greeks used to say. We are, as Frank Kermode stresses, "in the middest," and only by making stories, even if only provisional ones, can we get some hold on the meanings of our lives. The story form, then, is not a trivial thing meriting attention only if we are discussing fiction. It is a reflection of some fundamental mental structure. It is a basic intellectual tool we use in making sense of the world and experience.

The second preliminary point to note is that primary age children are normally readily engaged by stories with particular features. Most prominent among these features is that of binary opposites: good/bad, brave/cowardly, big/little, alive/dead, love/hate, fear/security, and so forth. An analysis of almost any classic story will reveal such binary opposites as central structural features.

When Bettelheim discusses the prominence of binary opposites in fairy tales he makes what seems an obvious point: "Before a child can come to grips with reality, he must have some frame of reference to evaluate it.[3] Analysis of children's stories and fantasy play shows that prominent among the means by which children develop a frame of reference—indeed, perhaps the commonest access to generating such a frame of reference—is the establishment of binary opposites, between which meaning can be established.

If we consider how children learn and conceptually elaborate something fairly straightforward like, say, the temperature continuum, we see that they often begin by learning "hot" and "cold." This does not mean that they cannot feel an infinite continuum of temperatures; it is simply that the polar opposite concepts are learned first. Thereafter, children learn "warm," a mediating concept between the poles. They then learn concepts that mediate between, say, "hot" and "warm"—"pretty hot"; and "warm" and "cold"—"cool." The meaning of these terms is relative to the child's body temperature: for example, this feels hotter, or much hotter, than my body; this feels colder than my body. Later still children learn the temperature continuum as a set of arbitrary numbers. This does not displace the concepts of "hot" and "cold" and the rest; rather, it embeds them in a context removed from the personal referent of body temperature and indicates that when "hot" and "cold" are used their meaning has to be seen as relative to something. Similarly, the initial "good" and "bad" polar opposites are good or bad relative to the child's feelings— the daddy who insists that they stop playing Smurfs and wash their hands for lunch is "bad daddy," meriting a smack on the way past if they think they might get away with it. The poles become conceptually mediated by the acceptance of characters and events that are neither bad nor good but in between. Again, the concepts "good" and "bad" do not disappear as this moral continuum becomes increasingly elaborate, but they become embedded in moral schemes more or less removed from personal pleasure and pain. Some people[4] and a number of other structuralists as well as neo-Hegelians of various stripes argue that this binary opposites/mediation process reflects a fundamental predisposition of the mind in making sense of the world. We need hardly go so far to recognize it as a common process, and one that is rather effective at establishing and elaborating the meaning of all kinds of phenomena. It is hardly a mysterious process, as we all use it continually. If we hear of a evolution in some distant state we orient our response to the news by initially fitting it to binary categories. These will usually be derivatives of that most powerful pair good/bad. Were the revolutionaries C.I.A.-backed or did they get their weapons via Cuba? After this initial orientation we might be ready to mediate between our binary opposites, recognizing perhaps that the good/bad Marxist government was corrupt/noble but broke. And so on.

If our concern is meaning, then, we would be wise to consider in more detail those intellectual constructs to which children seem to have most direct access and to reflect on some of their prominent features.

Let me then move toward an example of a unit planned following the model outlined earlier and see whether it leads us to give more prominence to educationally more important matters than the currently dominant procedure.

The Planning Model Put to Use

I am recommending that teachers approach a unit on North American Indians as a story that is to be told rather than as a set of objectives to be attained. We need to remember that stories can be true as well as fictional and that shaping events into a story form may involve simplifying events but need not involve falsifying them. We also need to remember that in a well-wrought story there is room for detailed knowledge, inference, and discovery processes together.

The first task, then, is to decide on the most important and profound meaning that is to be conveyed. First we identify importance. We will not be concerned with a story in the sense of following a fictional "Little Talker" or "White Cloud" through a cycle of the annual activities of a tribe—though if written using the principles sketched here thesé could form a part of our unit. Rather we are looking for the story in the sense that a newspaper editor asks, "What's the story on this?" What is it that is important about it, and—for our next step of finding binary opposites—how is that importance brought out in the clearest and most dramatic way? Any complex content will involve many stories so we must make choices about which to tell.

These first two procedural steps will usually be taken close together. The first directs us to think at the outset about what is truly important about this content. The related second step of finding binary opposites directs us to try to see the content through the prominent conceptual forms whereby the child can have the most meaningful access to it.

In the case of our unit on North American Indians, we must ask first, What is important about this topic for young children? What are we teaching to them? Why should it matter to them? How do we deal with Indians of North America in a manner that engages children affectively? We decide that what is important is learning something about what a culture is and why there are different cultures. We cannot deal with all aspects of this nor provide the complexity of answers social anthropologists seek to express. We must focus on a part, but it must be a central and important part of the answer. Our choice will need to be expressed in the binary opposites we find in order to articulate our story. Let us, then, take as binary opposites ''survival/ destruction'' and tell our story on those. What we are choosing thereby to teach children about cultures, and about a North American Indian culture in particular, is that they are, as it were, machines designed to maximize chances for survival against the various threats of destruction that face them. This is not, of course, all that is to be said about cultures, but it is important and will allow us to say much else as well. Also our choice of binary opposites provides us with a principle for the selection of relevant content. (In cases where the range of content is undetermined, any standard technique, such as concept mapping or webbing, can be used.)

Now we need to set about organizing the content in a story form. There are two parts to this. First is the choice of a particularly vivid example of our binary opposites in order to provide direct access to the heart of what we intend to teach. We must look at the range of content that falls within our topic and consider what can be used to show the culture of a particular North American Indian tribe most dramatically as a struggle for survival against destruction. We should choose an aspect of the life of the tribe that will vividly exemplify the struggle. We could begin with a dramatic account of Plains Indians hunting: They took a food supply that could last for three days and it is the third day; the hunters grow weak, the village waits for fresh meat—what will happen? Or we might dramatize the problems of Cree Indians facing a brutal and late winter, waiting to move south. Our beginning, that is, will be designed to engage children's affective response in a struggle between survival and destruction that they understand profoundly at the level of our basic animal existence.

The second stage of building the story is the longer activity of building the content onto the binary opposites that provide our story line. The abstract story line, stretching between our binary opposites, allows us a precise principle for determining exactly what aspects and details should be included and what excluded. The key to telling a good story, as Aristotle tells us in *The Poetics*, is that the incidents should be carefully chosen to carry forth the plot in a causal sequence.

Having chosen the basic structure of our story as the binary opposites survival/destruction, we must tie the rest of the content to the structural line that they offer. Thus, when we examine ''shelter,'' we will be concerned to see the particular shelters of our chosen tribes as parts of the struggle to survive against the particular threats of destruction that the tribe faces. This will constantly focus our attention on the limits of the protection offered. In the case of shelter, we will focus on each feature that protects against particular threats, and so we will see the form of their shelters as a part of a system in part determined by natural threats. We will thus consider, for example, against how many weeks of what winter temperatures such shelters would protect their inhabitants. The teacher might look up weather reports for the area and see if or how often during the period for which we have records lower temperatures prevailed for longer periods. Similarly when discussing food, our focus will not simply be on what was available at what time of year. The typical account of North American Indian life in textbooks at present suggests a harmonious and rhythmic swing through a mostly leisurely year. Our focus will be on what food supplies were available in the context of what is needed for health and survival. The relatively brief normal life span of North American Indians needs to be tied in to what was usually an insufficiently varied and inadequate diet. We will again focus on the limits of the food supply to provide for survival. What happened when a particular crop was late or diseased or killed by late or early frosts? How often did such weather conditions prevail?

That is, we choose the content that can be fitted to our binary opposites and that the binary opposites in turn weld into a coherent order. Each element is tied to this basic structural feature, and there are no ''episodic'' elements that do not further that particular story line. We do not decide to include a section on, say, the particular designs they weave into mats or baskets just because that is a part of their culture. If we want to include such a topic we have to tie it into our story line. Perhaps the designs have religious significance and represent charms to enhance the contributions the baskets or mats make to the survival of the tribe. Perhaps we will focus on the survival function of the baskets and show the designs incidentally to that. If we cannot find a plausible and clear relationship between a topic and our organizing binary opposites, we should leave it out. Otherwise it will slacken interest and dissipate the lesson we are teaching. If we cannot attach it to our story-line structure but nevertheless think it is important that children should learn it, we should use different binary opposites to organize our unit: binary opposites that would enable us to include such other topics.

We cannot teach everything about any tribe of Indians in North America. Our choice of binary opposites involves a choice of what to include and what to exclude. It is a choice that provides a clear principle for making decisions about inclusion and exclusion. The trouble with using the traditional model is that it provides no such principle. Any things that seem relevant may be included, and there are no strong and clear structural relationships built into the array of content to ensure that it is being made meaningful to children. When each element is tied to the same powerful structure and that structure is made from binary opposites that are affectively engaging, we have an organizing tool that can add clarity and ease of access to the content.

By using the survival/destruction binary opposites, children will learn that Indian cultures consisted of a sense of systematic, inter-related activities, all of which were closely tied to survival techniques in particular environments, and also that, for most tribes most of the time, survival was won often tenuously and at the cost of brutal and unremitting hardship. This particular, important lesson is brought to the fore by the choice of the survival/destruction organizers. I am not arguing here that this is the most important or the only way of organizing a unit on North American Indians. It is one useful way, however, because it allows us to deal with a great amount of the content of their lives and focuses attention on something very important to learn about a culture. Cultures are not sets of arbitrary differences in human behavior; they are in large part responses, and elaborations of those responses, to particular threats from nature and other peoples. If other lessons about Indian life are considered by any teacher as more important, they may be focused on by the choice of different binary opposites. One could use the survival/destruction organizers for one unit and choose, say, cooperation/competition or adventurous/conservative or other binary opposites to exemplify other aspects of a tribe's life or to compare different tribes.

Good stories do not just stop; rather, they reach some kind of resolution of the conflict that started them off. Similarly our unit should not simply peter out but must find some way of either resolving or moving toward mediation of the binary opposites that have provided the story line so far. In true Hegelian fashion we might use our mediated conclusion as one pole of a binary pair on which we can begin our next unit.

There are a number of alternative ways of concluding the kind of unit I have sketched here. One way might be to consider what happened to the Indian tribe(s), whose way of life we have been studying, with the coming of the White Man. In so many cases this is unrelievedly tragic. Such historical facts, however, fit precisely and meaningfully into the unit as structured so far. The conclusion, then, is an examination of ways in which the survival techniques of particular Indian cultures were unprepared for, and inadequate to, the threats presented by a rapacious, land-hungry, expansive culture with a developing technology. The cultural defenses broke down in the face of displacement for cultures tied closely to particular environments, of diseases against which there was no immunity, and of the U.S. cavalry.

In some cases, the conclusion is not so tragic. We may reach mediation in some tribes' persistent attempts to survive and maintain their culture in alien environments. The particular conclusion in the above cases would depend on the history of the particular tribe. An alternative is to reach a mediation by developing the concept of *equilibrium*—whether one uses that term or not—between culture and environment. It would be an image of the culture accommodating, with more or less success, to a somewhat unstable environment. The greater the flexibility of the culture, the more able it is to deal with greater environmental threats and instability.

How does one evaluate a unit such as this? Does our principle provide us also with new forms of evaluation? I do not think it does. One might, however, pause to consider how one might evaluate whether "The Return of the Jedi" had been properly learned, understood, or appreciated. One could ask factual questions, record how well narrative themes were understood, seek clues about how much it was enjoyed. Much of that would be idle because we know that a typical child will successfully follow a well-crafted story.

What is entailed in following a story is the use of a variety of intellectual skills, having a sense of causality, understanding relationships and what underlying concepts were embodied in particular characters, and so on. If the meaning is clear and the content is articulated on binary opposites to expose and elaborate that meaning constantly, we feel fairly confident that children are "getting the message." We really do not worry if a detail of "E.T." is missed because the whole story carries the more profound message forward consistently. This is to suggest that in a well-crafted unit structured on clear binary opposites we might well be less concerned with elaborate evaluation procedures. We may seek in the process of the unit evidence that children are following the unit; that they see aspects of the Indian culture as parts of a machine against destruction.

Apart from that, evaluation may go forward however teachers or administrators wish it to go forward. The only caveat is that the procedures for evaluation should not assume such importance that they affect the organization of the unit or its teaching. If the evaluation procedures, for example, are inadequate to provide precise measures of whether children have followed the story, we do not simplify or dilute or degrade our teaching to the primitive level of available evaluation procedures. If we do this, there is no incentive to make evaluation procedures more sophisticated.[5]

Conclusion

I have focused in this chapter on the organization of units. The organization of each lesson within a unit could employ the same principles. It could begin with a vivid example of the binary opposites, elaborate them with content selected to best fit them, and conclude with some resolution or mediation of them. This principle is evident in typical soap operas, where each episode reflects in small scale the story structure of the entire series. The challenge for each episode of the soap opera is to keep the viewer engaged and to carry forward the general story. Similarly, the teacher has to use each lesson as an integral part of the unit. To take a lesson to introduce content that cannot be fitted to the theme selected by one's choice of binary opposites is akin to introducing an episode in the soap opera that is peripheral to the overall story. Interest is lessened because the meaning is being gradually dissipated.

I should perhaps conclude by noting that what I am recommending here is a systematization of principles that I observe in good teachers' teaching. They instinctively shape material into a story form as they teach. I am proposing here a framework that should allow us routinely to organize curriculum material for maximum meaningfulness; one that will perhaps assist those instinctively good teachers more consciously and clearly to see how they might further add to the communicative power of their teaching. It is a framework that might be of more value to those intending to be teachers, to allow them routinely to use principles that should enhance the success of their lessons and units.

Initially, organizing units and lessons by these principles might seem quite hard. It is easier to list objectives and line up the content according to some logical principle. These principles require a careful reflection on the whole unit and, as it were, a shaking of it to and fro until it exposes its most basic organizing structure. Of course no one will be able to sustain tight organization all the time, and much school work will remain tedious, but use of these principles should ensure that we will be able to show children more frequently why the tedium and work is worthwhile, that meaning is there, is real, and is accessible to them.

End Notes

1. Kieran Egan, *Teaching as Story Telling* (Chicago: University of Chicago Press, 1989).
2. Kieran Egan, *Educational Development* (New York: Oxford University Press, 1979); and Kieran Egan, Primary Understanding: Education in Early Childhood (New York: Routledge, 1988).
3. Bruno Bettelheim, *The Uses of Enchantment* (New York: Knopf, 1976), 117.
4. For example see Claude Levi-Strauss, *The Raw and the Cooked* (New York: Harper and Row, 1968).
5. Further examples of the use of this framework are available in Egan, 1988, 1989.

PART III

The Influence of Children's Development on Their Reading, and Vice Versa

Introduction: Their Reading, and Vice Versa

Young readers prefer the comics; adults read the editorial page. Hearing a story, children are naturally drawn to actions, while adults and even adolescents are more likely to look for general truths and themes. Arthur Applebee's studies have shown that.[1] Surely we must take children's level of maturity or development into account when we share and discuss literature.

As far as the philosopher Gareth Matthews is concerned, however, children are the most likely of all of us to ask the most philosophically interesting questions and to pose the most original answers to them.[2] While their thinking might be inspired by concrete events, they wonder about the origins of things, the rightness and wrongness of events, the what-ifs and how-comes of situations. The late psychiatrist Bruno Bettelheim was sure that young children derived lessons for their own lives from hearing fairy tales.[3] According to Bettelheim, their interest might be attracted initially by the actions in stories, but they end up profoundly moved by the implications of those actions.

While there are observable differences in children's responses to stories at different ages, we are still a long way from understanding what those differences mean. We don't always know what is going on inside the child at the moment when he or she hears a story, much less during the the days, weeks, and years afterward as he or she mulls the story over.

In her chapter in this section, Janet Hickman shows us at least what is observable in children's responses at different ages. She read the same story to three age groups of children and faithfully recorded the result. A children's author herself, as well as a prolific reader and critic of children's books, Professor Hickman has written some of the most

183

interesting classroom-based accounts of children's responses to stories. Her chapter in this volume is a good sample of her knowledge of children and books and her careful scholarship.

Then we turn the question around, and ask not how development influences children's reading, but how reading influences children's development. Consider this: the three most avid readers in an average second grade class read forty-six times as much as the three most avoidant readers. By the end of sixth grade, the three most avid readers will have read a lot of books; so many, in fact, that the reluctant readers, at their slow pace, would take 230 years to read as many! The reluctant readers would need sixty years to read as many as the average readers.

We learn from experience. These enormous differences in the quantity of children's literary experience suggest that a child's age—and, presumably, his grade level—tells us little about what he's read, what's familiar to him in literature, and, hence, what he's likely to get out of a book that he reads. These differences also suggest that we should do everything in our power to boost the amount of reading children do, especially the reluctant ones.

In his chapter in this section, Keith Stanovich shows us, first of all, what the range of actual reading is among school children. Then he proceeds to tell us what these differences mean, in terms of learning from reading. Professor Stanovich's piece gives strong support to literature-based reading programs. In fact, he makes the case more urgently than ever that our first priority should not be to teach skills, but to invite children to become avid readers.

End Notes

1. Arthur Applebee, *The Child's Concept of Story* (Chicago: The University of Chicago Press, 1975).
2. Gareth Matthews, *Philosophy and the Young Child* (Cambridge: Harvard University Press, 1980).
3. Bruno Bettelheim, *The Uses of Enchantment* (New York: Random House, 1977).

13

What Comes Naturally: Growth and Change in Children's Free Response to Literature

Janet Hickman

Janet Hickman teaches children's literature at Ohio State University. She has published books for children, has coauthored a successful text on the use of children's literature, and for many years has written a column reviewing children's books for *Language Arts*. Her ethnographic studies of children's responses to literature have been valuable additions to our understanding of how literature affects children. Here she samples the responses of three different age groups of children to the same book.

Children show us what they think and feel and know of literature in many ways if we give them reasonable freedom to respond. When Matthew, not quite five, got a new picture book, Rodney Peppe's *The Mice and the Clockwork Bus,* he stretched out on his stomach in the middle of the kitchen floor and hummed as he turned the pages. Not yet a reader of print, he stopped to study each illustration. Halfway through he came upon a picture of tiny mice climbing along a tiny spiral staircase, and his own fingers crept onto the page. "Climb, climb, climb," he sang softly, walking two fingers up and around the painted rungs. "Climb, climb, climb. . . . ."

In contrast consider Billy, nine-and-a-half, who also came upon a book about mice and machines, Beverly Cleary's *The Mouse and the Motorcycle.* At school, it was his choice for silent reading time, and when he was finished, it was again his choice for independent work. He told his teacher that he had decided to write a separate page about what happens in each chapter and to draw a picture for each chapter and put all these pages together into a book of his own. He said he thought it would take a long time.

These two examples could serve as evidence for a number of basic understandings about children's dealings with literature. One is that each child—reader, browser, listener—has personal, unique responses. A second is that the contexts of various situations—home or school, who's there, what's expected, what's allowed—help to shape the kinds of responses that are expressed. It is a third idea, however, that I want to explore here, the idea that as children grow older we can see changes in the free responses they make to literature.

Preschooler Matthew read pictures instead of text, seemingly undaunted by not knowing the author's version of the story. It is apparent that he used the book in his own way, making its illustrations a vehicle for imaginative play as he "walked" up the mouse-sized stairs. He seemed happy and thoroughly engaged in what he was doing. In this glimpsed interaction between young child and book, we see more of the child than of the book.

With Billy, who was able to read quite a long story for himself, we see a much more deliberate response, one that focused his attention, and will ours, on the book's content. He opted to represent what he had read through the use of recently acquired abilities in writing and in drawing pictures that look "real." While Matthew literally played with his book, using language (including body language) for his own purpose, Billy's involvement was less visible in process. In a different sense he may have also "played around" with the story, considering its elements as he constructed and illustrated his summaries. Even so, he was using language in a conventional way.

These two incidents are not necessarily representative of particular age levels, but they serve to illustrate the general direction of changes that teachers might observe as children go from early kindergarten to the end of elementary school. Those changes involve a shift in the most common modes of expressing response as well as some difference in approach to the challenge of making meaning.

Comparing Free Responses

In order to understand what we can reasonably expect of children when we ask them to respond, it seems sensible to look at what they are likely to do without prompting. In his paper for the Dartmouth Seminar, Harding[1] pointed out that young children make spontaneous responses such as using story characters in dramatic play, correcting an adult who misses a word in a familiar story, or moving to the rhythm and sound of words.

My own overview study of elementary children's response in a school setting[2] also showed how likely young children were to use their bodies to respond. While children from kindergarten to fifth grade occasionally applauded for a read-aloud story or chimed in on refrains, children in the kindergarten–first grade class almost always did so. These youngest students also frequently "echoed" the action of a story they were hearing, making motions to represent what a character was said to be doing. In their play corner, certain prototypical characters such as the wolf from "Little Red Riding Hood" and "The Three Little Pigs" made frequent appearances when those stories were current in the classroom.

Some response modes occurred across grade levels but revealed different perspectives or centers of attention. All the children shared discoveries about books, favorite bits, or items worth remarking with classmates, teachers, and sometimes visitors by reading together, pointing, or urging the other's attention to specific pictures or print. They commented freely about what was read to them or what they read themselves. In this mode, however, students in the second-third grade class spent more time sharing than did other children, and their comments frequently revealed a preoccupation with conventions of print, how books work ("Let's use the index!") and their own accomplishments as independent readers ("I read three chapters.").

Fourth and fifth graders were notable for the range of choices for response at their command. They were more practiced writers, more accomplished in oral presentation, and more skillful with paints and other media. They made more deliberate choices and were more aware of their own choosing than younger children. Finding out what sense a fifth grader was making of a story sometimes meant waiting to see a product. In contrast, the animated responses of kindergartners more often provided immediate clues to what they were thinking. As children grow older and their responses more informed, their free expression of it seems to become less free—less spontaneous, less physical, less on-the-spot visible.

In schools and classrooms where formal structure allows little variation in free response, teachers will not find changes with age in preferred modes of expression to be very noticeable. However, differences will still be observable in the mode that is common to all classrooms, regardless of structure, and that mode is talk.

If children are given a chance to make their own comments about stories before their attention is directed one way or another by focused questions, they will reveal perceptions and preoccupations that they bring on their own to literature. Certainly all readers share some common concerns in the process of making meaning from stories. Certainly, also, there are many differences attributable to culture, social context, and individuality. These are influences on children's response that have received little research attention, unfortunately. However, the relationship between children's age and what they are able to retell of or say about stories has been the subject of formal investigation by Applebee,[3] Rubin and Gardner,[4] Lehr,[5] and others.

Listening to Children's Talk

Anyone who wishes to explore in an informal way the relationship between children's age and free response through talk might simply take one book to an elementary school, read it aloud to children at different grade levels, invite them to say whatever is on their minds, and listen carefully. I followed this procedure when I read Pam Conrad and Richard Egielski's *The Tub People* to separate small groups of kindergarten, third grade, and fifth grade students at Wickliffe School in Upper Arlington, Ohio. As we read, the children were free to ask questions, examine illustrations, or make comments. At the end I offered an open invitation to talk and plenty of encouragement to keep going.

Conrad's story tells, in a carefully measured, serious tone, of seven wooden toy figures who stand in a line on the edge of a bathtub and play in the water at bath time. On the evening the Tub Child disappears "down the drain without a sound," his little wooden father cannot save him and his Tub Mother presses her face to the grating beyond which he has vanished. Finally someone comes to jiggle a wire in the drain, but when the Tub Child does pop out he is shut into a toolbox and taken away. Later all the Tub People are lifted up and placed "on a large, soft bed" where the Tub Child is waiting for them. When the quilt is bunched up, they play at mountain climbing; each night they stand in line along the window sill. Now however, each morning the Tub Child's position is different from the night before. When the sun comes up he is standing between his mother and his father. "And if you looked very, very closely, you would see they all had smiles on their small wooden faces."

As an adult reader, my own response to this book identifies it as a story of separation and reunion, made especially poignant by the helplessness of the wooden toys. Although neither the author nor the illustrator indicates who is responsible for their movement, I felt the presence of a human child putting them into action and giving them voices. All of that led me to think about the larger theme of free will: Who or what controls our lives? Sometimes, I thought, we seem to be as powerless in our own situations as the Tub People in theirs. I was also reminded as I read of the toys in Russell Hoban's *The Mouse and His Child,* who longed to be self-winding. And, as a parent, something kept me turning back to the powerfully simple illustration that lets the viewer look up through the grating on the tub drain to see the lost Tub Child's mother with her face pressed close.

What thoughts did kindergartners have about this story? One child took a moment to study the picture that had moved me so and demanded, with some exasperation, "Why don't they just go after him?" In general, this group of children took in the story page by page, making comments as the story progressed rather than volunteering general comments when it was finished except to say that it was "good." They chimed in as I read the frequent repeats of the order in which the Tub People stood: "the father, the mother, the grandmother, the doctor, the policeman, the child, and the dog." They counted the figures in the picture, making sure all seven were there. They scooted close on the carpeted floor and touched the pages. When the text described what each of the figures "like to play" in the tub, one child asked, "What does the dog like to do?" When the text reveals that the saddened Tub People "never winked at each other any more," one child's voice echoed that thought as we all looked at the picture: "They didn't wink." All these spontaneous responses seemed to function as checks and clarifications of content, affirmations of what actually was in the story (words and pictures) as it presented itself to children.

The small group of third graders who heard the same story were more intent as listeners, made fewer page by page comments, but had a wider range of things to say at the end. Some of these children were inclined to come close to study the book and touch it, but much of what they said as a result expressed admiration of the illustrator's work. They liked the toy figures and the swirls in the tub water, which "really look real." Examining the picture of the mother peering through the drain, some decided that her expression had changed slightly. One boy said he thought the Tub People's expressions "fit the mood." Then he flipped through the pages to the final picture in the book and pointed out that the Tub People had become "more close," which is literally as well as figuratively true, and were "lots more merrier now."

One third grader noted that the title "sounds like a silly story, but it isn't." Another suggested that it could be retold lots of different ways, and a whole chorus of voices joined in: "It could be on the ocean." "The Tub People find the Lost Treasure." "There could be a cat and a mermaid tub person." "We could do a series!"

In some ways, certainly, this group of children responded like the kindergarten students. They were interested, a condition that showed in their eyes, their faces, and their body postures as well as their comments. Like the younger children, they said the book was "good." However, their relationship to the story seemed to be on a different footing. While the kindergartners showed their efforts to "take in" this story, the older group stepped back to consider its merits. What seems even more interesting is the way they responded as producers of stories, both in their critique of the illustrator's talents and their suggestions of possible story variants and sequels.

Six fifth grade students listened with almost no comment to *The Tub People*, but when invited to talk afterward, they became quickly involved. They also made immediate references to the illustrations and to specific pictures. One child mentioned point of view in the picture that looks up through the tub drain into the mother's face. "I would never have thought of doing it like that," she explained. Another girl mentioned the cutaway view of the Tub Child lodged in the drain pipe. "It makes you wonder how he felt in there," she said.

"The policeman and the doctor don't have much character," one boy observed. "They're just there. And why was the dog there?" Another student suggested the dog was "like a symbol for the boy." "It's a simple story," said a boy who had already identified the illustrator as a former Caldecott Medal winner; "there's only one problem in it—not like *Hey, Al!*" [the award-winning book]. "I'm going to write a sequel," still another student said, "and the Tub People get sold at a garage sale."

Like the third graders, and to an even greater degree, these fifth graders stepped back from the book and considered how it was made. They were more inclined than younger children to speak as critics, questioning the function of specific characters; and as readers aware of their own relation to the story ("It makes you wonder how he felt. . .") and of the roles of author and illustrator ("I would never have thought of doing it like that").

Because no child in any group commented on the issue of power and control that had claimed so much of my own response attention, I did ask one focused question as each conversation came to an end: How do you suppose the Tub People moved around?

These are the kindergartners' answers:

> "They jump into the water and it makes them float."
> "The water is so heavy it pushes 'em."
> "The quilt moves because it's a water bed."
> "They have turners in their backs and people turn the other ones' turners."

It is important to note that these are intelligent and imaginative answers even though they deal only with the surface level of the question. The children seem to be struggling to make sense of the information they are given in light of what they know, fitting the world of the story into their own scheme of things.

When I asked the third grade children how the Tub People moved, the first answer was, "There are people in the bathtub playing with them." But other children in the group had different ideas. They suggested that the Tub People might slide down the side of the tub on soap or they might just fall down and roll to get from place to place. One noted the shape of the toy figure and said they would have to move slowly, like robots. The group did not return spontaneously to the first child's idea of a real person moving the toys, and he then seemed more interested in elaborating his classmates' suggestions than his own.

When I posed the movement question to fifth graders, there was immediate consensus that a real child was playing with the toys. Fifth graders also agreed that this child was a little boy, although the only reason they could supply was from one student who said his little brother play with small figures "like that," moving them around and giving them voices. Another student suggested that the unseen boy in the book had moved the Tub People to his bedroom because he had grown up and didn't need toys in the bath tub any more. Another disagreed, saying that it was to keep the Tub People safe. Interspersed with these comments were others that showed the children's fascination with the mechanical possibilities of toys moving. They pointed out that there were no ankle or knee joints shown in the pictures. "Their feet are connected!" one boy said, and he stood to demonstrate how difficult it would be to move under those conditions, thereby furnishing incidental evidence that older children as well as younger ones use their bodies to respond. In spite of general acceptance of the child-in-tub theory, some children wondered if the toys were somehow moving on their own "a little bit" in the story, especially at the end where their positions changed overnight on the window sill. On the whole, the fifth graders still showed interest in the literal aspects of this question, and, like the other children, it seems they were working to make the best sense possible of the story. On the other hand, they made inferences that younger children ignored and called up more evidence in their exercise of logic to solve the puzzles of the text.

It's probably fair to say that children's varying responses to this one book point to differences of degree within common domains. All of us—and I include myself among those who responded—constructed meaning in consideration of the whole as more than the sum of its parts. The youngest responders, however, paid less explicit attention to the whole and more to its parts as represented by individual illustrations or events and phrases within the story. Likewise, we all assumed a formative stance as critics or potential makers of story, ranging from affirmations of story content and implied reference to omission in the kindergartner's question about what the dog liked to do, through older children's comments about characterization and illustrator skill, to my own thoughts about the separation/reunion theme. Another of the common concerns that we shared was finding our own words with which to talk about story and illustrations. In some cases the younger children just didn't; instead they pointed and touched the pictures or borrowed the author's words to repeat a phrase in recognition, approval, or wonder. Not surprisingly, the number of conventional terms noted in students' responses rose with the age of the group.

Accounting for Differences

It would seem impossible to sort out all the influences that shaped these children's responses to *The Tub People*. It is probably safe to say, however, that the fifth graders in this group did not get to be more polished than kindergartners in their responses just by getting older. True, children go through physical changes and accumulate more experience of the world as they grow, all of which influences cognition, logic, world view, and the other lenses through which we see literature. But most people considering these children's responses will sense the presence of teachers along the way, feeling that children's experiences with stories and with language probably have the most to do with the changes in response that are visible here.

The students who talked with me about *The Tub People* have been particularly privileged in their experiences with literature. As a beginning, their parents are mostly professional people who value education, reading, and the importance of language. Their school expects children at all grade levels to read trade books rather than textbooks. Teachers read aloud regularly, discuss books with children, and share the attitude that children's ideas should be accepted and built upon rather than "corrected." And everyone writes. This rich environment nurtures the level of perception and degree of spontaneity I found in the children who shared their thoughts about *The Tub People*.

Obviously it is futile to try to assemble a response profile that would fit all preschoolers or eleven-year-olds or second graders everywhere, yet we do achieve a small measure of predictability by observing over time and in different locations. Even more important, we find that the direction of change is fairly consistent—from more to less motor involvement, from more to less focus on parts as a first level response, from unconscious delight to more self-aware and deliberate responses, to name a few of the patterns.

In sum, it's useful to know what modes of response come most naturally to kindergartners or what kinds of comments are likely to take the foreground in older children's discussions. The responses children offer without being asked are the foundation for the understandings and insights we hope to help them develop. We need to know how children think about books on their own so that as we plan more formal activities we will not expect too much, or too little. We also need to understand how children change so that we can work to preserve the spark that underlies the crucial early responses, such as Matthew's. When he finished "reading" *The Mice and the Clockwork Bus,* he snapped it shut and smiled. "Where's another one?" he asked.

End Notes

1. D.W. Harding, "Response to Literature: The Report of the Study Group," *Response to literature ed. James Squire* (Champaign, IL: National Council of Teachers of English, 1968).
2. Hickman, 1979.
3. Arthur Applebee, "Children's construal of stories and related genres as measured with repertory grid techniques," *Research in the Teaching of English*, 10 (1976) 236–238; Arthur Applebee, *The Child's Concept of Story: Ages Two to Seventeen* (Chicago: The University of Chicago Press, 1978).
4. S. Rubin, and H. Gardner, "Once Upon a Time: The development of Sensitivity to Story Structure," *Researching Response to Literature and the Teaching of Literature* (Norwood, NJ: Ablex, 1985).
5. S. Lehr, "The Child's Developing Sense of Theme as a Response to Literature, *Reading Research Quarterly*, 23 (1988) 337–357.

Children's Books Cited

Beverly Cleary, *The Mouse and the Motorcycle*. New York: William Morrow, 1965.

Pam Conrad, *The Tub People*. Illustrated by Richard Egielski. New York: Harper & Row, 1989.

Russell Hoban, *The Mouse and His Child*. New York: Harper & Row, 1967.

Rodney Peppé, *The Mice and the Clockwork Bus*. New York: Lothrop, Lee & Shepard, 1987.

Arthur Yorinks, *Hey Al!* Illustrated by Richard Egielski. New York: Farrar, Straus & Giroux, 1987.

14

Individual Development in Literacy
Kieran Egan

Research on children's responses to literature has tended to focus on the effects of intellectual development on what children are able, or likely, to respond to in stories. In this section, Janet Hickman has helpfully shown how younger and older children respond to the same story.

Kieran Egan has a different approach: He has looked at the reasons children turn to stories at different ages—the kinds of meanings they seek; or, as he puts it, "the environments of meaning within which children make sense of things."

His work can guide us in choosing books to share with children. The ideas he outlines in this chapter have been developed in two book-length treatments, *Primary Understanding* and *Romantic Understanding*.

Introduction

It has been confidently asserted that speech is biologically determined whereas literacy is not.[1] Thus learning to speak is easy and, given no relevant biological subnormality, is achieved universally, whereas literacy is relatively difficult and is achieved with ease and fluency by a relatively small proportion of the population, the proportion varying with the criterion of literacy used. We might, however, question the confidence with which this assertion is made. Children are brought up in oral language environments. They receive constant vocal stimulation in contexts where continual efforts are made to associate the sounds with things, people, and events of significance to them. Similarly, the sounds they make are constantly shaped to fit the conventions of the language group into which they are being initiated.

If children were brought up in a silent world we would hardly expect some biological determining mechanism to produce articulate speech. If children were subjected to the same intensity of stimuli to read and write from birth to age five, we would reasonably expect universal and fluent literacy. So to argue that speech is biologically determined whereas literacy is not as an explanation of difficulties in stimulating and sustaining the development of literacy is surely misguided. One might say that biologically we have the capacity for speech, and speech may be evoked and developed by appropriate interactions with an oral language environment. Equally one might say that biologically we have the capacity for literacy, and literacy may be evoked and developed by appropriate interactions with an environment in which reading and writing matter.

The focus for this essay is on the kind of environments that evoke, stimulate, and sustain the development of literacy. I don't mean the social environments. That middle-class children from homes where there is much pleasure gained from reading and writing tend to learn and to read and write better than children from homes where none of this goes on is now a commonplace observation. Nor do I mean the kind of immediate ''environment'' created by certain reading curriculum packages. There is a danger, evident in such packages and in some of the writing and research on literacy, of treating the achievement and development of literacy as narrowly technical problems to whose solution technical tools are paramount. This is a danger not because techniques of teaching reading and writing are not important, but because such a focus tends to disguise the much more important matter of more general environments in which the things read or written about are made meaningful and accessible. Thinking in terms of decoding and encoding may make us feel in command of a more scientific approach to our problem, but it can do so at the expense of a sense of proportion. We say, for economy's sake, that our aim is to teach children to read and write. We might try to remember that ''read'' and ''write'' are transitive verbs and that our aim is to teach children to read something or to write something. The difference between the intransitive and transitive sense leads to a subtle but potentially important matter of focus. By focusing on teaching to read and write, to decode and encode, we tend towards contentless techniques. By focusing on what we want to teach children to read or write, our focus tends toward what makes the achievement worthwhile, toward the appropriate environments for stimulating reading and writing.

A related observation is that in certain circumstances children tend to find some things more accessible, engaging, meaningful, and they

can more readily learn and remember such things in such circumstances. R.C. Anderson shows how what he calls 'schemata' determine what is seen as meaningful, what is learned most easily and
remembered longest, and so on.[2] If we can design reading and writing
materials to fit children's dominant schemata, it would seem to follow
we will be better able to aid their learning to read and write and to
improve their continued development of literacy.

Attempts to characterize such schemata or structures are of considerable interest to educators. One of the more obvious things about
children is that when they are engaged by something their learning
power is prodigious. We want some general theory about what turns
on that power.

Clearly some particular facts about, say, Roman history might be
of no interest to a particular child at age five but become quite fascinating at age fifteen, while they remain of no interest to some other
fifteen-year-old. What makes the facts meaningful and interesting
is affected by age, by what has already been learned, and by the particular child's attachment to some more general context within which
these particular facts "fit." To a child whose past learning, tempera-
ment, and the like, have produced a romantic engagement with heroes
and the struggle for freedom, the revolt of Spartacus will likely be
engaging. That child will want to learn about these events, will be
"motivated" to do so, will exhibit the kind of interest we find desirable
as both a stimulus to learning and a part of what we mean by the process of education. What we could well use in education, then, is a
theory that characterizes the general contexts of meaning that seem
to determine what particular things children will find first accessible and meaningful and then engaging and stimulating at different
ages or stages in their educational development. In what follows I
want to make an attempt toward sketching such a theory.

My concern with environments here is with the environments of
meaning within which children and students make sense of things.
An assumption in what follows is that what most matters in teaching
children to read and write things and in teaching them to become increasingly sophisticated readers and writers is that the things one
wants them to learn need to be embedded in contexts or environments
that are rich in meaning for them. I will characterize four distinct contexts of meaning, or layers of understanding—mythic, romantic,
philosophic, and ironic. These four layers of understanding are age-
conditioned and environmentally influenced.

These are necessarily unlike the kinds of stages one finds in
psychological theories, such as Piaget's. The psychologist is concerned
to establish what is the case about psychological development. The

educator is concerned to prescribe what ought to be done to bring about some ideal. Clearly the educator's prescriptions must not contravene whatever the psychologist establishes is the case.

The relationship between psychological theories and educational prescriptions, however, is a problematic one. Psychology is a relatively young field of study and perhaps for that reason has established very little about significant features of human behavior and development securely. How far should the educator feel constrained by insecure psychological theories? Of course each educator has to deal with particular theories as seems most sensible. While the educator needs to be constrained by what is the case, however, many of the educator's prescriptions work in areas that are rather remote from the kinds of questions with which psychologists deal. For example, in his seminal essay on "The Rhythms of Education"[3] A.N. Whitehead argues for the importance of romance in education. Neither a study of the nature or structure of knowledge nor psychological research would lead to such a concept; it is not a part of knowledge nor a necessary stage of psychological development. It is, rather, a quality of thought that can come about when we use knowledge for particular human purposes.

What follows is a little closer to Whitehead than to Piaget. It deals with what seem to me important and general matters that are central to education; it focuses on phenomena that are on the whole remote from areas where psychological theories provide either support or constraints; it prescribes what seems to me a desirable educational scheme; it embodies a complex logical progression; and it is supported empirically by a wide range of uncontentious observations.

The Mythic Layer of Understanding

This first stage is appropriate from earliest years to approximately age eight. If the scheme is to be empirically based on uncontentious observations, where might we begin looking for descriptive data? We might reasonably begin with those things that seem to engage typical children most—games and stories. Given that our topic is literacy, I'll focus on stories here. For purposes of theory-building we will need not only descriptive data but also some attempt at an explanation of what we find.

Two things are immediately evident about the stories whose appeal to young children seems most powerful. First, concerning their content, they are full of weird creatures like talking middle-class bears, monsters with human motives and emotions, ghosts, and so on; also, they tend to be set in exotic times and places—or no-times and no-places. Second, concerning their form, they seem to involve powerful and pure emotions and forces in conflicts that are clearly resolved: that is, they follow the pattern of the basic story form.

We have, then, two sets of questions to answer: First, what is a story, why are children so engaged by them, and what are they for? Second, why are young children's stories full of middle-class talking bears and other weird creatures? (For this first layer I will overlap a little with my other chapter in this book.)

Take the incident, "He took the book." We know in some vague sense what it means, but the sense is very vague because we don't know who "He" is or what the book contains, whether taking it is good or bad, or anything else about it. It has no significance for us by itself. By adding a context, a time and place and circumstances in which he is a clean-cut young man who is taking the book to help his grandmother, we add meaning to the incident. More significant, we begin to orient our feelings about his taking the book. We might extend the context further, such that he and his grandmother are drug-pushers and the book contains information about where to make their next drop. This widened context of meaning will cause us to reorient our feelings about the incident. Where we were, mildly, glad before, we may now feel sorry that he was able to take the book. The story-writer can play with our affective responses by adding to the context, which determines the meaning of the incident. The only unit in language that can ultimately fix the meaning of incidents is the story. We know we have reached the end of a story—not when it says "and they lived happily ever after," because if often doesn't—but when we know how to feel about all the incidents that make up the story.

A story is the linguistic unit that can determine the affective meaning of incidents. In history, for example, we do not know ultimately how to feel about an event. Horrible events sometimes lead to wonderful conclusions. Because history has not ended we can only provisionally feel glad or sorry about any event. Those who become certain of how they feel about particular events do so by converting history into a story in which they assert an end. In a sophisticated way this is what Marxists do. They can feel confident about the meaning of certain events because they have imposed a plot on history that asserts a particular end to the process. We have the same general problem with our lives. Until the end, we cannot be sure about the meaning of any part of them. We can falsify this experience, in the way Marxists falsify history, by imposing a plot on our lives that determines the meaning of particular experiences. The commonest way of doing this is by asserting a more general religious story whose context can fix the meaning of the events of our lives.

If a story is the machine we have for fixing the affective meaning of events, we may be approaching a reason why young children find them so engaging. In a world where the meaning of events and incidents must be often ambiguous and quite puzzling, the story offers a haven of clarity. But why the middle-class talking bears?

If, as we have been told by many educators, we should seek reading material that is "relevant" to children's own situations, we should notice that children tend to seek quite the opposite. A common impulse is to move toward the most exotic content. Early developmental theorists stressed that children could deal only with the most simple matters in their immediate experience. John Dewey suggested that we should move the child only gradually outward from their daily social experience. Piagetians have told us that children lack the concepts that enable them to handle abstraction, most logical connections, causality, geographical space, and historical time, and that only very slowly are these mastered. How, one must wonder, do children so easily have access to Darth Vadar, witches, talking dragons, and space warriors long ago in galaxies far away?

Consider how children develop the conceptual apparatus that enables them to articulate what they know about the temperature continuum. First they learn the concepts "hot" and "cold." They start, that is, with binary opposites. Next they mediate between these poles by learning the concept "warm." Then they mediate between cold and warm—perhaps "cool" or "quite cold," and between warm and hot—"pretty hot." After elaborating this continuum by mediating between poles they develop an abstract concept of a temperature continuum, on which meaning is established by acceptance of an arbitrary numbering convention.

And middle-class talking bears? What are the most basic, prominent, and powerful polar opposites in our environment? Surely nature and culture. So basic indeed that we tend to forget about it. While young children do not typically distinguish between such terms as *nature* and *culture*, they make the distinction in their observation that the guinea pig does nothing to make himself a table or chairs and the cat resolutely refuses to talk back. They know immediately when walking through the woods that the park bench is in a different category from the fallen tree, even if they cannot articulate the difference. If we mediate between natural and cultural objects what do we get? Talking bears, for one thing. A talking bear combines cultural capacities in a natural creature; it coalesces or mediates between the categories of nature and culture. A feature of the mythic layer of understanding is its attempts to mediate between polar opposites, and its energetic attempts to generate mediating categories between poles that we later learn do not have such mediating categories. That other great evident division, between life and death, also absorbs endless mythic energy in attempted mediation. In the shadow between life and death, worlds of gods, spirits, and ghosts, pullulate. A ghost has some of the qualities we associate with living things: It moves, can perhaps talk, has intentions, and so on, while it also has qualities we associate with dead things. It has, not least importantly, died, presumably doesn't eat, and so on. Ghosts, gods, and spirits, then, are things that are both alive and dead, just as warm is both hot and cold. We learn, or fail to learn, that life and death are discrete empirical categories that lack a mediating category.

If we consider these observations valid, however brief this look at them,[4] we might see how we can use them to guide us toward setting up a mythic environment to encourage early literacy. We would want to use mythic-type stories prominently: i.e., binary opposites in conflict, clear affective meaning, mediation between life/death, nature/culture, or other binary categories derived from features of the everyday world and children's experience in families: big/little; brave/cowardly; fear/security; good/bad; and so on. That is, the characteristics that we find prominent in the great fairy stories of the world, but hardly at all in typical basal readers. More important, we would want to borrow the story form. The form—as distinct from the fictional stories—seems crucial in helping children in their early years to make sense of things. The story form is a most important tool for making its contents meaningful. Thus any content we can organize in terms of young children's basic polar categories and put into a story form of binary conflict, elaboration, and resolution can be made meaningful. (This is elaborated in my other essay in the book.)

It is surely not coincidental that children master the story form about the same time as they master the sentence form. Indeed some scholars of poetics claim that the story is simply the sentence writ large; syntax and plot are the same mental function working in different levels of content.[5] Growing appreciation of the forms and conventions of stories would thus likely transfer to increased mastery of sentences. Mastery of story and sentence do appear to occur together: Nursery rhymes are incomplete, fragmented stories that appeal most strongly when children's sentences are mainly incomplete and fragmented; simple complete stories tend to be enjoyed when simple complete sentences are mastered; more sophisticated stories are appreciated when more sophisticated sentences figure in students' writing; and eventually we enjoy those exploding parodies of story and sentence in *Finnegan's Wake.*

Perhaps it should also be noted that learning to follow a story requires a sense of causality, problem solving, analyzing events and situations, forming hypotheses and reforming them in light of further content, and so on. Learning the conventions of increasingly sophisticated stories is learning such intellectual skills. Teachers occasionally have a tendency to talk about a story a great deal. Better to read a second story. We might think of these early years as a time for immersion in stories and any content we can organize within the story form.

What seems to follow for the promotion of literacy skills is that such exercises should as far as possible be put into the context of stories. Workbooks with lists of more or less discrete exercises will likely be much less effective than the same exercises organized into a story with the characteristics sketched earlier.

The Romantic Layer of Understanding

This period occurs in children between approximately ages 8 to 15. The stories that seem most to engage children during this next layer have significantly distinct features from those of the mythic layer. They share the story form, the basic sense-making tool, but the form is more sophisticated. In terms of content one new feature is paramount: The stories are realistic. They are not realistic in the sense of seeking to be literally true but are concerned always to be possible or plausible within a world that mimics reality. Even in stories such as Superman, there is considerable energy devoted to making him seem plausible. It would be insufficient in the romantic layer for him to have superhuman powers by magic in the way in which earlier children accept the arrival of a Fairy Godmother without needing to know about her means of locomotion or the powers whereby she changes mice into horses. In this later layer there has to be some explanation or account of the magic. So we know all about Superman's birth and escape from the dying plant Krypton and how the molecular structure of our sun gives him his special powers. (I may be a bit lazy on the details.)

Prominent in romantic layer stories are heroes and heroines, but they often have common and curious qualities. They live an ordinary life and can also in some way transcend ordinary life. Superman is also Clark Kent. These heroes and heroines are clearly figures with whom the student in the romantic layer associates in some important way.

In a romantic story a hero or heroine (or institution, nation, idea) with whom or which the student can form an association struggles against odds to a glory and transcendence over threatening nature (or persons, events, institutions, ideas, nations), in which glory the reader may then share. Such stories have more complex plots than mythic stories. They are concerned with realistic detail or plausibility, have clear and powerful heroes or heroines, and often have exotic, though realistic or plausible, settings.

The content of mythic layer stories often ignores the limits of what is possible. The crucial index of transition to the romantic layer is a concern with precisely what are the limits of what is possible. Associated with this is the beginning of a realistic mastery of concepts of historical causality, geographical space, and abstract logical relationships. Again contrary to what we are commonly told in education, students do not seem to focus immediately on the "relevant" everyday content of their environments and lives. Rather they seem to focus on the extremes, the limits, of reality, on the most exotic and romantic content. No longer are students immediately engaged by the mention of giants and monsters; their stronger interest during this layer is in who was really the biggest person, the most monstrous creature, the fastest, the slowest, the smallest. *The Guinness Book of Records* ideally responds to the dominant interest of the romantic layer. Romance, in this sense, is myth confined within reality. The mythic impulses are still evident, but they are in conflict with the intellectual desire to know where reality ends and the mythic begins.

One may say, then, that this romantic stage is concerned with the discovery of an autonomous world that lacks magic and works according to its own rules, regardless of what we might wish. This autonomy is threatening to the immature ego, which begins to be aware of itself as a part of the everyday world but also aware of itself as a rather powerless part. This threatening everyday world is countered by the student forming romantic associations with the forces that most clearly transcend the everyday world. Heroes and heroines appeal most powerfully to the imagination at this stage because they embody the power to meet and overcome those forces that the student is increasingly aware that he or she is subject to and determined by. That transcendent power is expressed in qualities such as courage, compassion, ingenuity, nobility, wisdom, and all the old virtues. If we embody these in characters who face and overcome the threats to which the flesh is heir, we have the kind of hero or heroine who most readily engages the romantic layer student.

These qualities, however, need to embodied not only in fictional characters in stories; they can also be embodied in the content of history, geography, physics, and so forth, in such a way as to engage the romantic mind.[6]

If our concern is with expanding students' literacy, such a characterization of the romantic layer of understanding suggests that certain forms of literature will best engage and carry forward students' educational development. The poetry we choose, for example, should be the most romantic, rather than that which is of the highest quality combined with simple expression. Thus, students are often introduced to poetry that celebrates nature in its quotidian forms, but however simple the language in which such sentiments are expressed, the meaning of such poetry is often not within the grasp of the romantic layer of understanding. The mountains of the moon and the valley of the shadow are more easily accessible than the daffodils by Ulswater. A strong narrative line, strong and clear rhythms appropriate to the theme, heroic actions, human qualities in extremis, high drama or humor, and sentiment verging on sentimentality seem the most engaging qualities of verse appropriate to engaging students in this layer.

Selecting such verse is not a matter of pandering to inappropriately crude interests. It is proper for the immature to be immature. There is no point trying to treat the immature as though they were mature. Reaching maturity is a process, and selecting the appropriate kind of verse, and stories and academic content, at each stage is intended to satisfy what is most engaging and to move the process along. Such verses as Macauley's *Lays of Ancient Rome* or A.E. Housman's or Kipling's more dramatic poems help, in this case predominantly male, students understand a little more what poetry is for; it also helps extend their appreciation of rhythms in language and develops a little further their sentiment and emotion.

Their writing should be expected to pursue similar themes, and they should be encouraged to write similar sentiment-full verse. They should be encouraged to write a great deal. It is a mystery that some teachers seem to expect students' mastery of literate expression to improve while giving them little practice, and much of that practice in the impoverishing context of workbook exercises.

The Philosophic Layer of Understanding

This layer appropriately begins, when it does begin at all, during mid to late adolescence, and continues into the twenties. The crucial feature of the move from the romantic to the philosophic layer is the realization that the world and experience are made up from complex processes of which the student is a part. The establishment of the individual's sense of identity can thus be no more achieved by romantic associations with transcendent qualities but rather by understanding his or her place within the complex processes that make up the world and experience. In the romantic layer one associates directly with whatever best supports one's developing ego—with heroes overcoming great odds or with much put upon but resilient heroines, to choose a couple of stereotypical examples. But the philosophic mind is most readily engaged by knowledge that promises to tell the truth about these general and complex processes. In history, then, the romantic events and great deeds of heroic characters are increasingly less engaging, and it is the general patterns of the historical process that engage the students' mind with increasing insistence. By knowing the nature of the historical process, philosophic stage students can establish their place in the process. Thus the Marxist may understand that the historical process is the progressive story of class conflicts leading towards a classless state. The Marxist students' identities are in part established by such a general scheme because it fixes their place within the scheme and tells them what they should do as agents within it. Similarly, the liberal-humanitarian scheme of late nineteenth century Western countries provided a general scheme, which was accepted by the philosophic layer mind as expressing the truth about the historical process and so establishing the proper role of the individual as an historical agent within it.

Interest in this layer, then, is on the general schemes that offer truths about history, psychology, science, sociology, and so on. Philosophic layer individuals provide the major market for the books that reach for very general truths about the human condition. The term "philosophic" is chosen to echo Aristotle's observation that poetry is more philosophic than history, because the former is concerned with what happens and the latter with what happened. The philosophic mind is attracted toward the general, the recurrent, the law, the general theory—toward the truth about what happens. The philosophic mind tends toward the reductive—trying to understand the whole within the clearest and simplest scheme possible. It is the stage at which ideologies and metaphysical schemes are most attractive.

The literature that attracts during this layer is largely a literature of ideas—even heroes become ciphers for ideas. Typical of such literature is Borges's *Inquisitions* or O. Henry's stories. Human particularity, the quirks of individual character, become less engaging, and there is a tendency toward a greater interest in theory than literature itself; poetics rather than poetry.

The curriculum that would advance literacy to and through this stage may be inferred from the general characterization suggested above. Very general concepts begin to proliferate in students' writing and conversation—"society," "culture," "the mind," "evolution," "human nature," and so forth. Poetry and fiction should perhaps tend to take a somewhat less prominent place in the philosophic curriculum than matters of rhetoric. The philosophic is a stage of argument. The curriculum might be taken up with exercises in having effects. The essay is probably the "cutting edge" of literacy development through this stage. Essays should be written constantly—all aimed out into the world in order to have an effect on it. The essays may be in the form of letters—to newspapers, politicians, advertisers, manufacturers, and the like. Students should learn the arts of persuasion through words. Formal debating might also further this.

Ironic Layer of Understanding

This is the stage of maturity, and the significant index of the move into this layer from the philosophic is the individual's realization that the general schemes that were so engaging because they offered to tell the most profound truths are seen at last as not open to truth tests. Their generality ensures that they evade falsification. The ironic layer sees the return to particularity but also to seeing the necessity of general schemes for creating more general meaning for those particulars. However, the general scheme is seen not so much as true or false as useful, beautiful, or elegant, or their opposites.

Education is a cumulative process, so these layers are not layers one leaves behind. Rather, each one contributes something to the developing understanding. Properly, the mythic layer contributes imagination; the romantic layer contributes a vivifying association with knowledge; the philosophic layer contributes the tools for searching for more general meaning, for pattern and theory construction; and the ironic layer represents the regulator of these, along with an appreciation that life and the world are made up of particulars and the coalescence of these into more general forms is the contribution of our mind. This maturity allows access to all forms of literature and the flexibility to express private experience in appropriate public forms.

Conclusion

Some of the above observations may seem sensible to some readers, but perhaps the scheme seems at least, shall we politely put it, epistemologically unclear. What kind of sketch of what kind of theory for what kind of use is the above supposed to be?

It is based on, and elaborated from, observations of common qualitative changes in children's and student's interests. It is an attempt to schematize these changes, recognizing four quite distinct layers in the process of becoming fully literate. It is indeed epistemologically unclear because it is unclear what an educational theory should be composed of. That is, while there obviously needs to be an empirical component, it is also clear that education is very largely a prescriptive matter. So while the above sketch obviously yields a variety of empirically testable claims, it is not only based on observations but also involves a prescription that the scheme outlined is one that ought to be followed. No empirical finding is relevant to the latter part of the claim—unless it is to show that what is prescribed is impossible—but rather it is properly open only to analysis and argument.

It is, then, a sketch of a prescription for how to become literate. Its use is as a guide to what ought to be read and what kinds of activities students ought to be engaged in order to become literate. Clearly, as it stands here, it is too brief to be more than suggestive. While many teachers might find elements of it, or even the whole of it, not according with their experience of children and students, it might at least serve the value of encouraging teachers to focus on what they see as the most energetic and imaginative intellectual engagements of students, and see how these may be used in building a more sophisticated literacy.

End Notes

1. See for example Eric Havelock, *Origins of Western Literacy* (Toronto: Ontario Institute for Studies in Education, 1976)
2. Richard C. Anderson, "The notion of schemata and the educational enterprise" *Schooling and the Acquisition of Knowledge* eds. Richard C. Anderson, Rand J. Spiro, and W.E. Montague (Hillsdale, NJ: Erlbaum, 1977).
3. Alfred North Whitehead, "The Rhythm of Education." *The Aims of Education* (New York: The Free Press,1922).
4. For a much more extensive treatment see Kieran Egan, *Primary Understanding. Education in Early Childhood* (New York: Routledge, 1988).
5. See Roland Barthes, "Introduction a l'analysestructurale des recites," *Communications 8* (1966); A.J. Greimas, "Elements pour une theorie del'interpretation durecits mythique," *Communications 8* (1966; Tzvetan Todorov), *Grammaire du Decameron* (The Hague: Mouton, 1969).
6. Kieran Egan, *Romantic Understanding: The Development of Rationality and Imagination, ages 8-15* (New York: Routledge, forthcoming and Kieran Egan. *Educational Development* (New York: Oxford University Press, 1979).

15

Are We Overselling Literacy?

Keith E. Stanovich

Keith Stanovich is a widely quoted experimental psychologist in the field of reading. His studies of "Matthew Effects" have shown how reading difficulties can snowball for a youngster and lead to pervasive school failure, and they have redirected our thinking about reading disability. In this chapter he looks at the amount of reading children do and shows us, first, as Wilson did in this volume, that there are enormous variations in the amount of reading done by school-aged children; and second, that these differences have powerful consequences for children's vocabulary and general knowledge. In short, reading, at least large quantities of reading, can be demonstrated to enrich the mind. His arguments are supported with tables of data that should persuade skeptics of the importance of developing avid readers as a prime goal of schooling.

We are in the middle of a perhaps unprecedented campaign by a variety of educational and reading organizations to increase children's experience with literature and to increase their exposure to print. Indeed, one of the few things that all segments of the reading education community can agree on is that exposing children to books early and in quantity is good.

In this chapter I am going to argue that print exposure has specific and unique cognitive benefits (in addition to the host of social and emotional benefits that are discussed elsewhere in this volume). Or, to put it another way, I am going to argue that encouraging children's free reading is good. Stated in this manner, my argument surely must raise the question of whether I am not belaboring the obvious. Is it not the case that everyone already knows and believes that emphasis on book reading is a good thing? And has not research proven beyond a doubt that print exposure leads to unique cognitive competencies? The answers to these questions are, respectively, "not really" and "not quite."

Does Everyone Agree That an Emphasis on Book Reading is Good?

In the academic community, there are actually those who do not share the high level of enthusiasm for children's book reading that currently exists in the reading education community. For example, there are the writings of the futurists who, with increasing frequency, are announcing the demise of reading. Advocates of the electronic media are quite ambivalent about the educational community's stress on reading. Indeed, many of these advocates would seem to welcome a decline in the prominence of print:

> What I am suggesting is that we are witnessing the demise of the written word as our primary means of storing and communicating information. By the time my four-year-old son reaches adulthood, there will be hardly any compelling reason for him to be able to read, write, and do arithmetic. He will have more—not less—access to the accumulated wisdom of the peoples of the globe, but the three R's will have succumbed to the influence of inexpensive, fast, reliable computers that call up information instantly in response to the spoken word.[1]

Although we are far from the nirvanas described in this quote, visual and electronic media advocates can point to some successes. The province of Ontario in Canada now has media literacy as a required component of the English and language arts curriculum.[2] In that province, a *Media Literacy Resource Guide* "stresses that teachers' attitudes toward the mass media and toward students as media consumers are crucial to the success of any program designed to develop media literacy. The media can be an important bridge between students and teachers, but only if teachers stress the positive features of the mass media rather than dwell solely on the negative" (p. 333). Teachers are told to exploit the teachable moments provided by "a new television series. . .a blockbuster film, or a television miniseries" (p. 333). In grades nine through twelve such studies in media literacy are supposed to account for one-third of the time in two mandated English courses.[3] Postman[4] describes efforts in the Philadelphia schools to have the curriculum sung to students who were to wear Walkman equipment playing rock music with lyrics about academic subjects. Then there is Christopher Whittle, the communications entrepreneur, who wants to donate free TVs and VCRs to school districts—if only they will have the children watch with advertisements that he puts on them. Whittle claims that "a mix of MTV-style graphics, news factlets and features on subjects like steroid-hooked teens [are the] perfect teaching tool for kids."[5] So far, 2,400 schools have signed up for his "perfect teaching tool" and, of course, the advertisements.

In some quarters of the academic community, the lack of book orientation among teenagers and college students is defended and, in some cases, seemingly welcomed. For example, two distinguished English professors argue in the *Chronicle of Higher Education*[6] that educators are "threatened by a changing student population, one more diverse and more in touch with 'televisual' culture." Or, in the *New York Times* Education Life Section, a professor at UCLA complains that "We have faculties that are very verbal, but students who cannot learn by reading. The computer screen seems to appeal to them. But it is hard to persuade the faculty to give up the chalkboard and textbook to do something different."[7]

Another source of hostility to book advocacy stems from concerns that literacy is a form of social oppression. For example, Wagschal[8] argues that "The printed word has always had a serious disadvantage—one which is reflected in our present worries over declining reading and writing abilities and in the continued failure of global literacy programs—the three R's are, by their very nature, tools of the affluent and elite" (p. 243). However, he neglects to present us with examples of technologies of communication that have not been more effectively used by those in positions of social influence. Certainly the computer technology that he champions is at least as much a tool of the elite as is reading.[9]

Nevertheless, Wagschal's opinions are not rare. They are echoed by other social scientists and humanities scholars within academia. As philosopher Robert Solomon[10] notes, "The arguments I hear these days, from some very literate and book-loving theorists, make it sound as if the love of books is nothing but self-serving, not just for writers and publishers but for the 'elite' who maintain their political superiority via pretensions of 'culture.' Literacy is a capitalist device to separate out the advantaged, some Marxists say. . . . Literacy is the ploy of a white, English-speaking elite to render 'illiterate' people from a different culture, with a different language and a different history, say some very learned educators" (p. 38). One need not look far to confirm Solomon's observations. A recent NEA publication complains that "There is an elitism in many schools that would place Loretta

Lynn, Harlequin Romances, and many other forms of art that are highly regarded and respected by many persons at the negative end of a 'cultural' continuum."[11]

In a book quite influential in literacy studies, Street[12] repeatedly intones that "The actual examples of literacy in different societies that are available to us suggest that it is more often 'restrictive' and hegemonic, and concerned with instilling discipline and exercising social control" (p. 4), and that "Schooling and techniques of teaching literacy are often forms of hegemony (p. 11). Although examples of such opinions could be expanded almost indefinitely,[13] many teachers are unaware of how influential these writings are in academic discourse and how thoroughly they infuse the teachings in present-day schools of education. It may come as a surprise to many teachers who are convinced of the efficacy of getting children "hooked on books" that the social spinoffs from their enthusiasm for print is seen as an oppressive force by some sociopolitical analysts.

It should be noted that the current radical critiques of literacy practices extend far beyond that of advocates of critical literacy such as Paulo Freire.[14] In fact, modern critiques argue that "key assumptions, goals, and pedagogical practices fundamental to the literature on critical literacy. . .are repressive myths that perpetuate relations of domination."[15]

Finally there are those who warn that we seem to be "overselling" literacy: "Literacy doesn't generate finer feelings or higher values. It doesn't even make anyone smarter. . . . What they read and write may make people smarter, but so will any activity that engages the mind, including interesting conversation."[16] Thus, the answer to our first question is an unadulterated "no." There are many social scientists and segments of the educational community that do not share the enthusiasm for print that is a direct consequence of the campaigns to saturate the environment of children with books. The uniform and universal "good" that is assumed in literacy and parental reading campaigns must be proven and not just assumed. Opinion on the matter is not uniform.

Have the Positive Cognitive Consequences of Print Exposure Been Demonstrated?

The second, more empirical, question of whether or not research has demonstrated that reading has positive cognitive consequences relates to the issue of whether or not we are "overselling" literacy. Here, it must be admitted that we have often been building policy more on assumptions than on demonstrated fact. The overselling charge, when directed at current campaigns to combat illiteracy, stem aliteracy, and foster early habits that lead to lifelong readers, strike home because there is a precedent for overselling literacy. That precedent resides in the international literacy campaigns conducted in nonindustrialized countries during the last three decades. There are lessons to be learned from this previous analogues situation—particularly at this time of such great enthusiasm, when we should be most cautious.

Unjustified enthusiasm was precisely the emotion that undermined the credibility of the international literacy campaigns. There was, in early writings, a tendency to attribute every positive outcome that was historically correlated with the rise of literacy—economic development, for example—to the effects of literacy itself. However, the potential for spurious correlation in the domain of literacy is quite high. Simply put, literacy levels are correlated with too many other good things. Thus, it was a mistake to attribute automatically everything that was historically correlated with the rise of literacy to the effects of literacy itself. For example, the link between economic development and levels of national literacy turned out to be much more complex than originally thought.[17] Literacy levels are as much a consequence of economic development as they are its cause.

The problem at the level of the individual reader is analogous to the problem of comparing the effects of different levels of literacy across different societies. Levels of print exposure are correlated with too many other good things. Avid readers tend to be different on a wide variety of cognitive skills, behavioral habits, and background variables. Attributing any particular outcome to print exposure uniquely is an extremely tenuous inference. This problem is a well-known one in research methodology, and it is not arcane. As the textbooks say, correlation does not imply causation. Early literacy theorists were guilty of overselling literacy by attributing to it every positive effect with which it was correlated. One cannot just assume a casual effect from the mere presence of a correlation. The relevance of this point to our discussion of the current enthusiasms for increasing children's free-reading habits and exposure to print should be obvious. We must be careful not to oversell literacy by attributing it as a cause of everything with which it is positively correlated.

Despite all of these caveats, I want to argue that, in the domain of individual cognitive effects, we are on firmer ground than were the earlier cross-national comparisons of literacy levels. My thesis is that, at the individual level, we will not get caught overselling literacy by wrongly interpreting spurious correlations. In short, at the individual level the claimed effects for print exposure are real. The argument above was meant to highlight the necessity of justifying claims about the efficacy of book reading, rather than just assuming such efficacy. I do believe that such justification exists.

Theoretical Reasons to Expect Positive Cognitive Consequences from Reading

There are certain very important cognitive domains in which there are strong theoretical reasons to expect a positive and unique effect of print exposure. Vocabulary development provides a case in point. Most theorists are agreed that the bulk of vocabulary growth during a child's lifetime occurs indirectly through language exposure rather than through direct teaching.[18] Furthermore, many researchers are convinced that exposure to print, rather than to oral language, is the prime contributor to individual differences in children's vocabularies.[19]

There are sound theoretical reasons for believing that print exposure is a particularly efficacious way of expanding a child's vocabulary. These reasons derive from the differences in the statistical distributions of words that have been found between print and oral language. Some of these differences are illustrated in Table 15-1, which displays the results of some of the research of Hayes and Ahrens,[20] who have analyzed the distributions of words used in various contexts.

Table 15-1. Selected Statistics for Major Sources of Spoken and Written Language (Sample Means)

	Rank of Median Word	Rare Words per 1,000
I. Printed Tests		
Abstracts of scientific articles	4,389	128.0
Newspapers	1,690	68.3
Popular magazines	1,399	65.7
Adult books	1,058	52.7
Comic books	867	53.5
Children's books	627	30.9
Preschool books	578	16.3
II. Television Texts		
Popular prime-time adult shows	490	22.7
Popular prime-time children's shows	543	20.2
Cartoon shows	598	30.8
Mr. Rogers and Sesame Street	413	2.0
III. Adult Speech		
Expert witness	1,008	28.4
College graduates to friends, spouses	496	17.3

Adapted from Hayes and Abrens[4]

The table illustrates the three different categories of language that were analyzed: written language sampled from genres as difficult as scientific articles and as simple as preschool books; words spoken on television shows of various kinds; and adult speech in two contexts varying in formality. The words used in the different contexts were analyzed according to a standard frequency count of English.[21] This frequency count ranks the 86,741 different words in English according to their frequency of occurrence in a large corpus of written English. So, for example, the word *the* is ranked number 1; the tenth most frequent word is *it*; *know* is ranked 100th; *pass* is ranked 1,000th, *vibrate* is 5,000th in frequency; *shrimp* is 9,000th in frequency; and *amplifier* is 16,000th in frequency. The first column, labeled Rank Median Word, is simply the frequency rank of the average word (after a small correction) in each of categories. So, for example, the average word in children's books was ranked 627th most frequent in the Carroll et al. word count, the average word in popular magazines was ranked 1399th most frequent, and the average word in the abstracts of scientific articles had, not surprisingly, a very low rank (4,389).

What is immediately apparent is how lexically impoverished most speech is, compared to written language. With the exception of the special situation of courtroom testimony, the average frequency of the words in all of the samples of oral speech is quite low, hovering in the 400–600 range of ranks. The relative rarity of the words in children's books is, in fact, greater than that in all of the adult conversation, except for the courtroom testimony. Indeed, the words used in children's books are considerably rarer than those in the speech on prime-time adult television. The categories of adult reading matter contain words that are considerably rarer than those heard on television.

These relative differences in word rarity have direct implications for vocabulary development. If most vocabulary is acquired outside of formal teaching, then the only opportunities to acquire new words occur when an individual is exposed to a word in written or oral language that is outside their current vocabulary. That this will happen vastly more often while reading than while talking or watching television is illustrated in the second column of Table 15-1. That column lists how many rare words per 1,000 are contained in each of the categories. A rare word is defined as one with a rank lower than 10,000; roughly, a word that is outside the vocabulary of a fourth to sixth grader. For vocabulary growth to occur after the middle grades children must be exposed to words that are rare in this definition. Again, it is print that provides many more such word-learning opportunities. Children's books have 50 percent more rare words in them than adult prime-time television and the conversation of college graduates have. Popular magazines have roughly three times as many opportunities for new word learning than prime-time television and adult conversation do. Assurances that "What they read and write may make people smarter, but so will any activity that engages the mind, including interesting conversation"[22] are overstated, at least when applied to the domain of vocabulary learning. The data in Table 15-1 indicate that conversation is not a substitute for reading.

It is sometimes argued or implied that the kind of words present in print but not represented in speech are unnecessary words—jargon, academic doublespeak, elitist terms of social advantage, or words used to maintain the status of the users but that serve no real functional purpose. A consideration of the frequency distributions of written and spoken words reveals this argument to be patently false. Table 15-2 presents a list of words that do not occur at all in two large corpora of oral language[23] but that have appreciable frequencies in a written frequency count.[24] The words *participation, luxury, maneuver, provoke, reluctantly, relinquish, portray, equate, hormone, exposure, display, invariably, dominance, literal, legitimate,* and *infinite,* are not unnecessary appendages, concocted by the ruling class to oppress those who are unfamiliar with them. They are words that are necessary to make critical distinctions in the physical and social world in which we live. Without such lexical tools, one will be severely disadvantaged in attaining one's goals in a technological society. As Olson[25] notes:

> It is easy to show that sensitivity to the subtleties of language are crucial to some undertakings. A person who does not clearly see the difference between an expression of intention and a promise or between a mistake and an accident, or between a falsehood and a lie, should avoid a legal career or, for that matter, a theological one. A person who does not see the oddity of "I know you'll change your mind" should, perhaps, avoid a career in logic or linguistics. A person who does not clearly see the difference between an explanation and a description should avoid a career in science (p. 341).

The large differences in lexical richness between speech and print are a major source of individual differences in vocabulary development. These differences are created by the large variability among children in exposure to print. Table 15-3 presents the data from a study of the out-of-school time use by fifth graders conducted by Anderson, Wilson, and Fielding.[26] From diaries that the children filled out daily over several months the investigators estimated how many minutes per day that individuals were engaged in reading and other activities while not in school. The table indicates that the child at the 50th percentile in amount of book reading was reading approximately

Table 15-2.

Examples of words that do not appear in two large corpora of oral language (Berger, 1977; Brown, 1984) but that have appreciable frequencies in written texts (Carroll, Davies & Richman, 1971; Francis & Kucera, 1982):

display	literal
dominance	legitimate
dominant	luxury
exposure	maneuver
equate	participation
equation	portray
gravity	provoke
hormone	relinquish
infinite	reluctantly
invariably	

Table 15-3. Variation in Amount of Independent Reading

	Minutes of Reading Per Day			Words Read Per Year	
Percent	Books	Text	All Reading	Books	Text
98	65.0	67.3	90.7	4,358,000	4,733,000
90	21.1	33.4	40.4	1,823,000	2,357,000
80	14.2	24.6	31.1	1,146,000	1,697,000
70	9.6	16.9	21.7	622,000	1,168,000
60	6.5	13.1	18.1	432,000	722,000
50	4.6	9.2	12.9	282,000	601,000
40	3.2	6.2	8.6	200,000	421,000
30	1.3	4.3	5.8	106,000	251,000
20	0.7	2.4	3.1	21,000	134,000
10	0.1	1.0	1.6	8,000	51,000
2	0.0	0.0	0.2	0	8,000

Adapted from Anderson, Wilson, and Fielding (1988).

4.6 minutes per day, more than six times as much as the child at the 20th percentile in amount of reading time (less than a minute daily). To take another example, the child at the 80th percentile in amount of book reading time (14.2 minutes) was reading more than twenty times as much as the child at the 20th percentile.

Anderson et al. estimated the children's reading rates and used these, in conjunction with the amount of reading in minutes per day, to extrapolate a figure for the number of words that the children at various percentiles were reading. These figures, presented in the far right table, illustrate the enormous differences in word exposure that are generated by children's differential proclivities toward reading.

For example, the average child at the 90th percentile in print exposure reads almost two-and-one-half-million words per year outside of school, more than 46 times more words than the child at the 10th percentile, who is exposed to just 51,000 words outside of school during a year. To put it another way, the entire year's out-of-school exposure for the child at the 10th percentile amounts to just eight days reading for the child at the 90th percentile. These are the differences that, combined with the lexical richness of print, act to create large vocabulary differences among children.

Methodologies for Studying the Consequences of Different Degrees of Print Exposure at the Individual Level

It is one thing to speculate on how these differences in exposure to print may result in specific cognitive consequences in domains like vocabulary; it is another to demonstrate that these effects are occurring. In our research, we have sought empirical evidence for the specific facilitative effects of print exposure—effects that do not simply result from the higher cognitive abilities and skills of the more avid reader. As part of this research program, our research group[27] has pioneered the use of a measure of print exposure that has some unique advantages in investigations of this kind.

In all, we developed two measures for adults' exposure to print and one for children's exposure. Briefly, the children's measure (I refer the reader to the above-cited works for descriptions of the adults' measure) requires children to pick out the titles of popular children's books from a list of titles that includes equal numbers of made-up titles. This task is easy to administer to large numbers of children, it does not make large cognitive demands, and its results are reliable—it is not possible for children to distort their responses toward what they perceive as socially desirable answers.[28] Because the number of wrong answers can be counted against corrected ones, it is possible to remove the effects of guessing from the results (I refer the reader to Cunningham and Stanovich, in press; and Stanovich and West, 1989, for a full description of these instruments and a discussion of the logic behind them).

Of course, a score on the Title Recognition Test (TRT) is not an absolute measure of children's exposure to print, but it does provide an index of print exposure. Having this index enables us to ask what effects print exposure (rather than general reading comprehension and word decoding ability) has on intelligence, on vocabulary, on spelling, and on children's general knowledge about the world. In short, it enables us to answer the question, Are we overselling literacy?

The titles appearing on the TRT were selected from a sample of book titles generated in pilot investigations by groups of children ranging in age from second grade through high school. In selecting the items that appear on any one version of the TRT, an attempt was made to choose titles that were not prominent parts of classroom reading activities in these particular schools. Because we wanted the TRT to probe out-of-school rather than school-directed reading, an attempt was made to avoid books that were used in the school curriculum. Of course, versions of the TRT constructed for other classrooms will necessarily differ somewhat in item content. In short, if the TRT is to be used as a measure of out-of-school print exposure it must be considerably more individualized than the adult measures.

The list of children's titles appearing on one version of the TRT is presented in Table 15-4 along with the percentage recognition for each item in two different third and fourth grade samples. The correlation between the percentage recognition of the items in the California and the Michigan samples was very high ($r = .87$). The foil titles are listed at the bottom of the table, but on the actual TRT forms they were interspersed with the real titles. Table 15-5 presents the titles and percentage recognition for another version used with fourth, fifth, and sixth graders in a different school system.

As I said above, the TRT for children is a proxy measure of reading activity. It is obviously not intended to measure absolute levels of print exposure, as are the time studies of children's activities[29] that attempt to estimate actual time spent reading. Instead, the TRT was designed as a measure reflecting relative individual differences in exposure to print, all that is needed in order to uncover correlational relationships.

Data on the TRT as a Measure of Children's Print Exposure

Does the TRT distinguish the performance of children? Table 15-6 presents the data from a study of fourth, fifth, and sixth grade children who were classified as high or low in print exposure (within each grade) based on their performance on the TRT. The table indicates that the group that scored high on the TRT displayed significantly superior performance on a variety of other cognitive tasks. There was a small difference in their favor on Raven's Progressive Matrices, a measure of nonverbal cognitive ability, and larger differences on a phonological coding (decoding) task and a spelling task. The group scoring high on the TRT was considerably better at a check-list task that measured word knowledge and on a verbal fluency

Table 15-4.

	Percentage Recognition California Sample	Recognition Michigan Sample
Title Recognition Test Items:		
Jackaroo	11.2	3.9
The Kid Who Only Hit Homers	30.0	47.1
Call of the Wild	30.0	45.1
The Chosen	10.0	5.9
Tales of a Fourth Grade Nothing	77.5	92.2
Soup	17.5	15.7
The Secret Garden	76.2	51.0
The Cybil War	38.7	17.6
Just Between Us	37.5	33.3
Heidi	37.5	49.0
Freedom Train	30.0	17.6
James & the Giant Peach	78.8	64.7
Ballet Shoes	22.5	9.8
Superfudge	73.8	88.2
Dr. Dolittle	50.0	37.3
Strawberry Girl	18.8	13.7
When Hitler Stole Pink Rabbit	23.7	13.7
The Boxcar Children	32.5	29.4
Becky's Horse	22.5	25.5
The Great Coverup	18.8	7.8
Misty of Chincoteague	18.8	15.7
Henry and the Clubhouse	47.5	25.5
Slammer	6.2	9.8
Harriet the Spy	42.5	33.3
Jabberwocky	7.5	15.7

Foils:

It's My Room
Hot Top
Don't Go Away
The Hideaway
The Missing Letter
The Rollaway
Sadie Goes to Hollywood
The Schoolhouse
He's Your Little Brother!
Ethan Allen
The Lost Shoe
Skateboard
Curious Jim

Table 15-5.

	Percentage Recognition
Title Recognition Test Items:	
A Light in the Attic	75.2
How to Eat Fried Worms	64.7
Call of the Wild	51.9
The Chosen	17.3
Tales of a Fourth Grade Nothing	88.7
The Polar Express	32.3
The Indian in the Cupboard	73.7
The Cybil War	24.8
Homer Price	26.3
Heidi	56.4
Freedom Train	49.6
James & the Giant Peach	85.7
By the Shores of Silver Lake	32.3
Superfudge	67.7
Dr. Dolittle	58.6
From the Mixed-Up Files of Mrs. Basil E. Frankweiler	45.9
Island of the Blue Dolphins	80.5
Ramona the Pest	75.2
Iggie's House	21.1
The Great Brain	25.6
Misty of Chincoteague	6.0
Henry and the Clubhouse	22.6
Dear Mr. Henshaw	69.9
Harriet the Spy	42.9
The Lion, the Witch and the Wardrobe	68.4
Foils:	
Joanne	
It's My Room	
Hot Top	
Don't Go Away	
The Hideaway	
The Missing Letter	
The Rollaway	
Sadie Goes to Hollywood	
The Schoolhouse	
He's Your Little Brother!	
Ethan Allen	
The Lost Shoe	
Skateboard	
Curious Jim	

**Table 15-6. Means for Children High and Low on the
Title Recognition Test**

Variable	Low TRT	High TRT	
Title Recognition Test	.246	.524	**
Raven Matrices	37.5	40.3	*
Phonological Coding	.445	.605	**
Spelling	8.3	11.3	**
Word Checklist	.640	.807	**
Verbal Fluency	15.2	19.1	**
Peabody Picture Vocabulary Test	16.9	18.5	**
General Information	10.8	12.4	**

* = difference favoring High TRT, $p < .05$
** = difference favoring High TRT, $p < .01$

task that assessed the accessibility of verbal labels in memory. Performance was also superior on a set of items taken from the Peabody Picture Vocabulary Test, a confirming indicator of a vocabulary advantage for the group high in print exposure. Finally, a test of general information indicated that the high TRT group had a larger general knowledge base.

We are, however, faced with an issue of experimental logic: the problem of spurious correlation. We attacked this issue by employing the following methodological controls. The question is: Do children exposed to more print display superior vocabulary and knowledge when they are matched with the low-print children on general cognitive ability? The data in Table 15-7 address this question. Here, two groups of children high and low on the TRT have been equated on their performance on Raven's Progressive Matrices. Thus we can examine whether subjects high and low in print exposure look similar in vocabulary and knowledge when they have been equated, at least to some extent, on general cognitive ability. The results indicate that these subgroups were still differentiated on every other variable in the study. The differences were particularly large on the spelling task, the checklist measure of word knowledge, and the verbal fluency measure. However, significant differences still obtained on the Peabody measure of vocabulary and on the indicator of general information.

The results of a much more stringent test of whether exposure to print is a specific and unique predictor are displayed in Table 15-8. Here, two subgroups of high and low scorers on the TRT have been equated on their word decoding ability: Their scores on the phonological coding task are quite close. Here we ask the question of whether the TRT can differentiate two groups that are specifically

Table 15-7. Differences Between Subjects High and Low in Print Exposure Who are Equated on General Cognitive Ability

Variable	Low TRT	High TRT	
Title Recognition Test	.229	.484	**
Raven Matrices	39.0	39.3	
Phonological Coding	.460	.595	*
Spelling	8.0	11.0	**
Word Checklist	.644	.802	**
Verbal Fluency	15.1	19.2	**
Peabody Picture Vocabulary Test	16.9	18.2	*
General Information	10.8	12.3	*

* = difference favoring High TRT, p < .05
** = difference favoring High TRT, p < .01

Table 15-8. Differences Between Subjects High and Low in Print Exposure Who are Equated on Decoding Ability

Variable	Low TRT	High TRT	
Title Recognition Test	.244	.500	**
Raven Matrices	37.7	39.5	
Phonological Coding	.528	.539	
Spelling	8.6	10.4	
Word Checklist	.642	.783	**
Verbal Fluency	15.3	18.6	**
Peabody Picture Vocabulary Test	16.5	18.1	**
General Information	10.3	12.1	**

* = difference favoring High TRT, p < .05
** = difference favoring High TRT, p < .01

equated on their decoding ability. They have obtained the same level of a reading subskill essential to fluent reading,[30] yet the TRT indicates that they exercise their reading abilities to differing degrees. Does the exercise of the skill have any cognitive consequences? The answer is yes. The data in Table 15-8 indicates that the high TRT group displayed superiority on all of the verbal tasks. The differences on the word knowledge measure, verbal fluency, Peabody, and general information measure were all statistically significant. The high TRT group also obtained a higher spelling score, but this difference did not attain significance. These results are particularly impressive because they drive home the necessity of distinguishing the presence of skills and abilities from the exercise of those abilities.

An additional way to illustrate the importance of print exposure is to examine the consequences of a mismatch between general cognitive ability and print exposure. Can, for example, print exposure compensate for modest levels of general cognitive abilities? The comparisons presented in Table 15-9 address this issue. The children in the sample were classified according to a median split of performance on the TRT and on the Raven Progressive Matrices. The resulting 2 × 2 matrix revealed 58 children who were discrepant: 28 who were high on the TRT but low on the Raven (HiPrint/LoAbility) and 30 who were low in print exposure but high on the Raven (LoPrint/HiAbility). These two groups were then compared on all of the variables in the study. Of course, there were significant differences on the variables that had defined the groups: the TRT and the Raven. However, the LoPrint/HiAbility group did not attain higher scores on any other variable in the study. In fact, the HiPrint/LoAbility group actually scored significantly higher on the verbal fluency measure. In short, exposure to print seems to more than compensate for lack of general ability in the domains of knowledge and vocabulary.

Table 15-9. Differences Between Children High in Print Exposure but with Low Ability (N = 28) and Children Low in Print Exposure but with High Ability (N = 30)

Variable	LOPRINT/HIABILITY	HIPRINT/LOABILITY	
Title Recognition Test	.476	.271	*
Raven Matrices	34.7	43.8	#
Phonological Coding	.518	.560	
Spelling	10.0	9.4	
Word Checklist	.744	.743	
Verbal Fluency	19.2	16.0	*
Peabody Picture Vocabulary Test	17.3	17.3	
General Information	11.2	11.0	

\# = significant difference favoring HIPRINT/LOABILITY
* = significant difference favoring LOPRINT HIABILITY

Table 15-10 displays an analysis that pits print exposure against decoding ability. The sample was classified according to a median split of performance on the TRT and on the phonological coding measure. The resulting 2 × 2 matrix revealed 51 subjects who were discrepant: 25 who were high on the TRT but low in decoding (HiPrint/LoDecoding) and 26 who were low in print exposure but high in decoding (LoPrint/HiDecoding). These two groups were then compared on all of the variables in the study. Of course, there were significant differences on the variables that had defined the groups: the TRT and the phonological coding measure. Also, not unexpectedly, the spelling

Table 15-10. Differences Between Children High in Print Exposure but with Low Decoding Ability (N = 25) and Children Low in Print Exposure but with High Decoding Ability (N = 26)

Variable	HiPrint/ LoDecoding	LoPrint/ HiDecoding	
Title Recognition Test	.511	.269	*
Raven Matrices	38.5	41.0	
Phonological Coding	.309	.777	#
Spelling	9.0	11.7	#
Word Checklist	.739	.796	
Verbal Fluency	17.0	17.3	
Peabody Picture Vocabulary Test	18.1	16.7	
General Information	11.6	10.9	

\# = significant difference favoring HiPrint/LoDecoding
* = significant difference favoring LoPrint/HiDecoding

performance of the LoPrint/HiDecoding group was superior. However, this group was not superior on any of the other verbal measures in the study. In fact, a vocabulary difference on the Peabody favoring the Hi/Print/LoDecoding almost reached statistical significance. This analysis indicates that, as regards the acquisition of knowledge and vocabulary, exposure to print seems to compensate for lack of specific decoding ability. Low ability need not necessarily hamper the acquisition of vocabulary and knowledge as long as the individual is an avid reader. Finally, these results are further indications of the validity of the TRT as a measure of print exposure for children.

The "Overselling" Issue Revisited

The data I have presented go a long way toward answering potential charges that we are overselling literacy in our efforts to get parents and teachers to realize the importance of getting children hooked on books. While it is true that avid readers will differ from reluctant readers on a variety of other cognitive abilities, in a host of analyses presented above we have demonstrated that the effects of print exposure are separable from general cognitive ability. This has been the logic of our research program: to show that amount of print exposure is not just tracking good reading ability; that it is more than just another indicator of verbal skill.

Of course, another way to view what these analyses are illustrating is to conceive of them as illustrations of rich-get-richer and poor-get-poorer effects in educational achievement.[31] Other things being equal, more reading leads to more rapid growth in vocabulary and other knowledge bases. However, other things are not equal. Better readers read more.[32] The greater reading volume then leads to precisely the things—more differentiated vocabulary, language awareness, and knowledge—that serve to make subsequent reading easier and thus more enjoyable, thereby leading to even higher levels of print exposure which in turn, etc. etc. . .

Thus, a mechanism is set up whereby those already ahead in educational achievement will increase their advantages through behavioral self-selection.[33] These rich-get-richer, poor-get-poorer effects are probably one source of the seemingly negative comments about reading made by radical social theorists.[34] These theorists are reacting to the paradox that reading, though often valued as an unequivocal good, is a major contributor to increasing achievement disparities as schooling progresses.

Nevertheless, although print exposure tracks ability to some extent, the two are not totally overlapping. This was the point of several of the analyses presented above, which demonstrated significant effects of print exposure even after abilities had been equated. In short, exposure to print is efficacious regardless of the level of the child's cognitive and reading abilities. We do not have to wait for "prerequisite" abilities to be in place before encouraging free reading. Even the child with limited reading skills will build vocabulary and cognitive structures through immersion in literacy activities. An encouraging message for teachers of low achieving children is implicit here. Rather than despair of "raising ability levels" perhaps an educational emphasis on things we know to be malleable, habits and attitudes, will itself raise the "abilities" that teachers often despair of changing.

Finally, I think it worth considering whether the argument that reading "doesn't even make anyone smarter"[35] might really be wrong. If by "smarter" we mean having world knowledge and vocabulary in addition to the abstract reasoning skills usually assumed to be encompassed within the concept of intelligence ("smarter" in the colloquial), then reading does make people "smarter." In fact, there is ample precedent for considering intelligence to encompass knowledge, vocabulary, and verbal skills. Since the beginning of modern scientific interest in the concept known as "intelligence" many different theorists have included verbal comprehension, verbal fluency, and knowledge as components of their construct.[36] Laymen and teachers, to whom Smith's Kappan article is addressed, concur with intelligence theorists in viewing verbal facility as part of intelligence.[37]

Thus, to the extent that we emphasize verbal ability in our conceptualization of intelligence, reading does "make people smarter," and it becomes doubly imperative that we not deny reading experiences to precisely those children whose verbal abilities are most in need of bolstering. Allowing the reading activities of those already low in ability to decline further sets up a particularly perverse poor-get-poorer effect whereby we attribute negative habits ("this child doesn't like to read") to abilities ("no wonder, he has low ability"). It is the very act of reading, however, that could foster precisely the verbal abilities that are employed as an explanation for lack of reading!

The key point that must always be recognized is that print exposure is both a consequence of developed reading ability and, as we have seen above, a facilitator of further development of aspects of verbal intelligence. I have previously discussed[38] how the failure to recognize such reciprocal effects characterizes practices in the field of special education, where educational designations—learning disability being the most salient example—are created based on a discrepancy between achievement in reading and ability (intelligence). Theoretically, these reciprocal effects serve to undermine the logic of discrepancy measurement in special education because they destroy the distinction between aptitude and achievement. Practically, such reciprocal effects raise the issue of whether we really want to withhold certain types of educational treatments from children whose poor reading is accompanied by equally subpar aptitudes or abilities when we know that the poor reading may at least in part be a direct cause of the low verbal abilities.

Consider a further implication. The research reported here supports the increasing concern voiced by reading educators that we have focused our attention too much on reading comprehension viewed as an ability rather than on the habits and acts that surround literacy itself. Simply put, there are increasing indications that we are producing children who can read but simply choose not to do so. Thus, we are producing what might be called a second-level disability, sometimes called aliteracy. As far as unlocking the world's storehouse of knowledge, many people might as well be having basic ability problems—they appear to be so little better off for having the skills. In short, we are teaching the basic skills of reading as well as we ever did,[39] but our performance in the domain of fostering positive reading habits and attitudes falls short. The importance of treating the latter as an indicator variable is reinforced by the data presented above showing that the positive consequences of print exposure can occur independently of ability.

Finally, from the standpoint of teacher morale, a focus on fostering reading habits seems motivated. Reading education has been dogged by indicators that are minimally sensitive to instructional effects. Reading comprehension tests constructed in the typical manner are a case in point. Conceiving reading as a stable cognitive ability, they are not designed to track more malleable instructional effects.[40] Treating reading habits as an indicator variable would give teacher efforts a fairer chance to be reflected in assessment.

In summary, the push to immerse children in literature and to increase their amount of free reading is already an ongoing educational practice. Teachers often look to researchers for evidence to justify current trends. In the domain of print exposure they appear to have such justification. We are not overselling literacy.

End Notes

1. P.H. Wagschal, "Illiterates With Doctorates: The Future of Education in an Electronic Age," *The Futurist* (Aug. 1978): 243.
2. T. McConaghy, "Media Literacy Mandated in Ontario English Curriculum," *Phi Delta Kappan* 70.5 (1989): 332–333.
3. McConaghy 1989: 333.
4. Neil Postman, *Amusing Ourselves to Death* (New York: Penguin Books, 1986) 94.
5. Joshua Hammer, "A Golden Boy's Toughest Sell," *Newsweek* 19 Feb. 1990: 52.
6. Scott Heller, "Press for Campus Diversity Leading to More Closed Minds, Say Critics," *Chronicle of Higher Education* 8 Nov. 1989: 22.
7. Robert Reinhold, "Losing the Race," *New York Times* 7 Jan. 1990: Sec. 4A: 22.
8. Wagschal 1978.
9. Michael Apple, *Teachers & Texts*, (New York: Routledge, 1988).
10. R.C. Solomon, "Literacy and the Education of Emotions," *Literacy, Society, and Schooling*, eds. S. deCastell, A. Like, and K. Egan. (Cambridge: Cambridge University Press, 1986) 37–58.
11. P. Hasselriis, and D.J. Watson, "Language Arts Basics: Advocacy vs. Research," *Whole Language: Beliefs and Practices, K–8*, eds. G. Manning, and M. Manning. (Washington, D.C.: National Education Association, 1989) 28.
12. Brian Street, *Literacy in Theory and Practice*, (Cambridge: Cambridge University Press, 1984).
13. For example see J. Sledd, "A Basic Incompetence in the Defining of Basic Competencies," *English Journal* 75.7 (1986) 26–28; see also Street 1984.
14. Paulo Freire, *Education for Critical Consciousness* (New York: Seabury Press, 1973); Paulo Freire, and Donaldo Macedo, *Literacy: Reading the Word and the World* (South Hadley, MA: Bergin & Garvey, 1987).
15. E. Ellsworth, "Why Doesn't This Feel Empowering? Working Through the Repressive Myths of Critical Pedagogy," *Harvard Educational Review* 59 (1989): 298.

16. Frank Smith, "Overselling Literacy." *Phi Delta Kappan* 70.5 (1989): 354.

17. See J. Edwards, and K. Gorman, "Does Rising Literacy Spark Economic Growth? Commercial Expansion in Mexico," *The Future of Literacy in a Changing World,* ed. D.A. Wagner (Oxford, England: Pergamon Books, 1987); J.P. Gee, "The Legacies of Literacy: From Plato to Freire through Harvey Graff," *Harvard Educational Review* 58 (1988): 195–212; D. Olson, "Literate Thought," *Understanding Literacy and Cognition: Theory, Research, and Application,* eds. C. Leong, and B. Rundhawna (New York: Plenum Publishing, In Press); and D. Wagner, "Literacy Futures: Five Common Problems from Industrializing and Developing Countries," *The Future of Literacy in a Changing World,* ed. D. Wagner (Oxford, England: Pergamon Books, 1987) 3–16.

18. See G. Miller, and P. Gildea, "How Children Learn Words," *Scientific American* 257.3 (1987): 94–99; Robert Sternberg, "Most Vocabulary is Learned from Context," *The Nature of Vocabulary Acquisition,* eds. M. McKeown, and M.E. Curtis (Hillsdale, NJ: Erlbaum, 1987); W. Nagy, and R. Anderson, "How Many Words Are There in Printed School English?" *Reading Research Quarterly* 19 (1984): 304–330; and W. Nagy, P.A. Herman, and R. Anderson, "Learning Words from Context," *Reading Research Quarterly* 20 (1985): 233–253.

19. See D.P. Hayes, "Speaking and Writing: Distinct Patterns of Word Choice," *Journal of Memory and Language* 27 (1988): 572–585; D. Hayes, and M. Ahrens, "Vocabulary Simplification for Children: A Special Case of 'Motherese'?" *Journal of Child Language* 15 (1988): 395–410; W. Nagy, and P. Herman, "Breadth and Depth of Vocabulary Knowledge: Implications for Acquisition and Instruction," *The Nature of Vocabulary Acquisition,* eds. M. Mckeown, and M.E. Curtis, (Hillsdale, NJ; Erlbaum, 1990); W. Nagy and R. Anderson, 1984; and Keith Stanovich, "Matthew Effects in Reading: Some Consequences of Individual Differences in the Acquisition of Literacy," *Reading Research Quarterly* 21 (1986).

20. Hayes and Ahrens 1988.

21. J.B. Carrol, P. Davies, and B. Richman, *Word Frequency Book* (Boston: Houghton-Mifflin, 1971).

22. Smith 1989: 354.

23. See K.W. Berger, *The Most Common 100,000 Words Used in Conversations* (Kent, Ohio: Herald Publishing House, 1977); and G.D. Brown, "A Frequency count of 190,000 Words in the London-Lund Corpus of English Conversation," *Behavior Research Methods, Instruments, and Computers* 16 (1984): 502–532.

24. W.N. Francis, and H. Kucera, *Frequency Analysis of English Usage: Lexicon and Grammar* (Boston: Houghton-Mifflin, 1982).

25. D. Olson, "Intelligence and Literacy: The Relationships Between Intelligence and the Technologies of Representation and Communication, *Practical Intelligence,* eds. R. Sternberg, and R.K. Wagner (Cambridge: Cambridge University Press, 1986).

26. Richard Anderson, Paul Wilson, and Linda Fielding, "Growth in Reading and How Children Spend Their Time Outside of School," *Reading Research Quarterly* 23.3 (1988): 285–303.

27. See A. Cunningham, and K. Stanovich, "Assessing Print Exposure and Orthographic Processing Skill in Children: A Quick Measure of Reading Experience," *Journal of Educational Psychology* (In Press); and K. Stanovich, and R. West, "Exposure to Print and Orthographic Processing," *Reading Research Quarterly* 24 (1989): 402–433.

28. See Philip Ennis, *Adult Book Reading in the United States*, National Opinion Research Center Report No. 105 (Chicago: University of Chicago, 1965); D.L. Paulhus, "Two-Component Models of Socially Desirable Responding," *Journal of Personality and Social Psychology* 46 (1984) 598–609; and A.T. Sharon, "What Do Adults Read?" *Reading Research Quarterly* 9 (1973–1974): 148–169.

29. For example see Anderson et al., 1988; and V. Greaney, "Factors Related to Amount and Time of Leisure Time Reading," *Reading Research Quarterly* 15 (1980): 337–357.

30. See Charles A. Perfetti, *Reading Ability* (New York: Oxford University Press, 1985); Keith Stanovich, "Toward an Interactive-Compensatory Model of Individual Differences in the Development of Reading Fluency," *Reading Research Quarterly* 16 (1980): 32–71; and Stanovich, "Matthew Effects."

31. Stanovich, "Matthew Effects."

32. Anderson et al., 1988; C. Juel, "Learning to Read and Write: A Longitudinal Study of 54 Children from First through Fourth Grades," *Journal of Educational Psychology* 80 (1988): 437–447; and Stanovich, "Matthew Effects."

33. See S. Scarr, and K. McCartney, "How People Make Their Own Environments," *Child Development* 54 (1983): 424–435; Stanovich, "Matthew Effects"; and R. Sternberg, *Beyond IQ: A Triarchic Theory of Human Intelligence* (Cambridge University Press, 1985).

34. For example see Street 1984.

35. Smith 1989: 354.

36. See A.B. Cattell, *Abilities: Their Structure, Growth, and Action* (Boston: Houghton Mifflin, 1971); E. Hunt, "The Next Word on Verbal Ability," *Speed of Information-Processing and Intelligence*, ed. P.A. Verron (Norwood, NJ: Ablex, 1987); J.B. Sincoff, and R.J. Sternberg, "Two faces of Verbal Ability," *Intelligence* 11 (1987): 263–276; L.L. Thurstone, *Primary Mental Abilities* (Chicago: University of Chicago Press, 1938); and P.E. Vernon, *The Structure of Human Abilities* (London: Methuen, 1971).

37. See M. Chen, J. Holman, J. Francis-Jones, and L. Burmester, "Concepts of Intelligence of Primary School, High School and College Students," *British Journal of Developmental Psychology* 6 (1988): 71–82; R.J. Sternberg, "Implicit Theories: An Alternative to Modeling Cognition and its Development," *Formal Models in Developmental Psychology*, eds. J.

Bisanz, C. Brainerd, and R. Rail (New York: Viking, 1988); and R.J. Sternberg, B. Conway, J. Ketron, and M. Bernstein, "People's Conceptions of Intelligence," *Journal of Personality and Social Psychology* 41 (1981): 37–55.

38. Keith Stanovich, "Cognitive Processes and the Reading Problems of Learning Disabled Children: Evaluating the Assumptions of Specificity," *Psychological and Educational Perspectives on Learning Disabilities*, eds. J. Torgensen, and B. Wong (New York: Academic Press; 1986); and Keith Stanovich, "Has the Learning Disabilities Field Lost Its Intelligence?" *Journal of Learning Disabilities* 22 (1989): 487–492.

39. L. Stedman, and C. Kaestle, "Literacy and Reading Performance in the United States, from 1880 to the Present." *Reading Research Quarterly* 12 (1987): 8–46.

40. D.R. Cross, and S.G. Paris, "Assessment of Reading Comprehension: Matching Test Purposes and Test Properties," *Educational Psychologist* 22 (1987): 313–332.

41. Hayes and Ahrens 1988.

16

Culture, Curriculum, and Canon

E.D. Hirsch, Jr. and James D. Watkinson

E.D. Hirsch, Jr. established a solid reputation as a literary scholar with his influential books *The Aims of Interpretation* and *Validity in Interpretation*. He made his mark in the field of college composition with his book *The Philosophy of Composition*. He became a force for elementary and secondary educators to reckon with, however, when he began his campaign for cultural literacy. His books *Cultural Literacy* and *A Dictionary of Cultural Literacy* are mass-market bestsellers. He has traveled tirelessly promoting his ideas and lately has established the Cultural Literacy Foundation to institutionalize his efforts to get more information into the school curriculum. Here Mr. Hirsch and James Watkinson, who is director of the Cultural Literacy Foundation, explain why cultural literacy should be a central goal in literacy education, and then argue that we should choose books for children to read in service to the goal of cultural literacy.

Is there, or should there be, a literary canon for children? The same question, asked at the level of higher education, has been the cause of fierce debate and has yielded little satisfaction for anyone involved in the discussion. While there has long been the assumption that institutions of higher education should be, in the words of Ezra Cornell, places where "any person can find instruction in any study," thus almost begging canonical debate, few have doubted that children can and should be told what they will learn and when they should learn it. Is there any point, then, in even posing the question with regard to elementary education in America? Not really.

233

Schooling rests on the assumption that there are certain things all children should know. To engage in a debate over a literary canon would obscure a more important issue. In the first place, when one speaks of a canon—whether it be Biblical, Straussian, or literary— all of the choices made in establishing it are necessarily arbitrary and only encourage further, often futile debate. Time is wasted, little is solved. Second, there is already far too much emphasis on fiction in the language arts. A literary canon for children would simply encourage this wrong-headed scheme. What is more important is that children have the background knowledge to understand fully and appreciate any literature or learning with which they might be presented. If anything, then, children need a canon of information, not a canon of literature.

At present, many of America's schoolchildren, especially those from so-called disadvantaged homes, do not have this knowledge, nor are our schools providing it. The curricula in American schools are too fragmented to remedy this situation, let alone help to formulate a canon. If America is no longer to be "a nation at risk," if all children are to have an equal opportunity to obtain a quality education, curricular change is paramount. Curriculum reform can provide the requisite knowledge. Once this reform was in place, if a school district felt the urge, some canon might be generated. Until that basic curricular change can be instituted, however, discussion of a canon is premature and harmful.

The decline of American literacy and the fragmentation of the American school curriculum have been chiefly caused by the growing dominance of romantic formalism in educational theory during the past half century. We have too readily blamed shortcomings in American education on social changes (the disorientation of the American family or the impact of television on reading and study) or incompetent teachers or structural flaws in our school systems. But the chief blame should fall on faulty theories promulgated in our schools of education and accepted by educational policymakers.

Consider William Raspberry's comments on test results that show that black students score 35 to 45 percent lower than white students in standardized achievement tests. And while the most recent tests have shown minority gains, they still lag far behind white scores.

The news hits like a series of bombshells as one suburban school district after another reveals that black children are significantly behind their white counterparts on standardized achievement tests. . . Whose fault is it that blacks tend to get lower scores? I don't know all the answers to that one. Surely a part of it is the simple fact that those children who come to school already knowing a good deal of what the society deems important to know tend to find it easier to learn more of it. The more you know, the more you can learn.

We know that Raspberry is right, not only about achievement tests but also about reading and writing ''skills.'' ''The more you know, the more you can learn.'' What does his judgment imply for schooling? Some children, he says, enter school already possessing the information needed to make further advances in the literate culture, while others come to school lacking the information.

Why have we failed to give them the information they lack? Chiefly because of educational formalism, which encourages us to ignore the fact that imparting the information a child is missing is most important in the earliest grades, when the task is most manageable. At age six, when a child must acquire the knowledge that is critical for continuing development, the total quantity of missing information is not huge. As Dr. Jeanne Chall has pointed out, the technical reading skills of disadvantaged children at age six are still on a par with those of children from literate families. Yet only a year or so later, their reading skills begin to diverge according to socioeconomic status, chiefly because low-income pupils lack elementary cultural knowledge. More recently, in the *Handbook of Reading Research,* data have come to light that reinforce Dr. Chall's conclusions and Mr. Raspberry's intuitions. The graph in figure one tells a sad tale, as you can see.[1] Under present school arrangements, children who start kindergarten with a low oral vocabulary fall increasingly behind their more advantaged classmates as they progress through school. American schooling, rather than narrowing the reading and learning gap between the haves and have-nots, widens it.

Consider for a moment why the graph looks this way. We have noted that knowledge begets knowledge, that literacy and knowledge depend on each other. If you already know a lot and have a relatively large literate vocabulary, you can understand what teachers and the texts are saying. If you don't have a large literate vocabulary, you can't understand the teacher's remarks well enough to learn much that is new.

The widening gap represented in this graph is the consequence of a snowball effect. The minds of children with a small literate vocabulary are like smooth beach balls rolling through the snow of literate speech that surrounds them in school. They don't pick up as many new flakes as children who have a thicker covering of literate culture and accumulate ever more knowledge and vocabulary in the course of the school day. So the gap in literacy and learning skills between the groups begins to snowball.

Supplying missing knowledge to children early is, therefore, of tremendous importance for enhancing their motivation and intellectual self-confidence, not to mention their subsequent ability to learn new material. Yet schools will never systematically impart missing background information as long as they continue to accept the formalistic principle that specific information is irrelevant to language arts skills. And what good is a language arts canon if a child cannot understand it?

Consider, too, this important but little-known fact: The reading ability of a normal child becomes approximately equal to his or her listening ability by the seventh grade—no matter what methods have been devoted to the teaching of mechanical skills. By grade seven, the limiting factor in reading (and therefore learning) ability is not mechanical but intellectual. A child with a broad literate vocabulary will understand written language as effectively as spoken language. By the same token, a child with a small literate vocabulary will understand them both equally badly. The limiting factor in reading and learning is vocabulary. And, since words stand for things, the limiting factor in vocabulary is knowledge.

Perhaps the main flaw of educational formalism is that it assumes that the specific contents used to teach language arts do not matter so long as they are closely tied to what the child already knows. This developmental approach ignores Raspberry's important point that different children know different things. Current schoolbooks in language arts pay little systematic attention to conveying a body of multiculturally significant information from grade to grade. Their developmental approach contrasts sharply from textbooks from earlier decades and ignores reputable research by cognitive psychologists. Texts now used to teach reading and writing are screened not for the information they convey but for their readability scores and their fit with the sequence of abstract skills that a child is expected to acquire. On this skills model, the ideal method of language arts instruction would be to adjust the reading curriculum to the interests and competencies of each child. When this formalistic approach was developed, the information explosion seemed to make the mere assimilation of facts a fruitless, even cruel exercise. It appeared to be highly enlightened not to stuff children's minds with traditional facts that had no interest for them nor any direct bearing on their current lives.

If this nontraditional approach had worked, we should emphatically wish to follow it, for it would be at once both pleasant and motivational. The approach has, however, failed miserably. In recent years, according to a comparison made by the IEA, educational achievement in the United States has steadily declined and has placed dead last among the developed nations not just in science but in all other subjects tested. Diane Ravitch and Chester Finn demonstrated the pronounced lack of knowledge about the humanities among high school juniors. Recently, the Secretary of Education was forced to admit the lack of geographic literacy among American students.

The nontraditional approach has caused American educators to miss the opportunity of teaching young (and older) children the traditional materials that make up literate culture. This is a tragically wasteful mistake that deprives them of information they would continue to find useful in later education and life. The inevitable effects of this fundamental educational mistake have been the precipitous decline of American students' performance when compared with the rest of the world. It has also caused a gradual disintegration in our cultural memory, causing a decline in our ability to communicate.

There is, however, a way of reversing the decline. What is needed is to instill in the minds of our youngest students what was called at the beginning of this essay a canon of information. The responsibility for reversing the downward trend falls necessarily to the language arts teachers in the elementary grades. Language arts has now grown so large as to incorporate much of what is learned in early schooling. The language arts teachers have America's schoolchildren for the majority of their first four years in school. If progress is to be made in all subject areas, language arts itself—which encompasses most subject areas in elementary education—must be fundamentally changed. Again, there's far too much emphasis now on fiction and far too little on fact.

When I [Mr. Hirsch] wrote *Cultural Literacy,* I rejected the phrase *core curriculum.* This has since been rethought and now the term is embraced, as better describing what was originally called the *extensive curriculum.* A school's curriculum should be still be thought of as consisting of two complementary parts: a core curriculum—a canon of information—that takes up to 50 percent of teaching time and is shared nationwide, and a local curriculum that emphasizes whatever the school or teacher believes should be stressed in addition. The core consists of the traditional, multicultural literate knowledge—the information, attitudes, and assumptions that literate Americans share and that all American schoolchildren need to learn. This core must not be taught just as a series of terms or disembodied facts but as a vivid system of shared associations. The name John Brown should evoke in children's minds not just a simple identifying definition but a whole network of lively traits, the traditionally known facts, and values.

The nature of this world knowledge as it exists in the minds of literate adults is typically elementary and fragmented. People reliably share just a few associations about canaries, such as yellow, sing, kept in cages, but not much more. Literate people know who Falstaff is, that he is fat, likes to eat and drink, but they can't reliably name the Shakespeare plays in which he appears. They know who Eisenhower was and might recognize "military-industrial complex," but they can't be counted on to state anything else about Eisenhower's Farewell Address.

If a high school teacher today wishes to have his or her students read Martin Luther King's "Letter from the Birmingham Jail"—that powerful document of the civil rights movement—the teacher must pause and consider whether or not the students have the wherewithal to grasp what is being said. Within the first two pages Dr. King makes reference to St. Augustine, St. Thomas Aquinas, Paul Tillich, Martin Buber, Nebuchadnezzar, and Adolf Hitler. To whom was Dr. King writing? He was certainly not addressing solely his old theology professors. No. He wanted to reach Americans, black and white, young and old, and assumed that most of his readers would be able to grasp the allusions he made that helped make this document so powerful.

Or consider the problem of the teacher from a northern Virginia high school who appeared on a talk show with Maya Angelou. The teacher sadly noted that he found it almost impossible to teach *I Know Why the Caged Bird Sings* because most of his students could not understand the allusions Ms. Angelou employed in her book.

Students' possession of the limited information mentioned here is a necessary preliminary to their acquiring more detailed information. Thus to understand the full text of Dwight Eisenhower's Farewell Address and the historical circumstances that gave rise to it, they have to know who Eisenhower was and what a farewell address is in the American tradition. To understand Dr. King's letter students must know who Martin Luther King, Jr. was and, since he was a preacher, that he used the Bible and biblical references intensively when writing or speaking. The core curriculum would be designed to ensure that our students are given this information, over time, from the earliest grade.

But the core curriculum is not a sufficient basis for education by itself. It is simply a minimal description of the elements that should be included in every child's schooling, no matter what form the schooling takes. The core curriculum can be taught in a highly formal traditional school or in a more informal progressive school. Any kind of school can find ways of incorporating these contents in its course, given a determination to do so and coordination among grade levels in deciding on the appropriate times for introducing particular aspects of particular subjects.

The other half of the curriculum—the intensive curriculum—though different, is equally essential. Intensive study encourages a fully developed understanding of a subject, making one's knowledge of it integrated and coherent. It coincides with Dewey's recommendation that children should be deeply engaged with a small number of typical concrete instances. It is also that part of the curriculum in which great flexibility in contents and methods can prevail. The intensive curriculum lends even more pluralism to our proposal, because it ensures that individual students, teachers, and schools can work intensively with materials that are appropriate for their diverse cultures, ethnic backgrounds, temperaments and aims.

This concept of the two-part curriculum, then, while suggesting that children do need to learn some of the same things, avoids the idea of a canon, if that is taken to mean that all high school students should study, say, *Romeo and Juliet.* A proper curriculum should ensure that students have some information about *Romeo and Juliet,* but in their intensive curriculum they might study *Twelfth Night* or *The Tempest* in detail. If a school decided that all of its students should read two Shakespeare plays, or two works by Toni Morrison, most language arts/English teachers would have a hard time deciding which plays or works should be read. Schools can find the means of imparting core knowledge side by side with intensive knowledge without imposing an arbitrary canon.

Unlike children of today, the Major-General in Gilbert and Sullivan's *Pirates of Penzance* had plenty of core knowledge; it was the intensive he had missed:

> I am the very model of a modern Major-General,
> I've information vegetable, animal, and mineral,
> I know the Kings of England, and I quote the fights historical,
> From Marathon to Waterloo, in order categorical.

These "cheerful facts" are all the Major-General knows, and they were the intellectual baggage possessed by every literate schoolboy in nineteenth-century Britain. Everyone in Gilbert's audience knew those same facts, and this extensive information made them no better at military strategy than it made Major-General Stanley:

> When I have learnt what progress has been made in modern gunnery,
> When I know more of tactics than a novice in a nunnery:
> In short, when I've a smattering of elementary strategy,
> You'll say a better Major-General has never sat a gee.

Instead of being able to name the fights historical, if the Major-General had studies at least a battle or two in some detail—Austerlitz or Waterloo—he might have developed a coherent idea of nineteenth-century warfare. Thereafter, any new fact about battles that he encountered could have been accommodated to the mental model that he had gained from intensive study of the Battle of Waterloo. To understand how isolated facts fit together in some coherent way, we must acquire mental models of how they cohere, and this can some only from detailed, intensive study and experience.

Almost any battle will do to gain a coherent idea of battles. Any Shakespeare play will do to gain a schematic conception of Shakespeare; it doesn't matter whether the play read in ninth grade is *Macbeth* or *Julius Caesar.* Our choice of canonical materials can vary with circumstances and should depend on many grounds for choice, including student and teacher interest, local and community preferences, and the aims that predominate in particular schools or classrooms. There is a limit, however, to the flexibility of the intensive curriculum. If we want people to have a conception of Shakespeare drama, then a play by Amiri Baraka is not a satisfactory substitute for a play by Shakespeare, or vice-versa.

All of the foregoing should make clear that talk of a literary canon for elementary or secondary schools is, for the most part, irrelevant, though many seem fascinated with the idea of a canon. If schools or districts choose to create a literary canon for their students, they must realize that their choices will necessarily be limited by the preparatory background knowledge they have provided their children. Otherwise, any canon of literature will be lost upon them. It does little good to insist that a child read Martin Luther King's speech in which he proclaims, ''I have been to the mountain top, and I have seen the promised land . . . I may not get there with you, but . . . as a people, we will get to the promised land,'' unless the child knows about Moses, for it is the end of the story of Moses that gives King's words their peculiar resonance. Similarly, it does no good to refer to Harriet Tubman as ''Black Moses'' while teaching unless the students know the same story.

Without the core curriculum to give all children the requisite background knowledge, Shakespeare, Morrison, Melville, Hurston, Hemingway and any other authors one chooses will be poorly understood and perhaps irrelevant. A greater waste of children's minds and teachers' time can hardly be imagined.

When asked to write a piece for this book, Professor Temple was good enough to send along some drafts of other papers that were to be included. We were particularly struck by the piece by Joy Moss, and not necessarily because of the discussion by precocious nine-year olds about Icarus, Pegasus, and biblical references such as ''pride before the fall.''[2] Rather, we were taken by her assertion that ''literary, literacy, and content learning are complementary and interrelated when fiction and nonfiction are integrated in content area learning." Ms. Moss and the subjects of her study are on the right track, as is evidenced by the nature of the students' comments during the discussion. However, her further contention that "literature serves as the springboard for inquiry and discovery about the human experience, the arts and science, the world we live in" gives too much credit, we fear, to fiction. If she means, however, that canonical information can be conveyed through narrative, in the manner suggested by Kieran Egan in his book *Teaching as Story Telling*, then we agree wholeheartedly.[3] This is the path we must take in the language arts curriculum—narrative to convey a canon of information. Let's forget about a "kiddie kanon."

End Notes

1. Graph appears in T.J. Sticht and J.H. James, "Listening and Reading," ed. P.D. Pearson, *Handbook of Reading Research* (New York, 1984) 293–308.
2. See Joy Moss, "Literature in the Elementary Classroom: Making Connections & Generating Meaning," in this volume.
3. Kieran Egan, *Teaching as Story Telling: An Alternative Approach to Teaching in the Elementary School*, (Chicago: University of Chicago Press, 1986).

17

Firing Canons and Maintaining Boundaries

Jill May

Jill May teaches children's literature at Purdue
University and is the past Publications Chair of
the *Children's Literature Association Quarterly*. Trained as a children's librarian, she has been
a central participant in professional debates
about what constitutes good or lasting children's
literature, arguments that sometimes take the
form of debates over a literary canon or a core
list of great works in children's literature.

When I was asked to determine whether children's literature had a
canon of literary works and, if it did, to discuss how these works might
be taught to children, I was both delighted and perplexed. Trained
in literary analysis at a time when English professors stood in front
of classes and taught undergraduates how to "read the text" in the
correct way, I have a history of uneasiness with the scholarly pursuit
of excellence. Although I was too inexperienced and naive to question the professor's reading of the text or to ask him how he had chosen
what it was that I should be reading at the time, I was old enough to
suspect that what he was presenting was largely his opinion. Since
I never asked, I never discovered that his choices had largely been
predetermined for him by others and that his interpretations were
a reflection of his acceptance of traditional standards that evolved
from cultural values.

Even then I had unanswered questions about the texts we were
reading: I wondered why women had not written more important
works; I wished that every novel's plot was not somehow consumed
with war, love, and marriage, intensified by woman's dependence on

others or willful wickedness towards men; I sensed a need to devise private schemes of analysis that made me uneasy because I knew if I shared them on an essay exam I would fail the exam. In short, I felt out of place in my favorite field. The canon of literature boxed me in and made me feel somehow inferior to those males around me who immediately agreed with the professor that the texts being read constituted "culture" and that there was an absolute interpretation for a particular text.

In those days, university professors didn't tell you that there was a canon of literature. They didn't talk about their trips to conferences to hear scholarly papers about the books considered to be empirical. And so, the typical literature student had no inkling about the field's privileging of knowledge. We knew that Washington Irving and F. Scott Fitzgerald were minor writers, not really worthy of serious study, because we had been told they were. Rarely were women mentioned; in fact, not one of my classes mentioned the contributions of Virginia Woolf or Jane Austen, gaps that seem strange to me now when I remember that my concentration for study was British literature. Since we didn't have to read any of the above authors and compare them to Henry James or Tobias Smollett, we didn't consider how they differed from Tennyson or Dickens; how we, as new readers of the classics, felt when we read authors from different eras who had caused a sensation when their books were first released and who continued to be published and read throughout the years. We were told what the hidden meanings were for the texts we read and then we considered why the author placed the symbolism into his text, but we never were allowed to question if the text worked for us. We were learning about works, not determining their values for ourselves. Professors could consider students the vacant vessels ready to be filled with literary standards. In turn, the students would one day pour their acquired knowledge into another generation of novices.

When I entered graduate library school I was given the dubious task of weeding the historical collection at Madison's Children's Book Center, and I was on my way to my first exercise in canon formation. I relied on the catalog from the Osbourne Collection in Toronto. I consulted Meigs's *A Critical History of Children's Literature: A Survey of Children's Books in English from Earliest Times to the Present*, Arbuthnot and Sutherland's *Children and Books*, and books like Gillian Avery's *Nineteenth Century Children*. If the author, artist, or book was mentioned and described, I would place the book in the proper place on the shelves. Otherwise, out it went. I was not asked to read the books or to consider what would happen once the books were lost to future scholars. My opinions were not considered relevant since earlier scholars in the field had already decided how I should react. All that was needed was reference work to discover what others had decided.

I was looking for group consensus from those who had already determined what was worth remembering. I was defining the boundaries of greatness, but I was not considering why certain books were being privileged, others were being discarded. At that time, I was not concerned about the authors who were being burned in the basement. Since I had been trained by English professors to discard the minor poets, I assumed that my job was a necessary one if children's literature was to become a legitimate subject for literary study. I was firing off my first canon, but I was not making intellectual choices.

My studies in English literature had convinced me that I could not make literary decisions on my own. Since it was never suggested that I should read the books and determine their values for myself, I did not consider that there might be arguments about what was canonical. As a long time recipient of past knowledge who had been taught not to question "the right interpretation," I felt my job was to identify and preserve the materials that others had labeled as quality reading for future generations.

I was ignoring the concept that all literature might fit into a canon because I assumed the list had already been set, that I was simply identifying the books that belonged. I was not questioning literature. Recently, however, I had been given the right to question the rules of cataloging. My cataloging teacher was an Arab who refused to be bound by the Library of Congress. What if, he maintained, we had to establish rules that would be acceptable to varying cultures in the world? This man was demanding that we read cataloging theory from around the world, that we consider why American rules would not work for everyone. Although I did not appreciate his teaching, largely because he resigned himself to the attitude that we would probably all work in America and therefore had to know American standards while at the same time preaching against the system we were using, I learned that diversity in thinking did exist. Even in cataloging there were renegade systems.

I no longer believe that books on canons should be chosen because they have been placed on past critical lists of excellence. Surely, each generation needs to reevaluate greatness for itself. I have traveled beyond my beginning years as a student of English; I will not accept someone else's opinion of what is great. And, I no longer believe that teachers, librarians, or university scholars have the right to choose materials based on their experiences alone. I am afraid that they will reify their favorites, naming them the "literary masterpieces" that everyone should read and discuss, while they ignore mine. I would argue that everyone has the right to choose books that speak to them; that cause them to think in new and different ways.

Yet, I know that canons have inevitably evolved for children's literature. Lists do exist, and teachers in elementary schools do depend upon them. Note that I said canons and lists; unlike Shakespearian studies, experts in children's literature do not agree on one list of books. Yet, each list is taken quite seriously by a specific group of professionals who study and write about children and their literature. The lists reflect the diversity found within the field of children's literature.

The Newbery Medal award list, which began in 1922 under the auspices of the Children's Services Division of the American Library Association, reflects librarians' concern that they recognize the best contemporary United States authors. The list was not consciously created to establish what should be shared and taught, but indirectly it seemed to do just that. These books are selected for their "distinguished contribution to literature for children published in the United States during the preceding year by an author who was a United States citizen or who lived in the United States when the book was published." Thus, the listing can be interpreted as a catalog of what is best in contemporary United States children's literature during a particular year.

When I was in library school, I was told that any children's librarian worth her salt would order the books on the list as soon as it was released. These books were exemplary, and they should be the backbone of any children's library collection, I was informed. Once again, standards were being set without firm guidelines to follow. Since each year's committee membership varied, the lists varied.

The Newbery list was so successful that a second list was established in 1937 for picture book illustration. The Caldecott Award had the same stipulations about publication and residency as the Newbery, and as an award for illustration it acknowledged the importance of artistic design in children's books. Again, it became a standard ordering list for children's librarians.

As a field, elementary education has paid little attention to the placement of books in the curriculum, yet it has always supported the idea that good books should be shared and has relied heavily on librarians to help them find those books. Teacher educators seem to accept these lists. Oftentimes, teachers teach units in their language arts classes about the medals and have the students read a title from the lists. College professors in education teach their children's literature classes with units on the Caldecott and Newbery awards.

The lists are traditionally placed in appendices at the end of children's literature textbooks intended for future teachers and librarians. In most textbooks the lists are simply presented, suggesting that they are canons of literature.

Once established, these lists seemed to reflect what a group of trained professionals deemed most valuable in the field, but no one was exactly sure why these books were better than the others in the library. The committees who have selected the books have never been forced to discuss their choices, and so the lists have created contemporary "classics" based upon taste. Like all canons, the lists receive criticism.

Children's librarians complain that they cannot get children interested in the award winning books. Teachers suggest that the vocabulary and theme emphases of the Newbery books are not consistent with the literary and emotional development of children in elementary schools. Critics argue that the list does not acknowledge all genres equally; that minority literature is basically ignored, that the list is chosen by a select group of people who have all been trained to think in one way. However, neither ALA nor the world of children's literature has abandoned the lists. Teachers seem to like the idea that they will be teaching "quality" literature when they share these books.

There are other organizations that have established contemporary lists. The British and Canadian library associations have their own national lists of award winners and runners-up. Other lists concentrate upon an author's complete body of works. These lists are usually also found in children's literature textbooks.

Each year, committees make choices, and new sets of winners emerge. Thus, there is a continual updating of unofficial canons, which privilege certain authors and artists in the field of children's literature. The lists establish trends in children's publishing because they are recognized trendsetters in writing and illustrating for children. However, the books are chosen with little regard to the interests and attitudes of the children who will read them. They are lists of "good books" that some librarians and teachers feel every child should read. The lists, then, are designed and maintained to support the publishing industry and to show teachers what is best for children.

In the 1970s professors in English and foreign language departments began to teach children's literature. They felt that the lists only reflected current book selection practices of identifying "the right book for the right child at the right time." Traditionally trained as scholars who studied archetypal literature and who sought to explain how these books influenced the field of literature, they sensed a need for a classical canon. As members of the Modern Language Association, they sensed that literary authority came only to those areas of study that had a canon.

In his 1978 Children's Literature Association's presidential address ChLA's first president, Jon C. Stott, argued:

> . . .we still do not have a basic canon of works, something possessed by all other fields. I think that the ChLA could provide an invaluable service to teachers and researchers alike by working to establish a canon. . . . The establishment of a basic list would serve as a basis for a relatively uniform curriculum in university courses, something lacking now. We know that if a student takes an American fiction course, he'll have read Hawthorne, Melville, Twain, James, and so forth. What will a student who has taken children's literature have read?[1]

Stott went on to say that such a canon "is the sapping out of the field of scholarship and criticism" and thus suggested that canons set the perimeters of what should be studied and discussed. ChLA was firing off a purposeful canon of books that were important literary experiences.

Stott's argument called attention to the fact that literary canons are carefully maintained lists that encourage professors to teach similar books in similar ways. His arguments for a canon and for some standards in the field, while valid, caused some anger among librarians and educators. They had never studied canons or their formations, and they were uneasy about the call for a new list. Many had experienced literature in college classes like those I remember. To them, the call for a canon was an elitist call from English professors who wished to redefine children's literature as a scholarly field of study quite unlike it had been in the past. As novices to the idea of critical theory, they resented that there was a need to restructure the teaching of children's literature.

When the call came for a literary canon, I was teaching children's literature to education majors at Purdue University and was a member of the Children's Literature Association. Criticism had opened up in English departments, and new ideas were being discussed among its members. Because I attended ChLA meetings and listened to conference presentations that piqued my interest, I had read Northrop Frye and Louise Rosenblatt; I was aware of Virginia Woolf; I knew about the theories of Norman Holland, Alan Purves, and Richard Dorson. I listened to conference presentations about folklore by Priscilla Ord, a scholar actively involved in the American Folklore Society, and I argued theory and story reception with ChLA's past president, Jon Stott, and with Perry Nodelman, the recently appointed *ChLA Quarterly* editor.

I taught in a department of education while most of my ChLA friends taught in English departments, and I realized that our ultimate goals for literary studies might be slightly different. I assumed our divergence was healthy and so I dared to argue with people I perceived as authority figures, to try out new ideas about literature, its conventions, and its values in the school on new colleagues. I picked new children's books to share with my college students at the beginning of each year, feeling certain that I could learn as much as I would teach when my students and I discussed our interpretations and reactions to the books we read. In short, I felt very much at home in my favorite field.

This call for a canon seemed regressive because it seemed to suggest that there might be a set of books that everyone should read, a way to approach the literature that everyone should adhere to, and that frightened me. It seemed to me a call against my newly acquired freedom of thought. My first reactions, then, were ones of conflict.

In the 1980s Perry Nodelman wrote that ChLA's canon search came from a sense of responsibility. There should be a list of books everyone in the field would know, he claimed. However, Nodelman argued, canons were not usually created by committees in meetings. They have evolved from the literature itself. He concluded,

> What has become clear to me is that, in the long run, we are trying to "develop" a canon. In fact, we seem to be acting in faith that a canon already exists, that we already know which books belong in it but we simply have never got around to making ourselves conscious of our choices.[2]

This canon firing was a conscious act, based on someone's perceived standards of excellence, yet no one on the committee seemed interested in sharing those standards so that I could reconsider the veracity of the choices. Even as he worked on the canon formation committee, Nodelman acknowledged that the standards were not clear. He wrote: "There are lots of good books; but how can we distinguish between the merely good ones and the very good ones, between the merely important and the essentially significant? I have no answers to those questions."[3]

If a committee is allowed to establish standards without having to come to grips with its decisions, it is given too much power. Those who choose for the future of literary studies must define what the boundaries mean. Consideration must also be given to minority opinion. Too often in the past, once boundaries are set, academia has been more prone to maintain them than break them down. If titles were accepted as the books to read, professors could teach those books without considering other choices.

Wasn't this what I had earlier experienced as an undergraduate? What would stop the next generation of children's literature professors from teaching their subject the way I had learned English literature? Nodelman maintained that the canon already existed; it simply had to be consciously chosen. That bothered me since it implied that this empirical "we" (to which I was not a privileged member) already possessed some sort of special knowledge, which I did not. Once they shared it, did I have a right to disagree? Could I break down the boundaries, or were they always to remain the same?

And yet, I wanted a canon. How else could the literary arguments that I enjoy and wanted to share with my college students and with elementary school students exist? Didn't we need shared texts, some understanding of literary patterns and genres, famous authors and artists in order to agree to discuss our perceptions of any text? Couldn't we best discuss new titles if we recalled past shared experiences and compared our earlier reader's responses to those more recent ones that depended upon the earlier books we read?

In the end, I accepted the committee's argument that the list would stimulate discussion. I acknowledged their need to change the list from a canon to a "touchstones list" because it seemed less offensive to those teaching and working outside of English departments. As the first publications chair for ChLA, I supported the venture to issue a pamphlet, published in 1984, which would include an annotated list of the books selected as touchstones, supplemented by a listing of "Some Other Noteworthy Authors and Illustrators." I also backed and supervised the publication of a three volume set of essays entitled *Touchstones: Reflections on the Best in Children's Literature* and edited by Nodelman.[4] The set contained an essay for each work or author or illustrator chosen to be on the list on the grounds that everyone ought to know what was chosen and why what was on the list might have been selected. I was reassured that there were some standards when Nodelman wrote in the first volume's introduction,

> A touchstone has to be unconventional enough to draw attention it itself, to cause controversy, perhaps to encourage imitators; it cannot be merely another excellent book of a conventional sort, another good historical novel, another fine fantasy, another excellent picture book.

I was still concerned, however, that the group not become tied to its canon, and I hoped that it would not dominate our discussion once what "always was already there" was made official.

It is reassuring to discover that the Children's Literature Association has not taken its canon too seriously. Although its annual conference usually includes one or more papers on books found on their touchstones list, far more time and energy are devoted to the discussion of other books and authors. In fact, by the time the canon was fully in place, the leadership seemed to be moving away from archetypal criticism: Many were becoming identified with Marxist and feminist criticism; some were beyond canonical criticism, into the new literary movement to deconstruct the literary canons; as a whole ChLA was more interested in considering reader response theory as it applied to the child than in discovering a new way for college students to respond to a classic children's book. While ChLA had fired off a canon, it was disinterested in maintaining boundaries for reading. Members were unwilling to argue for one way of approaching literature, for one set of texts from which to teach. They were moving beyond canons and beginning to pursue the idea that literary methods cannot be institutionalized into a textbook approach.

In 1984 the Children's Literature Association's Board and The Growing Child sponsored a Symposium on Teaching Literary Criticism in the Elementary Schools. As chair and organizer of the symposium, I invited experts in children's literature who were active members in ChLA and who had expressed an interest in schoolwide programs of literary studies. Various fields of literary criticism were represented. I included Professor Jack Zipes, a recognized Marxist critic with positive leanings toward feminist criticism; Professors Perry Nodelman and Virginia Wolf, both advocates of the work of Northrop Frye; Professor Carol Gay, a strong proponent of reader response and feminist studies; Sonia Landes, a critic who was actively working in the schools with children; and Professor Roderick McGillis, an eclectic critic who was interested in deconstruction at the time of the meeting. Others were chosen for their leadership qualities or their ability to guide group discussion of diverse theories.

For three days the group met in small sessions and addressed a variety of philosophical ideals. In the end a subcommittee was directed to take the resolutions from the discussion groups and to draft a formal statement which held the stances we all agreed upon. That group's work was presented at the last meeting of the symposium, and members unanimously agreed that it held the sentiments the members felt were essential for future curricula planning.

At the end of the symposium, the group presented the formal call for change to the ChLA Board. The statement was endorsed by the Board. That statement has remained the official philosophical stance for the members of the organization. It asserts the following:

1. The study of literature offers various sorts of information, but its main purpose is always a better appreciation of literature itself. The focus of literary studies must be on the text, not on how to use literature to promote other forms of learning.
2. Current classroom practice allows children to make what they wish out of a piece of literature, without any attempt to channel their responses or to focus their attention. We should show

children that texts have specific meanings and attitudes to communicate, and that even though different readers may interpret those meanings and attitudes in different ways, close readings will help the individual reader gain the most knowledge and information from literature.

3. Each work of literature is unique; one of the goals of criticism is to help readers appreciate that uniqueness.

4. There are recurring themes and patterns throughout literature. Readers should know about them and make use of that knowledge.

5. The goal of any program of literary study is to develop discernment: to show students the difference between distinctive and mediocre literature and to broaden their ability to appreciate the distinctive as well as the mediocre.

6. Different children have different needs at different times. A curriculum should be eclectic enough in its approach to offer a variety of different approaches to be used at different times.

7. Literary study is a process, pleasurable less in its results than in the search for those results. We must try to teach children the pleasure involved in the search for understanding rather than focus on the goal itself. Those with a deep attachment to literature are almost never content with their conclusions about it.

The group failed to mention any particular list of books as essential to the learning process. Instead, it called for a well designed literature program that would allow students to consider their responses in light of the opinions of others and would encourage students to consider why they read and how they read. It demanded teacher planned programs that fit the needs of local communities, a definite break from canonical thinking. It suggested that the common reader had as much to gain from exploring literature as the college professor had.

ChLA's attitudes fit with the then current arguments of such literary critics as William E. Cain and Robert Scholes. Scholes warned against teaching students to have "an attitude of reverence before texts" and called for a critical approach that taught a "judicious attitude: scrupulous to understand, alert to probe for blind spots and hidden agendas, and finally, critical, questioning, skeptical."[5] Cain argued against the authority of a canon, maintaining that reading a narrowly defined group of books denies students "the crucial skills— as well as the pleasures—that can be gained" by engaging them in close readings of diverse texts.[6] Literary scholarship was changing. It was moving away from canons, arguing for change, for new ways of considering literacy. Critics were suggesting that readers must learn not to trust the texts they read but to scrutinize them for hidden pleasures and meanings. They were suggesting that teachers should not teach what to think but should concentrate on showing readers different ways of thinking. There were those English professors who denounced the new theorists as heretics, as people who had forgotten the standards they had been taught; but the new voices would not be stilled, however, and they gained support from their students. Of course, they were calling from their ivory towers, and few Americans outside of their college classrooms heard their pleas.

At the same time a cry for a new standardization of learning was resounding across the United States. Student test scores were falling, even in suburbia, and governmental and societal leaders were concerned. Alarmed about our fall from literacy, subgroups began to study the official teaching methods found within the schools. Armed with data of past failures and successes, education leaders began to call for a more traditional education. They based their plans for change less on idealism, more on pragmatism.

In 1985 the report of the Commission on Reading, *Becoming a Nation of Readers*, was released. Prepared under the auspices of the National Academy of Education's Commission on Education and Public Policy, the report called for a change in reading instruction. The report admonished textbook teaching that emphasized skills over inquiry, but it fell short of suggesting that books other than textbooks could be effectively used to teach reading skills. And it supported a way of looking at learning throughout their report. The commission insisted that the teaching of reading was possible through textbooks, and it focused its attention on the need for "controlling the difficulty and appropriateness of textbooks" and for building "bridges that help young readers make the transition from simple stories to more complicated reading material."[7]

Thus, while literary scholars were arguing among themselves about the importance of literary canons, the public was being told by experts in education that textbooks should be more standardized, more controlled in vocabulary and in ideology. For me, the split was all too obvious. Just when I had begun to feel comfortable with the idea that literature could bring enlightenment, I was hearing that reading could bring literacy. Instinctively, I knew they were not the same. One had to do with the reader's being able to discover meaning for himself or herself, the other had to do with the reader's understanding how to read the way I expected it. Suddenly I felt at home in my field but very uncomfortable with the popular concepts of its values to others. It seemed to me that educators were calling for a canon that they could control, and that made me nervous.

Then, in 1987, two perfectly respectable scholars published impassioned pleas for ''their canons'' of learning. E.D. Hirsch Jr.'s *Cultural Literacy*[8] told its readers that there were basic terms, facts, and books that were common in our culture (see Hirsch and Watkinson's paper in this volume). He went on to compile a list of 5,000 things Americans should know. Hardly anyone knew all the facts or had read everything on Hirsch's list, however, and so his list fell short of changing American education. Allan Bloom's *The Closing of the American Mind* had more effect in the long run. Bloom's book immediately became a best seller. It was praised by book reviewers for the *New York Times Book Review*, *The Wall Street Journal*, and the *Chicago Tribune*. It was an instant success with those who shape education. As I read Bloom I suddenly knew why I had troubles with canons and their maintenance in our education.

Bloom writes convincingly. He is fluid, though he seems scholarly enough to appeal to intellectuals. His arguments seem tempered and judiciously delivered. However, interspersed within his cry for the return of a civilized education is a public mocking of new theory and of minority opinion. At last, he claims that the only right education is one that relies on the past. Bloom argues:

> Of course, the only serious solution is the one that is almost universally rejected: the good old Great Books approach, in which a liberal education means reading certain generally recognized classic texts, just reading them, letting them dictate what the questions are and the method of approaching them—not forcing them into categories we make up, not treating them as historical products, but trying to read them as the authors wished them to be read.... A good program of liberal education feeds the student's love of truth and passion to live a good life.[9]

Suddenly I understood my *déjà vu*. I was back to cataloging, only this time I had to decide whether my cataloging professor was right of not. Weren't there other systems than ours? Shouldn't we strive to establish ways of learning that are acceptable to varying cultures? Shouldn't we consider why canonical books with their prescribed ways of interpretation cannot work for everyone?

By now I have read enough literary theory to say yes to all of my questions, yet, like my cataloging teacher, I had to decide what should be done. Should I try to raise the consciousness of my college students, or for that matter of small children, about the narrowness of canons and then teach them a canon that already was? Or, should I break away from traditional thought?

Reading *The Graywolf Annual Five: Multi-Cultural Literacy* gave me my answer.[10] As I read James Baldwin's angry discussion of the American failure to be honest with the black child, Paula Gunn Allen's reinterpretation of Anglo/Native American relations, Gloria Anzaldua's call for a new mythic base in literary studies, and Michelle Cliff's lucid description of her dichotomous experiences in majority and minority cultural relationships, I realized that I had an obligation not to give in to a canon with rigid boundaries.

I will not advocate that teachers concentrate on an Anglo/Christian canon like the one developed by the Children's Literature Association. It is too narrow, too self enclosed. I will not say that the books on the lists like the Newbery and Caldecott are the best in contemporary literature. These lists rarely recognize minority writers who are creating literature about minority cultures. I cannot support the boundaries that would privilege my reading over someone else's simply because the books and criticism I read hold the goals common to the "American dream." If there is not one canon to teach, however, then what can I propose that we teach about literature?

I can suggest that we teach children what "always was already there" in the study of literature. I can emphasize that if we teach children to deconstruct cultural texts and canons they will learn to appreciate what those canons hold, to understand how authors manipulate canons, and to seek stories that give them a sense of self-realization.

I would begin by creating a curriculum that emphasizes that *man* has always told stories to explain *himself*, his relationships with others around *him*, and *his* place within the world as he perceives it. I would want children to understand that the stories they most enjoy give them an appreciation of who they are by combining past experiences with their understanding of the world around them. I will need to promote a curriculum that will show children that all cultures contain legends that explain how or why something happens or happened in a particular way. Furthermore, I will want to emphasize that any teacher who is building a literature program in the classroom must be familiar with the myths, legends, and customs of the children she is teaching. Teachers must know how to choose books that give positive responses and contrast the legends of various cultures so that she can emphasize that stories are similar yet each group of tales is unique to its own culture. I would have them share the creation stories from several cultures, comparing what is similar and what is different.

Teachers could share mythic stories, including those from the Bible, and talk about the evolution of cultural tales from the originals through writers' and storytellers' retellings for new, less scholarly, and devout audiences. They can point out how the symbolism that religious leaders use in their stories is later manipulated by authors when they write new stories. They can have the students explore the histories and geographies of the cultures and can suggest that our surroundings influence the ways we tell stories. They can begin to explore the ideas of cultural truths and meanings by allowing the children to see how certain tales become privileged; how legends give meanings to rituals until they become official icons within a particular culture.

If teachers are honest, they must let children know that there is not one correct story pattern in literature, that there are variations of plot structure within the dominantly taught Anglo tradition, and that there are further story variations in other cultures around the world. For instance, they could show how stories evolve from our oral tradition by sharing the tales of the Brothers Grimm and discussing the typical folkloric patterns of European cultures. They could compare these tales to the more modern literary fairy tales of Hans Christian Andersen and Jay Williams to show how authors create unique tales using familiar motifs, heroes and heroines, and story patterns to cause their readers to feel that they are experiencing a familiar cultural tale when they are hearing an ironic tale that reveals society's failings. They could also introduce the stories of Isaac Singer to show how the tales that evolved from the Jewish Polish settlements differ in tone and humor and in symbolism to the tales from the surrounding Christian communities. They can explore the Japanese folktales found in today's picture books and discuss the feeling of reverence to elders and nature and philosophies of trusting miracles and accepting fate, which are central in the original tales. They should compare the illustrations by Japanese artists to the artwork found on earlier produced Japanese scrolls and in Japanese traditional painting and suggest that those who interpret a tale from the outer edges of a culture see the tales with different perceptions, look at the uniqueness of another culture's tales in different ways, or totally overlook what they cannot interpret according to their own experiences.

Of course, I need not limit teachers to the German tales in order to explore the Anglo/Christian patterns found in oral literature. I could just as easily emphasize the French tales of Charles Perrault or the British tales collected by Joseph Jacobs. I would also want them to understand that in a school with an Hispanic or black or Arabic population, they should substitute or complement the Japanese and Jewish tales with literature from those cultures. As I teach students how to design the curriculum for any situation, I must remember that stories are explanations of ourselves, our attitudes, our customs, and our beliefs. When teachers work with a group of children, they need to help those children find themselves within the literature shared.

Teachers need to share some of the cultural tales from the ethnic groups in their classes. However, they should stress the uniqueness within the tales chosen and make a conscious effort to research their literature presentations. They must become involved in the history, folklore, religion, and cultural attitudes of those with whom they work if they are to share stories with them.

I want teachers to stress the idea that all stories contain mysteries and that all readers pursue the stories they choose if they are tempted to try to unravel the plot, if they feel an affinity with the characters, and if they can experience the thrill of the plot's adventure.

As real readers, children seek story patterns that are similar to those they have heard in the past. They will enjoy the pleasures of the unusual tale if they are allowed to explore the author's narrative, remembering that authors create stories based on their literary experiences and preferences. Teachers need to help the children they work with see that black American literature has an underlying thread of protest, that Hispanic literature is often created with a sense of biculturalism, that Native American stories contain a good deal of spirituality that is not easily explained by science. Together, they need to consider how a new experience from another culture can heighten their and the students' appreciation of the author's sense of narrative and use of persuasive rhetoric.

Finally, I would promote a program that allows children to become critics with a voice of their own. Such a program will encourage young readers to trust their real reader responses when they are reading a story for the first time. It will promote second readings that allow them to concentrate on the author's clues to the plot's action, identify the author's relationship to the created characters and scenes, and the author's reasons for writing this particular story. Once readers begin to consider the writer and the writer's culture, they move from real readers to implied ones and begin to sympathize with the author, to appreciate the craftsmanship in the story's structure. They need not, however, agree with the author's conclusion. They have a right to disagree, to reshape the arguments for themselves until they have meaning for their lives.

If I advocate that teachers work together to create a program that helps each reader understand how each new story fits into the world of story, I will inspire teachers to encourage real readers to respond in unique ways without fear that they are not getting "the right interpretation." Those children will understand why reading is a pleasurable but complex act that can never be a passive activity. They will understand that the author, the text, and the reader are involved in an interaction, and that the text comes alive when readers sense its purpose, when they appreciate its meaning as an interpretation of themselves, the people around them, and the world they live in.

End Notes

1. Jon C. Stott, "Presidential Address." *The Children's Literature Association Newsletter* 99 (Spring-Summer 1978): 9–12.
2. Perry Nodelman, "Children's Literature Canon Comment," *The First Step: Best of the Early ChLA Quarterly,* compiled by Patricia Dooley (West Lafayette, Indiana: ChLA Publications, 1984) 40.
3. Nodelman 1984, 69.
4. Perry Nodelman, ed., *Touchstones: Reflections on the Best in Children's Literature* (West Lafayette, Indiana: ChLA Publications, 1985, 1987, and 1989).
5. Robert Scholes, *Textual Power: Literary Theory and the Teaching of English* (New Haven: Yale University Press, 1985) 16.
6. William E. Cain, *The Crisis in Criticism: Theory, Literature, and Reform in English Studies* (Baltimore: The Johns Hopkins University Press, 1984) 262.
7. Richard Anderson, Elfrieda H. Hiebert, Judith A. Scott, and Ian A.G. Wilkinson, comps. *Becoming a Nation of Readers: The Report of the Commission on Reading* (Washington, D.C.: The National Institute of Education, 1985).
8. E.D. Hirsch, Jr., *Cultural Literacy: What Every American Needs to Know* (Boston: Houghton Mifflin, 1987).
9. Allan Bloom, *The Closing of the American Mind* (New York: Simon and Schuster Inc., 1987) 344–345.
10. Rick Simonson, and Scott Walker, eds., *The Graywolf Annual Five: Multi-Cultural Literacy* (St. Paul, Minnesota: Graywolf Press, 1988).

Works Cited

Perry Nodelman, "Grand Canyon Suite," *In The First Steps: Best of the Early ChLA Quarterly,* compiled by Patricia Dooley. West Lafayette, Indiana: ChLA Publications, 1984.

"The Report of the Symposium on Teaching Literary Criticism in the Elementary Grades." Unpublished document found in the archives of the Children's Literature Association.

18

Time, Stories, and the Well-Being of Children

Marvin Bram

Marvin Bram is Professor of History at Hobart and William Smith Colleges. Professor Bram is deeply concerned about our culture and our children and is a devoted reader of children's literature. We asked him, not facetiously, to tell us what has been going on in story telling for the last 10,000 years. He nodded and set to work at once; he then called back and asked if it was all right if he went back 200,000 years. Here, in the admittedly difficult piece that resulted ("I'm afraid the reader will have to study this paper and not just read it," he told us), he shows how shapes of stories are caught up with shapes of societies. He argues that humans were once capable of feats of imagination that have now fallen into disuse. If we tell a different sort of story, we may learn to use more of our minds. If we don't, we may exterminate ourselves.

A first grade class and I were able to meet out-of-doors, a short distance from school, one morning in June. We sat in a circle next to a young magnolia tree. I thought we could tell stories about our pets. A boy started to tell about his puppy. A girl across the circle from him couldn't restrain herself; she began a story before he finished. In a few minutes, everybody, including me, was talking, pretty much at once. The circle began to close the more animated we became. The schoolbus arrived at lunchtime—too soon. Two things happened then that I can't forget. When we got up to go, the first boy to have spoken put his arms around the tree and said, "Bye, Mom." While we were walking toward the bus, I learned that each of the children had actually heard all the stories: what was cacophony to me was repletion to them.

We have been telling stories, listening to stories, embellishing and trading stories, as long as we have occupied this planet. Stories have been moving through human communities no less continuously and intricately than food has been moving through them—each, stories and food, as essential to health as the other. Genetically modern humans, precisely like us in capacities if not in dress, have lived here for 200,000 years, so stories have a very long history indeed. They have also come in a variety of kinds, and there has been a corresponding variety of motives for telling them. What we will need to make some sense of this span of time and these story types and story aims is a rough, pertinent anatomy of thought process and chronology of cultures.

Let us divide the 200,000 years into two unequal segments and identify three kinds of human community. From 200,000 years ago, plus or minus 50,000 years, in Africa, to about 6,000 years ago, everywhere in the inhabitable world, we *homo sapiens* lived mainly as "equilibrium-kinship" peoples—the first kind of human community that interests us. In such communities, everyday lives, in small bands or in self-sufficient agricultural villages, were concerned with doing what one's kinspersons required be done. Everyone saw everyone one knew every day; elaborate lines of authority and bonds of affection were clear to everyone. It was a complex, compact life.

Six thousand years ago or so, at the northwestern tip of the Persian Gulf, in present-day Iraq, equilibrium-kinship peoples were displaced by "disequilibrium-civilized" peoples, our second kind of human community, for the first time. The quickest nontrivial way to characterize the history of planet Earth in the last 6,000 years is to call it the history of disequilibrium-civilization's spread, from one point in the Middle East to the entire world. The new, disequilibrium-civilized communities, rather than retaining the existing networks of equilibrium-kinship duties, pleasures, obligations, sanctions, and rituals, began to create unprecedented, simpler social forms, which required the coerced break-up of equilibrium-kinship. These new social forms came soon to resemble what we would now call *formal hierarchies:* hierarchical political structures (cities, empires, later nations), hierarchical economic structures (markets, corporations), hierarchical spiritual structures (religions), and so on. As each new mode of life took hold, the equilibrium-kinship of band and village receded into secondary and tertiary status. Only fragments of equilibrium-kinship survived, vulnerable to every variety of hierarchical ordering in growing disequilibrium-civilized cities.

Sometime around the origin of cities in the Middle East, or somewhat before, a second kind of kinship split off from the main kind. We might call this rogue branch "disequilibrium-kinship," our third large class of human communities. Disequilibrium-kinship worked through extended blood relationships, like the older equilibrium-kinship, but it favored patriarchal and warrior values, just as disequilibrium-civilization did.

How disequilibrium-kinship came into the world is a mystery. It may have arisen as a by-product of disequilibrium-civilization: as equilibrium-kinship was violently being displaced 6,000 years ago, some part of that ancient culture may have survived in a distorted, patriarchal, and violent form. That has not been an uncommon pattern in more recent history. Or disequilibrium-kinship may have arisen in the western steppeland of Eurasia in response to unusual conditions there: Mounted herding life between perhaps 4,000 and 8,000 years ago may have shaded by small degrees into something like a light-cavalry military life. Equilibrium-kinship had depended on foraging or farming, not on herding. However it was that disequilibrium-kinship began, it remained a major force in worldwide conflicts until early modern times, when the technological prowess of disequilibrium-civilizations simply eliminated disequilibrium-kinship cavalries from the stage of world politics.

These are the three kinds of human community with which we will begin. One is 200,000 years old, has always been peaceful, and—for that reason—has virtually been obliterated by the other two. These latter, disequilibrium-kinship and disequilibrium-civilization, are some 6,000 years old. They are both violent—one of them driven by warrior clan headmen, the other by warrior politicians and businessmen. Each of the three kinds has stories to tell and its own reasons for telling them.

Children, Personcrows, and Stories

Human communities tell their most consequential stories to children. Small children are not equilibrium-kinship community members, or disequilibrium-civilized community members, yet. They are just children. Aristotle might have said they belong to the genus *small child*, not yet differentiated into the species *equilibrium-kinship older child*, or *disequilibrium-kinship older child*, or *disequilibrium-civilized older child*. It goes without saying that stories will be instrumental in moving children from their common genus into one, and only one, species.

The common genus suggests that there may be a single, deep-lying aspect of stories that will engage almost all children, at least small children, wherever they are in time or place. I think that there is such an aspect, a foundational layer, of stories. I'll call it the invitation to fuse with something.

The notion of fusion-with-something is not a familiar one to most disequilibrium-civilized adults—most of us. That it may be "deep-lying" suggests some sort of priority in the uses of the mind itself. Let us say that the mind normally proceeds on its way along one of two lines:

1. We make distinctions, or
2. We un-make distinctions.

Making distinctions eventually produces conceptual hierarchies (like modern school curricula) and social hierarchies (like cities, empires, and nations; markets and corporations; and religions; all of which we have seen before). It appears that making distinctions is the principal mental instrument of disequilibrium-civilizations, everywhere in such societies fine-tuned and rewarded. Un-making distinctions would appear, then, to promise the undoing of conceptual and social hierarchies. We would correctly expect the un-making of distinctions to be disconfirmed in disequilibrium-civilizations.

The terms "equilibrium" and "disequilibrium" are linked to the making and un-making of distinctions. The equilibrium-kinship world held exactly the making and un-making of distinctions in equilibrium. This co-presence, this equal weighting of the two modes of using the mind, is what grounded 200,000 years of human life. The disequilibrium of the two 6,000-year-old social forms is a disequilibrium of mental functions—before it is social inequality or violence. The unequal weighting in disequilibrium-kinship and disequilibrium-civilization always values distinction-making over distinction un-making.

Now the un-making, the elimination or dissolution, of a distinction is the means to fusion with a thing. How? A typical twentieth century person knows herself to be a human being. She sees a crow. One thing she certainly knows about a crow is that it is a different creature from her. It has wings; she has legs. It flies; she walks. And on and on. The distinction between her and the crow is unbridgeable. She may see the crow and react to it, but then she goes on with her life, not profoundly affected. However, if she were instead an equilibrium-kinship person of the fifteenth millennium before now, she might look at that physically so-different creature and then, with a force of imagination barely imaginable in the twentieth century, *eliminate* the distinction between person and crow. She would do that in order to become a "personcrow"—with legs *and* wings, large-bodied *and* small-bodied, smooth-skinned *and* feathered. It would be obvious to her that it was a good thing to have a doubled identity, to be two rather than one, to leave being merely human for a while and be something more. Doubleness might even define fun, or happiness, for her.

The stories her brothers and sisters, cousins, parents, and aunts and uncles told fifteen thousand years ago balanced asserting the differences among things with fusions of things, like the fusion of a woman and a crow. Stories like these made the children and grown-ups who listened to them smile—What kind of older cousin would want to make a young cousin frown?—and ask to hear them over and over. She told such stories herself and maintained the balance. Listening for the deep equilibrium, making it part of oneself, and telling it back: the circle of stories.

Six thousand years ago the work of terminating equilibrium-kinship and breaking that circle of stories began. To destroy equilibrium-kinship, one need only destroy the power-of-imagination that permits someone to eliminate the difference between herself and a separate thing. The un-making of distinctions is punished in powerless children, ironically by parents first and then by new institutions, characteristically schools, devoted to rewarding distinction-making and directly or indirectly eliminating distinction-unmaking from the mental equipment of the young. Equilibrium-kinship is thus crippled in the inner lives of growing children while the external lives of their parents are absorbed into hierarchical institutions. The hyper-development of distinction-making powers equips young adults to maintain the new institutions and to do little else. A new circle is created; life in the high civilizations becomes hyper-active in a single mode—which is to say, disequilibriated—and institutionalized, and grindingly boring, for all but a very few.

How will a typical disequilibrium-civilization absorb the genus *small child,* still possessed of both distinction-making and distinction un-making capacities and still supremely interested in life, into its tiresome arrangements, if typical disequilibrium-civilizations only recognize half of the human mental endowment, the distinction-making half, and are therefore too boring seriously to interest any healthy small child? The answer helps to explain one of the most important story-types in disequilibrium-civilized societies, the fairy tale or folk tale that brings together fusion and terror.

Stories and The Loss of Equilibrium

A disequilibrium-civilization goes about "civilizing" its children with stories by first hooking them where all children live—in their desire to be full, to have fun, indeed to fuse. Then, successfully engaged by a plot element that, say, fuses a person with a horse, children are colorfully terrorized by other plot elements, not excluding dismemberments and tortures. The penetration of distinction-unmaking by terror is repeated in story after story, until both the desire and ability to fuse are repudiated *by the children themselves.* Distinction-making is now the only kind of mentation left to them. It is perfectly understandable for children who do not want to be frightened repeatedly to say to themselves, "Being methodical and bored are awful, but imagining myself a fish and then asphyxiating in the air is worse. I'll take boredom."

Stories mixing fusion and terror are told at bed-time (!) by parents in disequilibrium-civilizations. Confirmations of distinction-making powers are the later charge of schoolteachers. Thus is formed the parent-teacher coalition that enculturates the young in disequilbrium-civilizations. The adult world exercises half of the child's mental life by the morally extraordinary means of stimulating children to self-reduction and exercises and rewards the other half of the child's mental life—stories and school. It begins to be evident that the adult world of disequilibrium-civilizations has a good deal to answer for.

The hundred or so stories Ovid tells in the *Metamorphoses* and the 200 the Grimms tell in their collection have made up the major compendia of disequilibrium-civilized and disequilibrium-kinship stories told to children in the (disequilibrium-civilized) West. They are joined by Hans Anderson and Charles Perrault, by stories from disequilibrium-civilized India and disequilibrium-kinship Arabia, and by stories from the particularly consequential disequilibrium-kinship Levant. Nearly all these stories mix fusions with truly terrifying scenes.

A special difficulty attaches to Grimm. Few children's stories have been given the production attention, so to speak, that *Snow-White* has had in recent times: Walt Disney's remarkable animated film; a new edition in book form, the illustrations for which have drawn admiration from an unusually wide reading public. We forget, or repress the fact, that *Snow-White* ends with the queen being forced to put on red-hot iron shoes and dance until she dies. Children have repeated nightmares about the same queen's requirement of the huntsman ordered to kill Snow-White—that he bring back her lung and liver as proof of having done the act. Another woman is shoved into an oven and loudly screaming is burned to death in *Hänsel and Gretel.* Of course there are psychoanalytic arguments about the cathartic or otherwise adaptive value of imagining grotesque violence on bad-mother introjects, but I do not find them convincing. *Rumpelstiltskin,* a story more about female incompetence than female evil, ends with the crooked little man ripping himself in two. Even *Cinderella,* with *Snow-White, Hänsel and Gretel,* and *Rumpelstiltskin,* the ubiquitous Grimms', with its charming fusions and interventions on the heroine's behalf, ends monstrously, with the false sisters having their eyes pecked out by Cinderella's protectress-pigeons. Such violence cannot be written off as "natural," or rationalized by cultural-relativistic arguments; it is the regrettable violence of a disequilibrium-kinship culture, made normative in disequilibrium-civilizations by being told to young children by their trusted parents.

If these parents persist in believing that such stories as the Grimms collected are the stories of our generalized ancestors and are consequently true to the life of all our predecessors, then it is no wonder children will finally choose modern adult life. Who would not? But the culture that produced the stories occupies a thin and pathological layer of the past; thus a serious historical mistake, mis-identifying and expanding that layer, becomes a much more serious moral mistake, raising our children in response to that layer's stories. Our authentic, far-from-pathological forebears are the equilibrium-kinship peoples of the 200,000 years. The trouble is that we have very few stories from them; disequilibrium-kinship and disequilibrium-civilized peoples have murdered them, systematically or by indirection.

The Language of Stories: Thinking Revisited

I would like to return to speculations about mental life in order to look further into the provenance, diction, plots, and intentions of stories.

Figure 18-1.

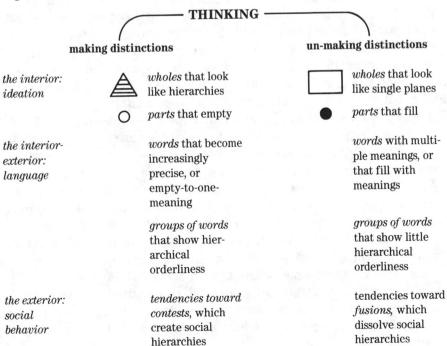

	THINKING	
	making distinctions	**un-making distinctions**
the interior: *ideation*	*wholes* that look like hierarchies	*wholes* that look like single planes
	parts that empty	*parts* that fill
the interior-exterior: *language*	*words* that become increasingly precise, or empty-to-one-meaning	*words* with multiple meanings, or that fill with meanings
	groups of words that show hierarchical orderliness	*groups of words* that show little hierarchical orderliness
the exterior: *social* *behavior*	*tendencies toward contests,* which create social hierarchies	*tendencies toward fusions,* which dissolve social hierarchies

We would expect leanings toward the left-hand, distinction-making constellation to create internal and external hierarchies. In an external, social hierarchy, the people living in the hierarchy exercise fewer and fewer of their abilities the more articulated the hierarchy becomes. For example, the typical employee of a big, hierarchically rationalized business has a narrower job definition than the typical employee of a small, less articulated business. The pertinence of this tendency to the nature of stories—and to the ways stories move pluripotential small children toward becoming equilibrium-kinship, disequilibrium-kinship, or disequilibrium-civilized adults—is surprising and profound because *languages* in the distinction-making constellation are "businesses," too. The parts of the very languages in which stories are told in a distinction-making world, the stories' words themselves, will reduce in function. The parts of social hierarchies, people, empty; the parts of language hierarchies, words, empty. The aim of the language hierarchy will be orderliness and efficiency. (One of the most influential CEOs of this century once called the aim of his business, one of the first hierarchically rationalized corporations in America, not making cars, or even making money, but being efficient.) Efficiency in the whole, single functions in the parts: the charter of distinction-making societies and their literatures.

So the deepest message communicated by a story told in a precise and orderly language will be to become precise and orderly. The manifest message may well be a different one, but the deep message will be that. When innocent-seeming contents, perhaps suggesting values other than precision and orderliness, adopt the precision- and orderliness-affirming forms of a distinction-making language, the resulting incongruency of content and form can put children into what Gregory Bateson called a "double bind." They hear one message and feel another, contradictory message, and go a little crazy.

Leanings toward the right-hand, distinction-unmaking constellation do not create hierarchies. The imperative here is to fill the parts of non-hierarchical wholes—to fill persons, or words, or moments. A person's substance can be doubled, for example, as the woman's substance was in the earlier example of fusing with a crow. If the whole in question is a language, rather than a society, and the part is a word, rather than a person, then, similarly, the task will be to fill the word with meaning. Efficiency in grouping words—into correctly formed sentences and paragraphs, into arguments with correct premises and conclusions—will not be pursued, as it is so energetically in distinction-making languages. Instead the distinctions among the referents of words will be weakened so that the words can refer to additional referents. In ancient Egypt, to which I'll return in a moment, the distinctions among a falcon, a river, and the sun can partially be dissolved, and one noun can mean all three. Such a noun, in ancient Egyptian, closely resembles a personcrow, in Native America. Both word and person are full.

Stories written in languages like ancient Egyptian usually have little plot, little movement, structure, suspense, or surprise. They would horrify Aristotle, who wrote the book on plot *et al*, and they would doom their authors in a modern college-writing program. What such stories would have is densely packed moments in no particular order. Readers or listeners would not be asked to move right along, through precise and quickly registered words, in order to see the larger structure; they would be given a single moment so layered with meaning that they would not want to move away from it. A stupendous poem in classical Chinese, to which I'll also return, has four words and takes hours to read. That is fullness.

Stories in the first constellation will often be about contests; stories in the second will often be about fusions. Second-constellation fusions are not like Ovid's and the Grimms'; they are not tinctured with such terrors as will cause the child to reject fusion. They are without ulteriority. Since plot and other structures matter less in the second constellation, fusions there go nowhere; they occur for their own sakes.

The two constellations can exist in equilibrium. In fact, equilibrium-kinship can be construed as our normal, even if now seldom encountered, state. There were also four "equilibrium-civilizations"—Egypt from 2700 B.C. to 1700 B.C., Minoa and Harappa from 2500 B.C. to 1500 B.C., and China from 800 A.D. to 1800 A.D.

Equilibrium-civilization is the fourth and last social form in our catalog. (It almost seems called for to remedy the asymmetry of two disequilibriated forms and only one equilibrated form.) The equilibrium-civilizations were, by and large, able in their own ways and each for about a thousand years, to judge when it was correct to be precise and orderly, to practice distinction-making and problem-solving, and when it was correct to be full and non-orderly, to practice distinction-unmaking and problem-dissolving.

What in the most practical terms made Egypt, Minoa, Harappa, and later China different from the run of the world's civilizations, disequilibrium-civilizations all, was precisely the evidence they presented of a full and balanced use of the mind. "Full and balanced use" speaks not only to mental life narrowly conceived, but to those day-to-day activities that we associate with personal happiness. For example, a mind working fully and harmoniously knows more pleasures than a mind only partly used—more kinds of pleasure, pleasures more often felt. There is a famous case in point from Minoa, brought to light with great force by the archeologist the United Nations chose to write the UNESCO history of archaic civilizations, Leonard Wooley. Wooley looked about at typical civilizations, again disequilibrium-civilizations, and noticed how depressed their behaviors were in religious observances. In Minoa between 2500 B.C. and 1500 B.C., on the contrary, the evidence of murals and portable sculpture reveals joyous, egalitarian, physical celebration as characteristic of spiritual life. A synthesis and intensification of pleasures, such as the Minoans knew, reminds one more of equilibrium-kinship than of any disequilibrium-civilization. Perhaps Henri Frankfort of the Oriental Institute at the University of Chicago best saw to the heart of equilibrium-civilizations when he said of ancient Egypt that it differed from other societies in having preserved its (equilibrium-) kinship past, not destroyed it.

Regaining Equilibrium Through Stories

We might ask if there are stories readily available to us in the twentieth-century West, a notably disequilibrated civilization, that show an Egyptian amplitude of meaning or Minoan joy in life. Such stories could stimulate the recovery of an equilibrium the West has not enjoyed since Minoa. Let me name five books, four for children that are enthralling instances of equilibrium, and one for adults that is so radically equilibrated that it is seldom recognized for what it is. *Alice's Adventures in Wonderland* and *Through the Looking Glass* are simultaneously brilliant handbooks of distinction-unmaking and elegant exercises in Victorian prose-writing, distinction-making to the hilt. The mixture is so fluid that readers regard the two books as relatively straightforward children's tales. On the contrary, they are monuments of equilibrium. If I.A. Richards was right that reading is a cure of souls, Lewis Carroll may have been the preeminent doctor of souls in English.

In this century, T.H. White and E.B. White have written stories that make distinctions and dissolve them in funny, worldly, and consoling ways. T.H. White takes on the Ur-story of the English-speaking world, the Arthur legend, and improves it. The boy Arthur, instructed by a Merlin only T. H. White could have imagined, fuses with animals in order to acquire the substance of the monarch Arthur. The first part of *The Once and Future King, The Sword in the Stone*, published separately in 1939, is the best manual on the subject of education I know. E.B. White's *Charlotte's Web*, as modest a book as *The Once and Future King* is magisterial, includes a moment that perfectly states the world-historical issue on equilibrium and disequilibrium: When the heroine's father justifies his intention to slaughter a baby pig of whom his daughter is very fond on the grounds that pigs are pigs and girls are girls, she says, ''I see no difference.'' There it is. The whole literary and moral force of E. B. White's great book derives from that assertion.

The fifth story, published in the same year as *The Sword in the Stone,* is similarly an epic, but unlike T. H. White's pellucid narrative, it is *the* heroically inaccessible epic. That is the pity, because James Joyce's *Finnegans Wake* may be the story of our time. It is only Joyce who tries actually to create a language of the distinction-unmaking constellation, pulling weight away from orderliness—the story can be begun anywhere and ended anywhere—and putting it into the words of the story themselves. By splicing pieces of words to each other, Joyce invents thousands of what Lewis Carroll called ''portmanteau words'' in *Through the Looking Glass.* Each portmanteau word has packed into it the meanings of every word from which the pieces of the new word come. It was an idea of genius, but it drove readers away. Perhaps more adults can suspend their excessive need for precision and orderliness as this century ends, go to *Finnegans Wake,* and permit it to begin the work of re-equilibrating their internal lives. Their children would be as much the beneficiaries as they.

Against the few, immeasurably important re-equilibrating stories in our lives and the lives of our children, stand the thousands upon thousands of crippling, frivolous-at-best, murderous-at-worst, so-called stories promulgated on television worldwide. Television has probably become the single worst enemy of equilibrium on the planet; it is the inverse of the long-ago planetary culture of equilibrium-kinship. Television, as it has actually devolved, not as an essentially neutral piece of hardware, erodes both distinction-making and distinction-unmaking, breaking down both constellations—an astounding accomplishment of television producers, writers, and sponsors. It has become the main cause, along with the automobile, of the destruction of the vestiges of equilibrium-kinship that survived into this century, and it has achieved this destruction through its ''stories.'' Again, the antithesis of a once worldwide equilibrium-kinship and its stories.

The contest between the stories of Lewis Carroll, T. H. White, E. B. White, James Joyce, their sometime allies like L. Frank Baum, the tragically few Native American, African, Asian, and Oceanic stories that come from an equilibrium-kinship past, these stories on the one hand, and the unending barrage of stories supplied by the electronic media on the other, is a continuous and unequal contest. The reason for conceiving an anatomy of thought-processes and then fitting the anatomy to a chronology of cultures is to give weight to the side of this contest with the fewer but authentically human stories to tell. Otherwise the other side will win, and the victims will be our children.

My class of 120 college seniors was within two weeks of finishing our history course and their undergraduate careers. I asked them to write a story to an imaginery eleven-year-old niece or nephew in which the wisdom they had acquired in college was somehow expressed. Of the 120, 112 wrote a story in the form,

"There are two kinds of people in the world, sharks and minnows. Don't you be a minnow, honey; be a shark."

Otherwise the other side will win.

Contributors

Diane Barone is an Assistant Professor in Language and Literacy at the University of Nevada, Las Vegas. She recently completed her doctoral work at the University of Nevada, Reno. Her dissertation centered on the written response of young children to independently read stories. Articles on this topic have appeared in *The New Advocate, The NRC Yearbook,* and *Language Arts.*

Marvin Bram received his Ph.D. from the University of Rochester. He is a Professor in the Department of History at Hobart and William Smith Colleges. His research has centered in what he terms "symbolic history."

Patrick Collins is an Assistant Professor of Education at Hobart and William Smith Colleges in Geneva, NY. A former elementary teacher, he holds an Ed.D. from Harvard University. In addition to teaching and writing about the role of theatre and drama in education, he has also done research on children's reading and writing and on the educational implications of the work of the philosopher Nelson Goodman.

Ariel Dorfman, born in Argentina in 1942, is a Chilean citizen who was forced into exile after the 1973 overthrow of Salvador Allende. Many of his books have been translated into English, including *How to Read Donald Duck, The Empire's Old Cloathes,* and *Some Write to the Future,* as well as several novels, a collection of short stories, and several plays. He is Research Professor of Literature and Latin American Studies at Duke University.

Kieran Egan is a Professor in the Faculty of Education at Simon Fraser University, British Columbia, Canada. He is the author of several books in education, including *Teaching as Story Telling* (University of Chicago Press, 1989), *Primary Understanding: Education in Early Childhood* (Routledge, 1990), and *Romantic Understanding: The Development of Rationality and Imagination, ages 8–15.*

Susan Hepler earned her Ph.D. at The Ohio State University. She is a consultant to schools interested in developing literature-based curricula and also teaches courses in children's literature and language arts for the Alexandria Virginia public schools. She is a coauthor with Charlotte S. Huck and Janet Hickman of CHILDREN'S LITERATURE IN THE ELEMENTARY SCHOOL and author of teaching guides for public television's "Long Ago and Far Away" series as well as of numerous articles and reviews.

Janet Hickman is an Assistant Professor of Education on the Faculty of Language, Literature, and Reading at The Ohio State University, where she teaches graduate courses in children's literature and conducts research on the reader response of children. She coauthored *Children's Literature in the Classroom: Weaving Charlotte's Web* (Christopher-Gordon, 1989) and is a coauthor of *Children's Literature in the Elementary School* (Holt, Rinehart and Winston, 1987), and has published four books for young readers.

E.D. Hirsch, Jr. received his Ph.D. in English Literature and Language from Yale University. He is currently William R. Keenan Professor of English at the University of Virginia, Charlottesville. He has published extensively, but is perhaps best known for *Cultural Literacy* (Houghton Mifflin, 1987), *Dictionary of Cultural Literacy* (Houghton Mifflin, 1988), *First Dictionary of Cultural Literacy* (Houghton Mifflin, 1989), and the recently published grades 1–6 series, *The Core Knowledge Series* (Houghton Mifflin, 1991).

Jonathan Lovell is an Associate Professor of English and Advisor for the Precredential (English Education) Program at San Jose State University. He also serves as the university-based co-director of the San Jose Area Writing Project. He holds degrees from Williams College, Oxford, and Yale Universities.

Jill May is an Associate Professor at Purdue University. She is an active member of the Children's Literature Association, the National Council of Teachers of English, and the Modern Language Association. She is the author of several books and has published numerous articles.

Joy F. Moss received her MA from the University of Rochester. She is a teacher at the Harley School in Rochester, NY, where she designed a literature program which has been the basis for her professional research and writing for two decades. She is also an Adjunct Associate Professor at the University of Rochester Graduate School of Education and a consultant and lecturer. She is the author of *Focus on Literature: A Conext for Literacy Learning* (Richard C. Owen, 1990) and *Focus Units in Literature* (NCTE, 1984).

James L. Plecha received his Ph.D. in Philosophy from the University of Virginia. He is a senior editor for the Great Books Foundation, publishers of Junior Great Books.

Stephen Simmer, M.A., Ph.D., M.S.W., is currently working as a therapist for children and families in Rochester, NY. He has previously taught at Hobart and William Smith Colleges and Syracuse University in Religion and Psychology. He has been on the editorial board of the *National Storytelling Journal* and has been a frequent lecturer on storytelling as well as Religion and Psychology.

Keith E. Stanovich is Professor of Psychology and Education at Oakland University, Rochester, MI, where he codirects the Reading Research Laboratory with Ruth Nathan. His research interests are in the areas of literacy studies, individual differences in reading, the cognitive consequences of print exposure, and literate intelligence. He is author of numerous articles and editor of *Children's Reading and Development of Phonological Awareness.*

Charles Temple received his Ph.D. in Reading Education from the University of Virginia. He teaches courses in literacy education and human development at Hobart and William Smith Colleges, where he is also chair of the Education Department. He is coauthor of five books in the areas of reading and language arts education, including *The Beginnings of Writing,* 2nd edition, *Understanding Reading Problems,* 3rd edition, and *Teaching Language Arts,* 3rd edition.

Frances Nolting Temple is a primary school teacher in Geneva, NY. She received her M.Ed. in Comparative and Community Education from the University of Virginia. She is coauthor of *The Beginnings of Writing,* 2nd edition and *Classroom Strategies: An Elementary Teacher's Guide to Process Writing.*

James D. Watkinson received his Ph.D. from the University of Virginia. He has taught at the University of Virginia as well as at the secondary level.

Paul Wilson received his Ph.D. from the University of Virginia. Currently at Western Michigan University, he was previously at the Center for the Study of Reading. His interests include language experience and integrated language arts, developing lifelong reading habits, and diagnosis and remediation of reading difficulties. At present, he is receiving teacher training in Reading Recovery, and is developing new guidelines for administering and interpreting informal reading inventories.

Index